MILTON STUDIES

X

MILTON STUDIES

X   *Edited by*

James D. Simmonds

UNIVERSITY OF PITTSBURGH PRESS

MILTON STUDIES

is published annually by the University of Pittsburgh Press as a forum for Milton scholarship and criticism. Articles submitted for publication may be biographical; they may interpret some aspect of Milton's writings; or they may define literary, intellectual, or historical contexts—by studying the work of his contemporaries, the traditions which affected his thought and art, contemporary political and religious movements, his influence on other writers, or the history of critical response to his work.

Manuscripts should be upwards of 3,000 words in length and should conform to the *MLA Style Sheet*. Manuscripts and editorial correspondence should be addressed to James D. Simmonds, Department of English, University of Pittsburgh, Pittsburgh, Pa. 15260.

Milton Studies does not review books.

Within the United States, *Milton Studies* may be ordered from the University of Pittsburgh Press, Pittsburgh, Pa. 15260.

Overseas orders should be addressed to Feffer and Simons, Inc., 100 Park Avenue, New York, N.Y. 10017, U.S.A.

Library of Congress Catalog Card Number 69-12335
ISBN 0-8229-3174-5 (Volume I) (out of print)
ISBN 0-8229-3194-x (Volume II)
ISBN 0-8229-3218-0 (Volume III)
ISBN 0-8229-3244-x (Volume IV)
ISBN 0-8229-3272-5 (Volume V)
ISBN 0-8229-3288-1 (Volume VI)
ISBN 0-8229-3305-5 (Volume VII)
ISBN 0-8229-3310-1 (Volume VIII)
ISBN 0-8229-3329-2 (Volume IX)
ISBN 0-8229-3356-x (Volume X)
US ISSN 0076-8820
Published by the University of Pittsburgh Press, Pittsburgh, Pa. 15260
Copyright © 1977, University of Pittsburgh Press
Feffer & Simons, Inc., London
Manufactured in the United States of America

CONTENTS

MILTON STUDIES

X

THE COMIC DIMENSION
IN GREEK TRAGEDY
AND *SAMSON AGONISTES*

C. A. Patrides

I

THERE IS nothing new under the sun. Or so we tend to hold, inclined as we are to elevate familiar concepts into ultimate truths, and known modes of thought into vast generalizations. There is comfort in such gestures, and much assurance, until the creators in our midst forcefully remind us that literature as a matter of course resists the dogmatic. The habit of mind that sustains the confident generalizations whether in Aristotle's *Poetics* or Sidney's *Apology for Poetry* is not necessarily pernicious, however. It must on the contrary elicit our sympathetic response and command our ample respect. Yet it is injurious all the same, since the impulse in each work is fundamentally toward the categorical, the definitive, the absolute.

The *Poetics* and the *Apology for Poetry* alike claim, with characteristic assurance, that what is tragic appertains to tragedy, and what is comic to comedy. We are of course amused by Sidney's dichotomy since his consequent censure of what he called "mongrel tragicomedy" was penned on the eve—and indeed on the very day—of the most imaginative transposition of his terms conceivable. Armed with hindsight, we have not failed to note that the practicing playwrights of his age, drawing on the rich experience of their medieval predecessors, habitually merged the tragic and the comic; and our recognition has yielded several investigations of the convergence of the twain in Marlowe as in Shakespeare.[1]

But Sidney's capital concern was not with his immediate contemporaries. The polemical nature of his *Apology* demanded that he should celebrate the distant past which, he decided, had consistently eschewed the confluence of the tragic and the comic. He also decided that the evidence was clearly present in the plays of "the ancients" who "never, or very daintily, match horn-pypes and

3

funeralls": a view not uncommon even today, our hindsight notwith-standing. But such a confident generalization was for him, as it is for us, a misjudgment of the first magnitude. True, Sidney merely echoed the opinions of the Italian critics who had themselves ex-tended—and, it must be admitted, relentlessly codified—tenden-cies implicit or explicit in Aristotle's *Poetics*. But in the very act of echoing his predecessors Sidney displayed a distressing infatuation with critical dicta at the expense of the actual practice in ancient Greek literature. The consequences are clearly to be observed. By endorsing a wrong dictum at the wrong time in the wrong country, he failed utterly to affect Elizabethan drama, but did contribute heavily to a serious misconception of Greek drama and consequently to the widening of the wide enough gulf between literature and criticism. The line of descent from the archetypical Aristotle to the codifying Italian critics and their imitator Sidney reaches to our time; and also encompasses, during the seventeenth century, Milton.

Or rather one particular Milton: not indeed the superb dramatist who composed *Samson Agonistes*, but the prosaic author who com-piled its narrow-minded preface. The prosaic author was of the unqualified opinion that to intermix "comic stuff with tragic sadness and gravity" is reprehensible in the extreme; but the dramatist promptly violated that dictum, cognizant as a creator that mere opinions—however sanctified by tradition—may be superseded in a play that aspires to reflect human experience. The discrepancy be-tween the preface and the play looms very large indeed; nor am I distressed by it since Milton the poet has always impressed me as an infinitely superior artist to Milton the left-handed prose-writer. In the pages immediately following, therefore, while my primary aim will be to demonstrate the correspondence between Greek drama and *Samson Agonistes* in terms of their jointly upheld "mongrel tragicomedy," a secondary but no less vital aim will be to maintain that the play's preface is monomaniacally polemical and may not be trusted as a categorical, definitive, or final judgment on the play itself. The parallel here, if I may appeal to the theologically inclined reader, is to the argument I ventured elsewhere, that Milton's pro-saic theological treatise bears *as literature* no conceivable rela-tionship to Milton's major poem: for while the prose of *De Doctrina Christiana* descends to theological grossness, the poetry of *Paradise Lost* is a window to the sun.[2]

But to my argument.

II

The intrusion of the comic upon the primary dimensions of *Paradise Lost* is no longer, I expect, a matter of dispute: the recognition of its presence in the poem appears to be widespread even if it is variously conceived and diversely articulated.[3] Not surprisingly; for the epic was regarded during the Renaissance as all-inclusive by definition, "the best and most accomplished kind of poetry" as Sidney unhesitatingly proclaimed. Mindful though Milton must have been of such critical pronouncements, he would have invoked the far more significant precedent which was Spenser's actual deployment of the comic in *The Faerie Queene*.[4] Yet he would have been no less prepared to invoke Homer.

Our own knowledge of Homer is limited in that it is commonly filtered through Pope's version, and possibly even through Chapman's. But Milton, who had access to the original Greek, would have been alert to the comic in *The Odyssey* as in *The Iliad*. Penelope in the former epic, for instance, will upon consideration emerge neither as the ethereal prototype of the patient woman nor as the pitiful victim of the suitors' advances, but as the living embodiment of craft: the ingeniously inventive center of conspiracies which she herself initiates, and habitually wins. Her mode of existence is by no means singular, however. It is on the contrary reflected on one plane in Odysseus himself, and on another in the goddess Athena —both brilliant performers, both consummate actors, both superbly adroit.

The delightful good will that in *The Odyssey* envelops several characters and reduces a goddess to the level of mere humanity, is in *The Iliad* amplified so generously that not to discern the implicit comic dimension is seriously to misconstrue Homer's intentions. Certainly no account of Achilles may bypass his extreme solemnity which Homer so obviously sets at the other extreme from the amusement generated by Nestor, while a variety of intermediate positions are assigned to Agamemnon and Odysseus among the other warriors. But mere translations, it should be emphasized, can rarely if ever convey the wondrously intricate balance between amicable laughter and perpetual admiration, witness the moment when the poet describes how Odysseus "looks short when he stands up and tall when he is sitting down."[5] On the other hand, even the worst possible translation cannot fail to suggest the twofold aspect of the greatest of the gods. Zeus, it is obvious, is neither solely grave

nor simply amusing; he is both: "the supreme and awful sovereign of
all the universe," and yet a comic "nursery-rhyme Zeus."[6] This dual
attitude was later to inform Greek art as well, most explicitly perhaps
in the delightful statue of Zeus at Olympia, portrayed at the moment
when clutching Ganymede in one arm he is fleeing the disapproval
of Hera, his face the very picture of mischievousness. But *The Iliad*
reserves much the same treatment for the lesser Olympians, jointly
and justly described by one critic as *"agents provocateurs,* smart
propagandists, heated partisans."[7] The fuller account by the same
critic deserves to be quoted at length:

The quarrels and reconciliation of Zeus and Hera, the seduction scene in
which, armed with Aphrodite's magic ribbon, she manages to make a fool of
her husband, the scene where Zeus discovers his wife's trick as he wakes up
and threatens to push her off the heights of Olympus and let her hang
suspended in the ether, all these really belong to musical comedy. But here,
again, truth to human experience somehow moves this marital farce to a
plane of more substantial reality. There is Hera with her big stupid eyes, her
obstinacy more brutish than evil, and the real genius she shows while
subjecting Zeus to a successful "war of nerves", from which she always
comes off with the honors. There is Aphrodite, all smiles and whims,
enchanting and futile in her weakness, yet not so defenseless as she seems.
There is Pallas Athena, a warrior with a man's muscles, expert and treacherous, who can send Ares rolling to the ground with the force of a single
blow, who knows how to harbor a grudge and let rancor steep within her
until her revenge is brewed. These are the three goddesses involved in the
judgment of Paris, and each in her own way reveals the other side of the
eternal feminine whose tragic purity is embodied in Andromache, Helen,
and Thetis.[8]

Students of Milton should in addition be reminded that "the comedy
of the gods" which in the first book of *The Iliad* terminates in
uncontrollable laughter, is comic especially because the light-
hearted exchanges of the merry Olympians are couched in language
that remains throughout grave, solemn, "epic." Intentions apart, the
premeditated discrepancy between matter and manner at the heart
of the Homeric account parallels the equally premeditated one in
Milton's account of the relations within the infernal trinity of Satan,
Sin, and Death.

    It is not without warrant, then, that Milton would have invoked
Homer as a major precedent for the introduction of the comic dimension in *Paradise Lost.* But did he also adapt the Homeric antecedents
to the demands of *Samson Agonistes?* More important still, did he
discern analogous patterns in Greek tragedy, the claims of Aristotle
and Sidney to the contrary?

III

Post-Homeric thought and experience are so totally dominated by Homer that he is present even where he appears to be most evidently absent. Yet in the area under examination it would seem that his impact was minimal. Consider Aeschylus, solemnly proclaiming the primacy of Zeus, gravely espousing the cosmic relevance of divine law and justice, darkly evincing the reality of inherited guilt and its extension from generation to generation by individuals voluntarily implicated in its web. Could such an awesome poet-prophet be connected with the convergence of the tragic and the comic we have noted in Homer?

It should in the first instance be remembered, however, that Aeschylus was celebrated not only for his trilogies but for his satyr-plays. He had written fifteen such plays,[9] all presented during the City Dionysia when each morning's performance of a cluster of three tragedies—closely related as a trilogy in the case of Aeschylus but less often interconnected in the case of Sophocles—would be promptly followed by the performance of a robustly comic and pretentiously "epic" satyr-play by the same dramatist: in sum, not a trilogy but a tetralogy. Not many examples of the unique genre of satyr-plays survive: we possess the complete text of only one, *The Cyclops* of Euripides; the nearly complete text of another, *The Searchers* of Sophocles; and mere fragments from the rest.[10] But even these remnants suffice to indicate how stunning their impact must have been. "It is almost," we are told, "as if Shakespeare had written a *Punch and Judy* show to be presented as an after-piece to *Romeo and Juliet*"[11]—or equally, I think, as if he had written a gross parody of *King Lear*, penned in the same style and presented immediately after that tragedy terminates. No less suggestive is the odd way that satyr-plays anticipate the efforts of the Attic poets of the New Comedy who later parodied the ancient myths, and of the craftsmen who represented on vases not the winged Pegasus but a winged donkey! The involvement of Aeschylus in these productions astonishes, to say the least; but alerts us also, I believe, to a proper understanding of his formal tragedies.

For curious things occur even within those "tragedies." Evidently composed while Aeschylus was μεθύων, "in a state of intoxication,"[12] they embrace the Dionysiac element which we will have the opportunity to observe on other occasions as well. Should "tragedy" be conceived in Aristotelian terms, the practice of Aeschylus certainly defies categorization since *Philoctetes* and *The Eumenides* alike end happily, and so apparently did *The*

Prometheia.[13] The latter trilogy survives, of course, solely in its first play, *Prometheus Bound;* and Aristotle who must have sensed that it did not conform to his vision of tragedy, pointedly enrolled it among "tragedies depending upon spectacle" (*Poetics,* Chap. XVIII). Horace Walpole was at least more honest when he protested that the play's leading lady is a cow![14] However absurd a remark, it does prevent us from accepting Aeschylus' characters at their face value. Oceanus—the god of the ocean—will then be more readily admitted to be what he is, "plainly half-comic in intention."[15] In Robert Lowell's version of the play ("derived from Aeschylus"), Oceanus is not unjustly described as "a tall, fat god with a beautiful white curling beard—good-natured, but now and then, vexation and venom animate his great langour."[16] According to the same version he enters riding a swan, but it appears that he should rather be conceived as riding one of his more amusing marine monsters, probably the hippocamp.[17] His offer to intercede with Zeus should be seen (literally) in the light of our ocular view of him on the stage, hippocamp and all; for that offer is well meant but rather silly, not unlike the misguided endeavors of Milton's Manoa. Prometheus responds warmly to Oceanus, as respond warmly he must; yet he sees through him after a minimum of reflection:

> *Oceanus.*   Tell me, what danger do you see for me in loyalty
>   to you, and courage therein?
> *Prometheus.* I see only useless effort and a silly good nature.[18]

We are tempted confidently to generalize that the comic element in primitive Greek drama was gradually "extruded from the tragedies," to be confined thereafter solely to the satyr-plays and eventually to the "new and independent outlet" of the comedies.[19] But such an "extrusion" is as inadmissible about Greek drama as it would be about medieval or Shakespearean drama, given the presence of Oceanus in *Prometheus Bound* on the one hand, and of Noah's wife in the mystery plays or the gravediggers in *Hamlet* on the other. Great artists, prodigally creative, do not abide by theories elevated into dogmas. Intent upon realistic dimensions beyond the simply comic or the expressly tragic, they are wont as in the case of Aeschylus to deploy satyr-plays as entities directly affecting the "tragedies" to which they are annexed. A robustly comic *Proteus,* converting the trilogy of *The Oresteia* into a tetralogy, would have transmuted our response radically; and so would *Prometheus the Fire-kindler,* reported to have been postfixed to the three plays constituting *The Prometheia.*

As with Aeschylus, so with Sophocles: the reputed intensi-fication of the tragic atmosphere in the plays of the latter as in those of the former, has deflected us into neglecting the numerous excep-tions to the vast generalizations so freely ventured on both. Soph-ocles had like Aeschylus written several satyr-plays; and their very existence should as before raise certain expectations concerning the intrusion of the comic upon the tragic. Aristotle's comment on the chorus provides one avenue of approach. "The chorus," he declared, "should be regarded as one of the actors, as a constituent part of the whole, and should share in the action as Sophocles, and not as Euripides, has it do."[20] To share in the action as one of the actors means, of course, that the chorus must necessarily be a character endowed with a particular sensibility and therefore subject to the same oscillations as any of the other *dramatis personae*. This fact, so manifestly appreciated by Milton in *Samson Agonistes* as we will see, also led Sophocles to introduce a highly individualized chorus in each of his plays, varying their characterization to suit the circum-stances surrounding the given protagonist. The result is often comic, not indeed because the behavior of the chorus is ever amusing but because, as in *Samson Agonistes,* there is a discrepancy between the progressive movement of the play in one direction and the regres-sive movement of the chorus in another.

Additionally, however, Sophocles introduced several minor characters who oddly resemble their counterparts not so much in Milton as in Shakespeare. The first of two such characters is en-countered in the opening lines of *Electra*. He is the old servant who had once attended to the boy Orestes and now accompanies him and Pylades to Mycenae. As the play unfolds, he is brought before Clytemnestra whom he pretends not to recognize. Much to her delight, he reports the "pleasant news" of Orestes' death; and ques-tioned more closely, he embarks on a very long and eminently realistic account of Orestes' lamentable end (679–763)—save that the account is not true. This brilliant inversion of the usual messenger's speech is at the same time an equally brilliant deploy-ment of dramatic irony as Electra cries out in agony, Clytemnestra exults, and we knowingly await the next reversal which is to compel them to switch roles. But the comic dimension borne by the old servant in *Electra* is even more explicitly carried by the guard who in *Antigone* confronts Creon (223–331). The guard has the unenviable task of reporting to the autocratic king that Polyneices has been buried in violation of the royal decree. Within a few lines he reveals himself to be not a stereotype but an individual with traits decidedly his own:

> Lord, I can't claim that I am out of breath
> from rushing here with light and hasty step,
> for I had many haltings in my thought
> making me double back upon the road.
> My mind kept saying many things to me:
> "Why go where you will surely pay the price?"
> "Fool, are you halting? And if Creon learns
> from someone else, how shall you not be hurt?"
> Turning this over, on I dilly-dallied.[21]

The guard's "light and hasty step" is clearly neither light nor hasty; and the impatient Creon whose lack of *sophrosyne* has already been impressed upon us, now confirms his limitations all too prodigally. The guard eventually delivers his report, embellishing his meandering narrative with numerous irrelevant details and ending with the complaint that his mates elected him to appear before Creon: "So here I am unwilling, / quite sure you people hardly wish to see me." Creon responds in kind, and there follows this comic variation on the traditional stichomythia:

> Guard.   May I say something? Or just turn and go?
> Creon.   Aren't you aware your speech is most unwelcome?
> Guard.   Does it annoy your hearing or your mind?
> Creon.   Why are you out to allocate my pain?
> Guard.   The doer hurts your mind. I hurt your ears.
> Creon.   You are a quibbling rascal through and through.[22]

The guard represents a sophisticated application by Sophocles of the point discerned, however distantly, by Horace. To quote Jonson's version of *The Art of Poetrie:*

> The Comick matter will not be exprest
> In tragick Verse; no lesse *Thyestes* feast
> Abhorres low numbers, and the private straine
> Fit for the sock: Each subject should retaine
> The place allotted it, with decent thewes.
> Yet, sometime, doth the Comedie excite
> Her voyce, and angry *Chremes* chafes out-right
> With swelling throat: and, oft the tragick wight
> Complaines in humble phrase.   (121–29)

When all is said, however, it is in Sophocles' last play that the comic intervenes on a massive scale; so much so, indeed, that *Oedipus at Colonus* can by no stretch of the usual critical criteria be regarded as a "tragedy." It is not simply that Oedipus is by the end of the play transmuted into a "hero" presiding over Colonus. Far more trenchant is the way that the cumulative details are handled by Sophocles. The highly individualized chorus—"one of the actors"—is initially less than pleased to see Oedipus trespassing the inviolate sanctuary, and in fact makes it clear that his very presence in Athens is altogether unwelcome. But Ismene intervenes to report the oracle's prophecy that Oedipus' eventual burial place will sanctify the land on which it stands. The chorus, profoundly impressed, hurriedly reconsiders the situation and later reminds King Theseus how very useful Oedipus is to prove once he dies. Theseus, having to his credit already extended hospitality to Oedipus, now proclaims him a citizen; and the chorus, much gratified, breaks into one of the most beautiful—and ironic because it is so exquisitely beautiful—choral poems in ancient Greek literature (668 ff.). But the underlying comedy that so relentlessly exposes human selfishness proceeds apace. Creon who had also learned of the oracle's prophecy arrives to invite Oedipus back to Thebes with telling assurances that the erstwhile exile would now be most welcome (728 ff.); but Oedipus unerringly perceives the motivation and violently denounces the transparent change of heart. Polyneices also comes, this time with a plea that Oedipus join the Argives against the Thebans (1284 ff.); but Oedipus responds with a harsh and often misunderstood tirade which, within the play's context, is a pointed disclosure of man's greed. The death of Oedipus at Colonus emerges in the end as a parable likely to be misunderstood only by those who seeing see not, and hearing hear not.

Euripides' predilections should have yielded more satyr-plays than Aeschylus and Sophocles composed jointly, but in the event he wrote fewer than did either of the other two. *The Cyclops* is consequently not the rule but the exception. Instead, Euripides elected to project the terms normally reserved for satyr-plays to his drama at large. The result was confusion expertly confounded. *Alcestis*, for instance, can be defined rather negatively than positively. It is clearly not a tragedy; but neither is it a comedy, or even a tragicomedy, and may in the end only loosely be classed as a satyr-play. At the City Dionysia, at any rate, it was given the benefit of the doubt and performed as a satyr-play. The crucial factor must be presumed to be the presentation of Heracles who is conceived as a burlesque character with a sufficiently obvious progeny. He is on his way to cope with the mares of Diomedes—"a horse-stealing expedition," explains the most irrelevant critic of Greek drama[23]—but on visiting the household of Admetus he is confronted by Alcestis' imminent

departure for Hades in lieu of her husband. A servant who is assigned to look after the travel-weary Heracles is not at all impressed:

> I have known all sorts of foreigners who have come in
> from all over the world here to Admetus' house,
> and I have served them dinner, but I never yet
> have had a guest as bad as this to entertain.

The trouble is that the omnicompetent and legendary Heracles
indulges rather too freely in wine:

> [he] drank the wine of our dark mother, straight, until
> the flame of the wine went all through him, and heated him,
> and then he wreathed branches of myrtle on his head
> and howled, off key.[24]

Yet the comic dimension is not restricted to Heracles, not even after
he enters the stage half-drunk. It is extended to include the return of
the veiled Alcestis, the refusal of Admetus to consider "another"
woman, and their joyous reunion. Should the play appear less than
promising as a potential influence on other dramatists, we could do
worse than ponder T. S. Eliot's acknowledgment that *Alcestis* was
the "source" of one of his own plays, *The Cocktail Party*[25]—itself
subtitled, in a calculated gesture of defiance, "A Comedy."

The other plays of Euripides also challenge our obsession with
classifications. In *The Heraclidae*, for instance, the superannuated
Iolaus touches high comedy when an attendant helps him (more or
less) to prepare for his improbable battle against the Argives:

Iolaus.	All right, come on; but keep my things all ready.
	Now put the spear-shaft into my left hand
	And take my right arm so, to guide my steps.
Attendant.	Ye gods! Am I to nursemaid you to war?
Iolaus.	No, but we'll watch our step. To fall's bad luck.
Attendant.	If only you could do what you can dream.
Iolaus.	Hurry! I can't afford to miss the fight.
Attendant.	You are the dawdler, though you think it's I.
Iolaus.	But don't you see how very fast I'm walking?
Attendant.	I see the speed is largely in your mind.
Iolaus.	You'll change your tune as soon as I get there.
Attendant.	What will you do? I want to see you win.
Iolaus.	You'll see me smash clean through somebody's shield.
Attendant.	If ever we arrive there, which I doubt.[26]

Two other plays, *Helen* and *Iphigenia in Tauris*, deploy a device
which may be described as comic by osmosis. In the one, Helen

tricks King Theoclymenus so that she can escape with her companions from Egypt; while in the other, Iphigenia does as much with King Thoas of Tauris—but not before she has advised him most earnestly, "O King, beware of Greeks!" (1204). The mind at work on these occasions is veritably Homeric, and more specifically Odyssean, in that it mirrors the conduct of the versatile Odysseus, of his equally callid wife, and of their protector the vulpine Athena. It is therefore not impossible to claim that *Helen* is "comedy from beginning to end,"[27] provided that we are fully cognizant of the "comedy" we have in mind, and that we are not tempted to negate the gravity of Euripides' ultimate concerns. The dramatist has much fun in positing a real Helen in Egypt at the very time that the Greeks were sacking Troy to avenge the abduction of Helen's ghost! The deflation of the Trojan war is total: "O Troy, how you were brought down in vain!" (1220). In other words, if in Aeschylus and Sophocles the comic intrudes upon the tragic, in Euripides the tragic emerges from the heart of comedy—nowhere more movingly than in Helen's passionate lament over the ravages effected by the folly of aggression and war:

> Ah, Troy, the unhappy,
> for things done that were never done
> you died, hurt pitifully . . .
> Mothers who saw their children die,
> maidens who cut their long hair
> for kinsmen who were killed beside the waters
> of Phrygian Scamander.
> Hellas too has cried, has cried
> aloud in lamentation,
> beaten her hands against her head
> and with the nails' track of blood
> torn her cheeks' softness.[28]

It would appear, however, that Euripides at the end of his life abandoned his well-attested predilections in favour of a tragedy properly so called. But in regarding *The Bacchae* care must be had to understand—so far as it is possible to understand—the mystery of the presence which is the god Dionysus. Risible and harmless at first, but utterly potent and awful by the end, Dionysus possesses a chilling smile that haunts the self-confident Pentheus to destruction, μεθύων. The ambivalence of Dionysus in *The Bacchae* parallels that which in *The Iliad* resulted in a "nursery-rhyme Zeus" who is yet "the supreme and awful sovereign of all the universe." Is it possible in such circumstances to seek, and much less to establish with assurance, any strict lines of demarcation between tragedy and comedy? The question answers itself when we recall that the marks borne by Dionysus in *The Bacchae* are also borne by Dionysus in *The Frogs* of Aristophanes.[29]

IV

Samson Agonistes is a tolerant play. It has tolerated in particular a variety of critical claims, especially the large claims about the influence reputedly exerted on it by several Greek plays ranging from Sophocles' *Oedipus at Colonus* to Euripides' *Heracles*.[30] But since a dramatist responds to an aggregate of influences only in order to transmute them into novelties, we must remain skeptical of all singular claims that endeavor to reduce the larger framework or impoverish the richer texture.[31] The caveat applies equally to the preceding paragraphs where my tentative suggestions may have inadvertently appeared in the guise of categorical dicta. The given detail was in each instance intended solely to suggest the general, precisely as the presence in *Samson Agonistes* of a character like Harapha is meaningful only in relation to the predicament of the protagonist.

Harapha's entry is heralded by a trumpet blast from the Chorus:

> I know him by his stride,
> The giant Harapha of Gath, his look
> Haughty, as is his pile high-built and proud.   (1067–69)

Harapha may or may not be "the high point of the drama" in that his presence effects "the necessary reversal in Samson's attitude."[32] If he is of such major importance, however, is it not very odd that Milton should have provided him with a literary progeny which includes the braggarts in the comic literature of the Continental Renaissance?[33] The consequences, after all, are unmistakable. So far as the play's preface is concerned, Harapha's progeny flatly contradicts—and, at the very least, neatly subverts—the militant censure of "the error of intermixing comic stuff with tragic sadness and gravity." So far as the play itself is concerned, on the other hand, the question must necessarily be posed whether Harapha's comic antecedents are meant to alert us to the concurrent presence of other comic elements.

Manoa's endeavors to ransom Samson, we noted earlier, are "not unlike" the well-meant if silly efforts of Oceanus to intercede with Zeus. The parallel—in itself hardly novel[34]—should not be pressed too far, however, since Manoa will always remain a rather distant cousin of his "plainly half-comic" predecessor. But an awareness of Aeschylus' intentions in Oceanus obliges us to inquire more closely into Milton's aims in Manoa. The first speech of Manoa (340–72) emotionally contrasts his erstwhile great expectations concerning Samson and his present shattering disappointment over the actual turn of events. Presently Manoa even threatens to induce despair by questioning divine justice; and as Samson is spontaneously driven to defend the ways of God, the roles are abruptly switched. The one who should have been comforted is now himself the comforter:

> Appoint not heavenly disposition, father.
> Nothing of all these evils hath befallen me
> But justly.   (373–75)

Samson who is eyeless will eventually gain spiritual vision, but Manoa who possesses eyesight will remain utterly blind to the end. Pointedly he is made to carry the burden of the playwright's dramatic irony, anticipating the final outcome even as he himself is incapable of perceiving it. For instance:

> God,
> Nothing more certain, will not long defer
> To vindicate the glory of his name
> Against all competition, nor will long
> Endure it doubtful whether God be Lord,
> Or Dagon. But for thee what shall be done?   (473–78)

Just as the initial affirmation here forecasts the play's actual resolution, so the final question—emphatically induced by the dichotomizing "But"—proclaims the impossibility that sealed eyes such as Manoa's can ever be made to see. A prisoner of his senses, Manoa credits only what he can see or touch or feel, whether in commending the "friends" in the Chorus who are in fact Samson's most dangerous enemies, or in prosecuting his plan to free his son through "ransom"—the very word which, in its theological context, pertains solely to the redemption of man by God. Samson's death is an occasion for Manoa contentedly to observe that his son is "on his enemies / Fully revenged" (1171–72); and as his blindness persists, he voices Milton's crowning instance of dramatic irony in the play by asking that the "heroic" Samson be carried to "his father's house" (1733). But "heroism" involves much more than the slaughter of one's enemies, just as "Father" has more than the single point of reference upheld by Manoa.[35]

The comic element in Manoa, it might be said, centers on the discrepancy between his own immobility and the onward movement of the world about him. What might in that case be ventured of the Chorus whose movement is less an arrested than a regressive one?[36] In the previous paragraph I proposed that the "friends" who constitute the Chorus are Samson's most dangerous enemies; nor would I, now, wish that premise to be dismissed lightly. The Chorus—"one of the actors"—is as highly individualized by Milton as it was by Sophocles. But the personality that emerges is meant to generate considerable disquiet, generously confirmed as it is by echoes of the Book of Job where the three "friends" militantly espouse a patently mistaken view of divine providence. The pattern in *Samson Agonistes* is most obvious in that extraordinary choral song which misleads precisely because it echoes the ambition of *Paradise Lost* to justify the ways of God to man: "Just are the ways of God, / And justifiable to men" (293–94). But it is assuredly an error to equate an epic's invocation with a play's manifestly dramatic speech. As Milton himself observed on another occasion,

> we must not regard the poet's words as his own, but consider who it is that speaks in the play, and what that person says; for different persons are introduced, sometimes good, sometimes bad, sometimes wise men, sometimes fools, and they speak not always the poet's opinion, but what is most fitting to each character.[37]

That which is "most fitting" to the Chorus in *Samson Agonistes* becomes apparent in the stunning affirmation that the universe is under the control of an alarmingly authoritarian and capricious deity,

> Who made our laws to bind us, not himself,
> And hath full right to exempt
> Whom so it pleases him by choice
> From national obstriction, without taint
> Of sin, or legal debt;
> For with his own laws he can best dispense.   (309–14)

The speech can hardly be claimed to carry the approval of Milton whose own efforts were, throughout his life, a relentless attack on the sinister theory propounded here. The Chorus is permitted to sustain it because each of the play's *dramatis personae* is individualized largely in terms of his (or her) attitude to divinity, whether

positive as it is in most cases, or strictly negative as it is in the case of
Dalila. But should the implications of the speech not register on us,
Milton has other means to mark the vulgarity of the "friends." These
means are partly thematic, as in the Chorus's omnipresent and
vicious antifeminism,[38] and partly poetic—thus:

> God of our fathers, what is man!
> That thou towards him with hand so various,
> *Or might I say contrarious,*
> Temper'st thy providence through his short course.   (667–70)

It requires total insensitivity to poetry not to see that the line here
italicized constitutes an arrant deviation from the most basic canons
of poetic articulation; yet it is an insensitivity that the Chorus clearly
possesses. I darkly suspect, indeed, that the Chorus would have
responded with equal enthusiasm to Mrs. Browning's improbable
lines: "Will you oftly / Murmur softly?" But in time the Chorus's
regressive movement is inverted, bent toward that superb bene-
diction that marks a novel dimension in its experience:

> Go, and the Holy One
> Of Israel be thy guide
> To what may serve his glory best.   (1427–29)

Where *The Iliad* predicates a "nursery-rhyme Zeus" who is yet
"the supreme and awful sovereign of all the universe," and *The
Bacchae* maintains as much in connection with Dionysus, *Samson
Agonistes* reflects explicitly through its Chorus what is implicit in its
protagonist: a gradual transition from risible vulgarities to the noble
conception of a mysterious universe under the control of "th'
unsearchable dispose of Highest Wisdom" (1746–47). The comic
dimension is not thereby negated, however. It continues to illumine
the human condition in that our follies—the greed exposed in
Oedipus at Colonus, the martial endeavors condemned in *Helen,* the
self-confidence of inconsequential man denounced in *The Bacchae,*
the vulgarity of presumption censured in *Samson Agonistes*—such
follies are best perceived through laughter. But laughter, as Henry
More the Cambridge Platonist pointed out, is itself the gift of God,

whose Gayete and Festivity is also so conspicuous in endowing us with that
passion or property of Laughter, to entertain those lighter miscarriages with,
whether in manners or fortune: As if Providence look'd upon her bringing
Man into the World as a Spectatour of a Tragick-Comedy.[39]

Samson Agonistes sidesteps explicitness in that it is not a treatise but a dramatic poem. Yet it embraces the self-same mystery which a later poet also perceived when he wrote that "constellations indeed / Sing of some hilarity beyond / All liking and happening."[40]

University of York, England

NOTES

Editor's Note: This essay's occasionally unconventional punctuation represents the author's intentions.

1. On Marlowe, see Robert Ornstein, "The Comic Synthesis in *Doctor Faustus*," *ELH*, XXII (1955), 165–72; John H. Crabtree, "The Comedy in Marlowe's *Doctor Faustus*," *Furman Studies*, IX (1961), i, 1–9; Gerald Morgan, "Harlequin Faustus: Marlowe's Comedy of Hell," *Humanities Association Bulletin* (Canada), XVIII (1967), i, 22–34; Donna Bobin, "Marlowe's Humor," *Massachusetts Studies in English*, II (1969), 29–40; and others. On Shakespeare, see G. Wilson Knight, "Lear and the Comedy of the Grotesque," in his *Wheel of Fire* (London, 1930), chap. 9; Robert A. Watts, "The Comic Scenes in *Othello*," *Shakespeare Quarterly*, XIX (1968), 349–54; J. L. Simmons, "The Comic Pattern and Vision in *Antony and Cleopatra*," *ELH*, XXXVI (1969), 493–510; William E. Sheriff, "The Grotesque Comedy of *Richard III*," *Studies in the Literary Imagination*, V (1972), 51–64; Harry Epstein, "The Divine Comedy of *The Tempest*," *Shakespeare Studies*, VIII (1975), 279–96; and others.

2. "*Paradise Lost* and the Language of Theology," in *Bright Essence*, by W. B. Hunter, J. H. Adamson, and myself (Salt Lake City, 1971), pp. 165–78; also, "Milton and the Arian Controversy," *Proceedings of the American Philosophical Society*, CXX (1976), 245–52.

3. See Arnold Stein, *Answerable Style* (Minneapolis, 1953), pp. 19 ff., 45 ff., and passim; Roy Daniells, "Humour in Paradise Lost," *Dalhousie Review*, XXXIII (1953), 159–66; Carolyn Herbert, "Comic Elements in the Scenes of Hell in *Paradise Lost*," *Renaissance Papers*, 1956, pp. 92–101; Gregory Ziegelmaier, "The Comedy of *Paradise Lost*," *College English*, XXVI (1965), 516–22; Joseph H. Summers, *The Muse's Method* (London, 1962), pp. 46 ff.; and others.

4. See W. B. C. Watkins, "Spenser's High Comedy," in his *Shakespeare and Spenser* (Princeton, 1950), app. 1; Robert O. Evans, "Spenserian Humor: *Faerie Queene* III and IV," *Neophilologische Mitteilungen*, LX (1959), 288–99; John M. Hill, "Braggadocchio and Spenser's Golden World Concept: The Function of Unregenerative Comedy," *ELH*, XXXVII (1970), 315–24; James V. Holleran, "A View of Comedy in *The Faerie Queene*," in *Essays in Honor of E. L. Marilla* (Baton Rouge, 1970), pp. 101–14; Clyde G. Wade, "Comedy in Book VI of *The Faerie Queene*," *Arlington Quarterly*, 2 (1970), iv, 90–104; Linwood E. Orange, " 'All Bent to Mirth'; Spenser's Humorous Wordplay," *South Atlantic Quarterly*, LXXI (1972), 539–47; William Nelson, "Spenser's 'ludens'," in *A Theatre for Spenserians*, ed. Judith M. Kennedy and James A. Reither (Toronto and Manchester, 1973), pp. 83–100; and others.

5. *Iliad*, III, 209–11; here quoted in the paraphrase by W. F. Jackson Knight,

Greek Tragedy and Samson Agonistes 19

Many-sided Homer (London, 1968), p. 156. Pope's version obliterates the point altogether: "Erect, the Spartan most engaged our view; / Ulysses seated, greater reverence drew." But even Richmond Lattimore's responsible version (1951) falters here: "when these . . . stood up, Menelaos was bigger by his broad shoulders / but Odysseus was the more lordly when both were seated."

6. Knight, *Many-sided Homer,* pp. 114–15.

7. Rachel Bespaloff, "The Comedy of the Gods," in her *On the Iliad,* trans. Mary McCarthy (New York, 1947; rpt. ed., New York, 1962), pp. 71–79.

8. Ibid., pp. 75–76.

9. Gilbert Murray, *Aeschylus: The Creator of Tragedy* (Oxford, 1940), pp. 146–47. Fragments survive from six of these plays: *The Heralds* and *The Lion* (subjects unknown); *Proteus, Prometheus the Fire-kindler,* and *The Sphinx* (the satyr-plays annexed to the trilogies of *The Oresteia, The Prometheia,* and *The Oedipodeia,* respectively); and *Lycurgus* (the satyr-play of the lost trilogy centered on Lycurgus). See *Aeschylus,* ed. Herbert W. Smyth, Loeb Classical Library ed., (Cambridge, Mass., 1926), II, 419, 420, 453–54, 455, 460–61.

10. Translated by Roger L. Green in *Two Satyr Plays* (Harmondsworth, Eng., 1957). The Sophoclean satyr-play was first published in 1912; but the Euripidean one was extant during the Renaissance (see *inter alia* the Latin version by Melanchthon), and had been studied by Milton (see his marginal notes on it in *Works of John Milton,* ed. Frank Allen Patterson et al. [New York, 1931–38], vol. XVIII, pp. 314–15).

11. From Green's introduction to *Two Satyr Plays,* p. 11. For a useful glance at satyr-plays, see Peter D. Arnott, *An Introduction to the Greek Theatre* (New York and Bloomington, Ind., 1963), chap. 7.

12. "Obviously," warns Gilbert Murray nervously, "the phrase is figurative"! (*Aeschylus,* p. 147).

13. H. D. F. Kitto, *Greek Tragedy* (New York, 1955), p. 118.

14. A "mad cow" at that! (Letter to the Rev. William Mason, January 24, 1778, in *The Letters of Horace Walpole,* ed. Peter Cunningham [Edinburgh, 1906], vol. VII, p. 24). I am grateful to Professor Allen T. Hazen for his assistance in locating this reference.

15. E. T. Owen, *The Harmony of Aeschylus* (Toronto, 1952), p. 58.

16. Lowell, *Prometheus Bound* (London, 1970), p. 12.

17. Jonson, in a marginal note to his *Masque of Blacknesse,* reminds us of still another possibility: "The ancients induc'd *Oceanus* alwayes with a Bulls head" (*Ben Jonson,* ed. C. H. Herford, Percy and Evelyn Simpson [Oxford, 1941], vol. VII, p. 170).

18. *Prometheus Bound,* 381–83, trans. David Grene, in *The Complete Greek Tragedies,* ed. David Grene and Richmond Lattimore (Chicago, 1956), *Aeschylus: II,* p. 153.

19. George Thomson, *Aeschylus and Athens: A Study in the Social Origins of Drama,* 3d ed. (London, 1966), pp. 222–23. I owe this reference to Mr. Michael Moschos.

20. *Poetics,* chap. XVIII, trans. Preston H. Epps (Chapel Hill, N.C., 1942), p. 37.

21. *Antigone,* 223–31, trans. Elizabeth Wyckoff, in *The Complete Greek Tragedies* (1954), *Sophocles: I,* p. 166.

22. Ibid., 315–20.

23. Jan Kott, *The Eating of the Gods: An Interpretation of Greek Tragedy,* trans. B. Taborski and E. J. Czerwinski (New York, 1974), p. 91. Kott's study is often amusing, in spite (or rather because) of his great expectations. It is otherwise "tire-

some, silly and pretentious" (Hugh Lloyd-Jones in *Times Literary Supplement*, November 29, 1974, p. 1330).

24. *Alcestis*, 747–50, trans. Richmond Lattimore, in *The Complete Greek Tragedies* (1955), *Euripides: I*, p. 37.

25. In *Poetry and Drama* (London, 1951), p. 31. See also his further remarks on "my Greek originals"—especially *Alcestis*—in *Writers at Work: The "Paris Review" Interviews*, 2d ser., intro. by Van Wyck Brooks (1965), p. 103.

26. *The Heraclidae*, 727–40, trans. Ralph Gladstone, in *The Complete Greek Tragedies* (1955), *Euripides: I*, p. 144.

27. H. D. F. Kitto, *Greek Tragedy* (New York, 1955), p. 328.

28. *Helen*, 362–73, trans. Richmond Lattimore, in *The Complete Greek Tragedies* (1956), *Euripides: II*, p. 205.

29. The connection between Aristophanes and Euripides could be extended to encompass Aeschylus whose *Pentheus* (now lost) had anticipated the Dionysus-centered story of *The Bacchae*. Cf. the reference in *The Eumenides* to Dionysus who "in divine form . . . led his Bacchanals in arms / to hunt down Pentheus like a hare in a deathtrap" (25–26, trans. Richmond Lattimore, in *The Complete Greek Tragedies* [1953], *Aeschylus: I*, pp. 135–36).

30. On Sophocles, see Martin Mueller, "Time and Redemption in *Samson Agonistes* and *Iphigenie auf Tauris*," *University of Toronto Quarterly*, XLI (1972), 227–45. Earlier, William R. Parker in *Milton's Debt to Greek Tragedy in 'Samson Agonistes'* (Baltimore, 1937), chap. 17, was concerned to establish that Milton's play "most resembles" *Oedipus at Colonus* in technical details and mere parallels. Neither critic appears cognizant of the comic dimension in the Sophoclean play noted earlier (pp. 10–11). On Euripides, see Carole S. Kessner, in "Milton's Hebraic Herculean Hero," in *Milton Studies*, VI, ed. James D. Simmonds (Pittsburgh, 1974), pp. 243–58, who detects the "substance and spirit" of *Samson Agonistes* in *Heracles*, but gingerly bypasses several fundamental and diametrically opposed aspects of the two plays, i.e., that Samson is not annihilated by his experience as Heracles is, that the brutality of Euripides is not even distantly matched by Milton, that the resolution in *Heracles* centers largely on a merely human agent (Theseus), and so on.

31. It is perhaps necessary to remind ourselves that Milton's respect for Euripides is well attested: see Philip W. Timberlake, "Milton and Euripides," in *The Parrott Presentation Volume*, ed. Hardin Craig (New York, 1935), pp. 315–40. But the evidence should be interpreted cautiously since Milton's favorable comments on Euripides on several occasions and in diverse contexts do not preclude his equal respect for Aeschylus and Sophocles when he came to write a play himself.

32. Nancy D. Libbey, "Milton's Harapha," *South Atlantic Quarterly*, LXXI (1972), 521–29.

33. As D. C. Boughner conclusively demonstrated in "Milton's Harapha and Renaissance Comedy," *ELH*, XI (1944), 297–306.

34. Parker, *Milton's Debt*, chap. 9, remarks that Oceanus may not be ignored as "a possible parallel" since his part in *Prometheus Bound* is "too strikingly like that of Manoa." Oceanus' comic dimension, at any rate, is downplayed ("to some readers he appears comic, or at least undignified").

35. Obviously I endorse the reading by Nancy Y. Hoffman in "Samson's Other Father: The Character of Manoa in *Samson Agonistes*," *Milton Studies*, II, ed. James D. Simmonds (Pittsburgh, 1970), pp. 195–210.

36. The ensuing argument, it should be made clear, reflects my respect for John

Huntley's thesis in "A Revaluation of the Chorus' Role in *Samson Agonistes*," *Modern Philology*, LXIV (1966), 132–45. Huntley understood implicitly the practice of the Greek dramatists which is here made explicit.

37. *Pro populo anglicano defensio* (1651); in *Selected Prose*, ed. C. A. Patrides (Harmondsworth, Eng., 1974), p. 363.

38. The most decisive claim of the Chorus reads:

> God's universal law
> Gave to the man despotic power
> Over his female in due awe,
> Nor from that right to part an hour,
> Smile she or lour. (1053–57)

I admit to a lack of patience with those who detect here Milton's own voice. They have clearly never read his humane treatise *The Doctrine and Discipline of Divorce*, nor understood the presentation of Eve in *Paradise Lost*. Their reading is probably confined to the irrelevant novel by Robert Graves, *Wife to Mr. Milton* (London, 1943).

39. *Divine Dialogues* (London, 1668), vol. I, p. 180. Cf. his *Antidote against Atheism* (1653): "if we could pierce to the utmost *Catastrophe* of things, all might prove but a *Tragick-Comedy*" (in *The Cambridge Platonists*, ed. C. A. Patrides [London and Cambridge, Mass., 1969], p. 269).

40. W. H. Auden, *Horae canonicae:* "Compline."

MULTIPLE PERSPECTIVES IN *SAMSON AGONISTES:* CRITICAL ATTITUDES TOWARD DALILA

John B. Mason

A N EXAMINATION of Dalila's character in Milton's *Samson Agonistes* proceeds in spite of warnings from two of the play's critics. A. S. P. Woodhouse maintains that Dalila's motives are left deliberately obscure by Milton. "They do not matter: she is there for the sake of Samson and the action, not in her own right."[1] Merritt Hughes maintains that Dalila is not supposed to be any more interesting than Cecil de Mille made her and that serious consideration of Dalila's motives is merely the self-indulgence of modern psychological criticism.[2] Woodhouse and Hughes may be underestimating Milton's ability in characterization. The interest in Dalila shown by nearly all of *Samson*'s critics may be a reflection more of Milton's expertise in creating characters than of a modern sensibility. Most critics cannot easily dismiss Dalila. In attempting to clarify her motives they risk placing emphasis where it is not due; Dalila is certainly not the central character in *Samson Agonistes*. In their studies of Dalila, however, the critics are also responding naturally to Milton's invitation. Though Dalila's motives may be secondary to Samson's reactions to her, her motives seem to invite explanation from the reader.

Regarding Dalila's motives, Stanley Fish explains, "One can't help wondering, and wonder is finally a large part of *our* response to the scene [Dalila's encounter with Samson] and to the entire play."[3] How one responds to Milton's invitation and interprets Dalila's motives, in fact, influences one's interpretation of Samson's character and the play's theme. Woodhouse and Hughes insist upon the acceptance of Dalila as a function of the play's action, but the full significance of the action cannot be understood until one can understand Dalila's character. A. B. Chambers's conclusion that Dalila's character suffers from "malitia" or "a perverse love of causing harm"[4] is both a simplicity and a mistake. Bernard Spivack has successfully shown how futile it is to search for clear motives in Vice characters, even as they exist in late Renaissance drama;[5] but *Samson Agonistes* is not a psychomachia, and Dalila is not a motiveless malignity in search of a motive. The motives behind her actions are numerous. Milton's reader, even more than Samson, is placed in the position of Adam: he must exercise his will and intelligence to identify motive and to distinguish honesty from craft. Honesty, the reader discovers, is not always made of a single substance. Critics of Dalila too often misread the character and the entire play because they insist upon isolating *the* Dalila. There are three Dalilas in *Samson Agonistes*, each of whom must be recognized by the reader to understand Dalila's role in the action and theme of the play.

How readers view Dalila's motives depends upon whose viewpoint they choose to adopt: that of Samson, the Chorus, or Dalila herself. Most critics of *Samson Agonistes* view Dalila through Samson. Though careful not to let Dalila alone be blamed for his misfortune, Samson is full of condemnation of his mate. She is "that specious Monster," "Traitress," and "Hyaena." Samson's vituperations reflect traditional assessments of Dalila up to Milton's writing of *Samson Agonistes*. According to F. Michael Krouse, "she had a bad name in the tradition which was still alive and intact; she was well known from poem, broadside, and sermon as a deceitful, a treacherous, a dangerously clever sort of woman." This tradition, as Krouse describes it, had centered upon Dalila's betrayal of Samson rather than upon Samson's spiritual growth through his misfortune.[6] For Milton's Samson, however, Dalila's betrayal is not the sum of her character, and the names he calls her are conveniences for him during his outbursts of wounded pride.

Samson finds Dalila's character, not in the act of betrayal itself, but in her motives for the act. He does not place the blame for his fall directly on her: "She was not the prime cause, but I myself."[7] What concerns him about Dalila are the reasons for her treason. His entire conversation with Dalila is a series of reactions to her explanations of her behavior. He counters her interpretations of her motives with his own interpretations, and he has more than a little difficulty in deciding what caused Dalila to betray him. In his opening soliloquy, Samson describes Dalila's methods as those of "importunity and tears" (51). He gives no hint of her motives, however, until he reacts to Manoa's lament for Samson's loss of glory. Then Samson explains that Dalila had been "vitiated with Gold," or at least tempted with it (389–90). In the same speech Samson suggests that Dalila had more complicated motives:

> She sought to make me Traitor to myself;
>
> . . . .
>
> I yielded, and unlock'd her all my heart,
> Who with a grain of manhood well resolv'd
> Might easily have shook off all her snares:
> But foul effeminacy held me yok't
> Her Bondslave.   (401–10)

The suggestion is that Dalila, intentionally or otherwise, managed to rob Samson of his manhood, and his speech reflects the Renaissance view that any man out of character is not himself and cannot be himself until a proper order is restored. Later, when Samson meets Dalila in his cell, he charges her and her countrymen with undermining the natural order of marriage, in which the wife is subservient to the husband:

> Being once a wife, for me thou wast to leave
> Parents and country; nor was I their subject,
> Nor under their protection but my own,
> Thou mine, not theirs: if aught against my life
> Thy country sought of thee, it sought unjustly,
> Against the law of nature.   (884–89)

Samson does not clearly distinguish cause from effect, and he cannot readily identify Dalila's motives for violating natural law. Did she intentionally set out to rob him of his manhood (his "self"), or was his loss of manhood merely precipitated by her betrayal? Samson's strong rejection of Dalila's offer to nurse him suggests that he sees her intentionally threatening his manhood. "How wouldst thou use me now, blind, and thereby / Deceivable, in most things as a child" (941–42). Samson, however, adds other possible explanations of Dalila's motives. He repeats his accusation that gold bought her fidelity (829–31), and he also suggests that she was motivated by her religious dedication: "But zeal mov'd thee; / To please thy gods thou didst it" (895–96).

Critics have been quick to join Samson in condemning Dalila, and most have attempted to isolate a single motivation behind her initial betrayal of Samson and her visit to his cell. John M. Steadman and Thomas Kranidas see Dalila primarily as a threat to Samson's manhood. Steadman argues that Dalila casts herself as both the romantic heroine and the hero: "In her appeal to Samson, she employs many of the conventional lures of the romantic heroine. She offers sensual delight. She employs the conventional language and imagery of courtly love." Cast as the hero, Dalila would usurp

Samson's masculine role and succeed where he failed: she would deliver her country and save her god. "Dalila affects heroic virtue; she plays a role outwardly heroic, but as unnatural as that of the female warrior."[8] Kranidas studies the rhetoric of Dalila's appeal to Samson and concludes that her language shifts from wavering (feminine deviousness) to legalistic and masculine argument.[9] Marcia Landy also studies Dalila's rhetoric and sees that her lines are delivered in the context of martial and militant behavior. Landy concludes that "This dramatizes a reversal of masculine and feminine roles which betokens here . . . an inversion of the proper nature of things."[10]

A few critics have interpreted this role reversal as the outcome of Dalila's hyperactive passion. They see her in the masculine role of the seducer. Don Cameron Allen maintains that Dalila's contrition and remorse are real, but that her "real impulsion" is lechery. He holds that Dalila goes into a rage, not when Samson rejects her proposal to nurse him, but when he rejects her physical contact. "For a wife or mistress this must be the ultimate insult."[11] Charles Mitchell proposes that Dalila returns to Samson after his fall because she regards him as a sexual athlete, one who could satisfy her great appetite.[12] Kranidas risks being offensive and concludes that Dalila "had never treated Samson himself as more than an object, at best a valuable stud whose mountings were to be controlled by his mistress."[13] Kranidas and the other critics who emphasize Dalila's masculinity can easily find support for their interpretations, but most of the support is gathered as the critics view Dalila through Samson. Samson at times suggests that she is a threat to his manhood, but to accept her as only an Amazon is to ignore the fact that Samson himself is often unsure of her motives. Unsure of why Dalila would visit him in his cell, he presumptuously concludes that "God sent her to debase me, / And aggravate my folly" (999–1000). To accept only Samson's accounts of Dalila's motives is also to ignore the other views of the character offered in the play.

Few modern critics have chosen to accept the Chorus's assessment of Dalila. Eager to free Milton from charges of misogyny, many critics note that the Chorus delivers a diatribe against women in general (1010–60), while Samson limits his condemnation to Dalila and "every woman false like thee" (749). William Riley Parker completely frees Milton from the charge of misogyny by illustrating that the Chorus is modeled after the Sophoclean chorus. It is excluded from any real share in the action and is "far from ideal in its character in the dialogue." The words of the Chorus, explains Parker, are not gratuitous opinions interjected by the poet, but expressions of sympathy for the protagonist.[14] Because the Chorus is so sympathetic to Samson, its viewpoint is often Samson's—or what it assumes to be Samson's.

The Chorus's catering to Samson's emotional state is most clearly seen in its reaction to Dalila. When Dalila enters Samson's cell, the Chorus is awed. What comedy there is in the description of Dalila's entrance falls on the Chorus, because the Chorus is impressed, not amused, at the picture Dalila presents. She may have her "Sails fill'd, and streamers waving, / Courted by all the winds that hold them play" (718–19), but her entrance is something more than comic. As Kranidas explains, "The high comic color of the Chorus' remarks modifies but does not obviate the efficiency and thrust of her entry."[15] Dalila has come on serious business, and if she enters like a ship, the ship is "stately" (714). The Chorus's very choice of the naval imagery reflects its sympathy for Samson, who earlier described himself to the Chorus as one "Who like a foolish Pilot have shipwreck't / My Vessel trusted to me from above, / Gloriously rigg'd" (198–200). If Samson is a floundered vessel, Dalila, reasons the Chorus, must be a powerful battleship.

The extent of the Chorus's sympathy with Samson is also evidenced by the fact that the Chorus begins its elaborate condemnation of women only after Samson has assured it that his disagreement with Dalila goes beyond that of a lover's quarrel (1008–09). Even as the Chorus concludes its ode and chides Samson too for his failure to fulfill his role in marriage (1054–60), it is echoing Samson's earlier self-condemnation: "She was not the prime cause, but I myself, / Who vanquisht with a peal of words (O weakness!) / Gave up my fort of silence to a Woman" (234–36). The function of the Chorus, then, is not to evaluate character (or situation) but to echo and sometimes exaggerate the character evaluations it hears. The Chorus's propensity for exaggeration leads it from a condemnation of Dalila (997–98), to its ode condemning all women, to its comparison of Samson to the Phoenix, in legend a hermaphroditic creature.[16] Other aspects of the Phoenix legend are, of course, more central to the Chorus's presentation of Samson as the regenerated hero, but to the end of the play the Chorus continues what it assumes to be Samson's attitude toward women—that one would be much better off without them.

The Chorus's exaggerations serve a double function: they offer to Samson easy ways for him to avoid his mental struggle with his own guilt, and they call into doubt the character assessments which are exaggerated. If the Chorus, out of its sympathy for the hero, is tempting Samson with an easy morality (women are the Fall of Mankind), the poet may be tempting the reader to accept the Chorus's view and sympathize too strongly with Samson. Samson has been wronged by Dalila, but the poet is careful to present also a case for Dalila, lest one read into the play a simple dichotomy of good and evil.

Only a few critics have sympathized with Dalila. Fifty years ago James Waddell Tupper initiated a "defense" for Dalila by concluding that "The very fact that Dalila should betake herself to the prison where Samson is confined and beg his forgiveness when the other Philistines are celebrating the victory of Dagon should predispose us in her favor."[17] Tupper could not account for this favorable presentation of Dalila, and he suggested that Milton tried to depict her as a hypocrite but did not succeed.

Only in the last few years have critics searched for detailed evidence which might show that Milton was not simply relating the traditional view of Dalila as evil incarnate. Don Cameron Allen suggests that Dalila was overwhelmed by the prestige of princes, by church and state, and consequently betrayed Samson. Allen maintains that "the fragile resistance of her slender intelligence collapsed," and that the reader should grant Dalila "a little chivalrous indulgence."[18] His suggestion is dangerous. To grant Dalila "chivalrous indulgence" is to accept only one of Dalila's explanations for her act, that she was duped by Philistine power. Even Samson refuses to attribute Dalila's frailty solely to her sex. Dalila does hide behind her sex in one of her many attempts to defend her betrayal of Samson:

> it was a weakness
> In me, but incident to all our sex,
> Curiosity, inquisitive, importune
> Of secrets, then with like infirmity
> To publish them, both common female faults.   (773–77)

Samson, however, will not accept her explanation: "Weakness is thy excuse, / And I believe it, weakness to resist / *Philistian* gold" (829–31). Samson knows better than to attribute Dalila's actions to feminine weakness, but he is not sure what her exact motives have been. Avarice is only one of the possibilities he proposes.

Two critics have sought explanations for Dalila's motives without viewing her as either an Amazon or a half-wit. William Empson and Virginia Mollenkott see Dalila as a self-sufficient, intelligent woman. They do not attempt to defend her betrayal of Samson, but they attempt to show that, from her own point of view, her actions are the results of sensible and even admirable motives. While other critics have found satanic logic in Dalila's arguments to Samson, Empson has found in the same lines "one of the noblest speeches in Milton." Says Empson, "A similar attempt to prevent the division of India single-handed would perhaps be the nearest modern parallel." Empson sees nothing sinister in any of Dalila's arguments or in her offer to nurse Samson: "I need not deny that on her own account she has sounded at times a bit insinuating; so would most of us when trying to make contact with a dangerous lunatic, and it is fairly creditable to get through, as she did as far as we learn, without telling any lies."[19] Empson does not attempt to prove Samson is a nihilist and a lunatic; he merely suggests that Samson could appear as only that to Dalila. From her own point of view, Samson threatened the state and her religion. Moreover, Samson, according to his own account of his history, had married Dalila so he could murder her relatives. Despite Empson's exaggerated parallels between the world of *Samson Agonistes* and the world of modern politics, he does make a good case for Dalila, not as a noble character, but as a real one. Empson's thesis, that Milton created a paradoxical Dalila because he had lost a belief in heaven and a fear of hell, is puzzling and eccentric. One need not agree with Empson's thesis, however, to agree that Dalila can be viewed from more than one angle.

Mollenkott suggests that Milton was "too good a psychologist to deal with humanity in absolute terms." She maintains that Milton's absolutism is manifested only when the play's conflict reaches the level of God versus Dagon. On the level of human interaction, "Milton is placing an unusually modern emphasis upon the partial validity of everybody's point of view."[20] Mollenkott points to the multiple perspectives in *Samson Agonistes*, but she is too involved in describing Dalila's viewpoint to explore the reason for the presence of those many perspectives or their effect upon the reader. Her approach is somewhat like Empson's in that she attempts to determine Dalila's point of view by an analysis of the character's motives, and to determine the character's motives by a process of elimination. She agrees with Empson that Dalila cannot be trying to trap Samson, since he is no longer a danger to her. She dismisses the possibility that Samson's attractiveness draws Dalila to possess him. Dalila could, supposes the critic, find other attractive men. Mollenkott also dismisses Kranidas's theory that Dalila is motivated by a desire for glory. "Kranidas does not explain what glory accrues from nursing the worn-out hero of an enemy nation."[21] Mollenkott interprets Dalila's claim to glory as the face-saving device of a woman whose every advance has been scorned.

One can never be sure that Mollenkott uncovers Dalila's real motives simply because she succeeds in showing what Dalila's motives cannot be. She does introduce, however, a Dalila who is often overlooked, and she provides a valuable explanation of why Milton raised Dalila's moral stature above contemporary estimates of her. Mollenkott notes that in the *Cursor Mundi* (ca. 1320), Dalila remarried after Samson's blinding and that at her wedding to a Philistine Samson pulled down the building.[22] Milton, however, has Dalila remain faithful to Samson when she has no apparent need to. Milton also alters another tradition in the Samson stories by making Dalila Samson's wife rather than his concubine. This elevation of character, as Merritt Hughes maintains, stresses the depth of Dalila's treason,[23] but it also gives more strength to Dalila's own point of view. As Samson's wife, she is entitled to better treatment than to be used as Samson's means of destroying her nation and family.

Kranidas's contention that Dalila abuses her marriage by treating Samson as an object (to satisfy her lust) directly counters Mollenkott's contention that Samson abuses his marriage by treating Dalila as an object (to overcome her nation). Both contentions may be partially valid. The issues of lust and revolution, however, are not in themselves important. What is important is that Milton presents a "nonmarriage" in which both partners are incapable of accepting each other and communicating with each other. That Milton is on Samson's side in no way invalidates the picture the poet presents of an impossible relationship, and the reader is invited to look at the picture from several perspectives.

Samson can no more understand Dalila's values than she can understand his. In their scene together, both pose a number of questions for each other; but they consistently answer their own questions, and the reader is encouraged to question those answers and to suspend identification with either character. Dalila tries in every conceivable way to reach Samson on a verbal level, but he will not, or rather cannot, listen. The communication which concerns Samson is not that between a man and a woman. Samson's last words before Dalila's entrance are concerned with his despair, his "sense of Heav'n's desertion" (632). In his despair he longs for death, and he pleads that his prayer be heard (648–51). Dalila enters at that point when Samson is least sure of his ability to reestablish communication with God. As Marcia Landy explains, Dalila's expertise with language is not so much an indication of a satanic character as it is an indication that she approaches all problems on a verbal level. Landy maintains that "language for Dalila, in her commitment to Dagon and the Philistines, is reality, because her god is a temporal, historical entity." When one verbal approach with Samson fails, she tries another: "Dalila's rhetoric . . . seeks to convince not only by 'cunning' but also by the sheer weight of verbiage and sound which assault Samson and the reader."[24] Dalila's final eruption of anger is, in part, the result of her failure to bring Samson to her level of communication: "I see thou art implacable, more deaf / To prayers, than winds and seas" (960–61). Her complaint is not unlike that of Samson before her entrance; he too felt that his prayers were in vain. But he is waiting for a spiritual sign, she for a physical or verbal one.

Their only common verbal ground concerns reputation, probably the least stable and least meaningful of all verbal levels. He tells her that his misfortune will make him "to Ages an example" (765) and that her betrayal will make her an example of faithlessness (955–57). Dalila defends her reputation, insisting that fame is relative and that she will be known as a heroine among her people (982–83). The entire play, from one point of view, is a record of Samson's mental struggle to overcome his pride, his self-pity, and his presumptuous nature (presuming to predict God's will). Dalila enters at that stage of his development when he is still regarding reputation as a meaningful measurement of one's worth. But he is already on the path toward a nonverbal language in which he responds with action to an inner voice. Near the beginning of the play, Samson tells the Chorus, "I learn / Now of my own experience, not by talk" (187–88). Throughout his debate with Dalila one senses not so much his hatred for her as his desire that she just be quiet and leave. If the reader is tempted to sympathize with Dalila, it is not so much because Samson appears unforgiving and priggish, but because the reader too cannot share in Samson's inner struggle toward a nonverbal level. He can only witness and wait for a sign from Samson. From Dalila's point of view, if Samson were only less headstrong, she could get him home, where they could forgive and forget. She cannot reach him, but her plight can reach the reader, whose sympathies cannot be directed solely toward Samson. To sympathize or empathize solely with Samson, one would have to be as uncritical and unimaginative as the Chorus.

Milton invites the reader to use his imagination, to propose possible explanations of a wife's betrayal of her husband and a husband's intractability. Dramatically, this exercise engages the reader while Samson's inner struggle takes place "offstage." Throughout the scene between Samson and Dalila, Samson waits, Dalila waits, and the reader waits—all for different things. But the pace is quick, because each, even as he waits, is involved in frantic activity. Samson struggles to hear an inner voice despite Dalila's eloquent yet loud rantings. Dalila struggles to get Samson's forgiveness, or at least his attention. The reader struggles to make sense of a conversation that is not really conversation at all, because the two participants are speaking from vaguely defined motives and different value systems.

Dalila is not the hero of *Samson Agonistes,* but she is more than just Samson's means of rejecting lust, effeminacy, and ease. Milton provides for three ways of viewing the character. From Samson's point of view she is a confusion, something alien to him and to the mental struggle which has engaged him. As he grows spiritually away from the concerns of vanity and reputation, he has less and less connection to her. From the Chorus's exaggerated point of view, she is impressive but also evil. From her own point of view, she is forgiving, loyal, and sensible. Most of *Samson*'s critics adopt either Samson's or Dalila's point of view, and they are responding to alternatives made possible in the play. But to accept only one view of Dalila is to miss what Milton has to say about human communication: between people of contradictory systems of value, genuine communication is impossible. To accept only one view of Dalila is also to miss a certain richness in the play and to avoid the challenge that Milton presents to his readers. Milton would have his readers become, like Samson, heroes of action, not through the simple rejection of personified evil, but through the discovery of the multiple perspectives that we must assume to exercise our judgment and imagination.

Youngstown State University

NOTES

1. "Tragic Effect in *Samson Agonistes,*" *University of Toronto Quarterly,* XXVIII (1958–59), reprinted in *Milton: Modern Essays in Criticism,* ed. Arthur E. Barker (New York, 1965), p. 453.

2. See Merritt Y. Hughes's introduction to *Samson Agonistes* in his edition, *John Milton: Complete Poems and Major Prose* (New York, 1957), pp. 532–34.

3. "Question and Answer in *Samson Agonistes*," *Critical Quarterly*, XI (1969), 244.

4. "Wisdom and Fortitude in *Samson Agonistes*," *PMLA*, LXXVIII (1963), 318.

5. *Shakespeare and the Allegory of Evil* (New York, 1958).

6. *Milton's Samson and the Christian Tradition* (Princeton, 1949), pp. 102, 103.

7. *Complete Poems and Major Prose*, ed. Hughes, p. 557, l. 234. Further references are by line number and refer to this edition.

8. *Milton and the Renaissance Hero* (Oxford, 1967), pp. 133, 135.

9. "Dalila's Role in *Samson Agonistes*," *SEL*, VI (1966), 128.

10. "Language and the Seal of Silence in *Samson Agonistes*," in *Milton Studies*, II, ed. James D. Simmonds (Pittsburgh, 1970), p. 185.

11. *The Harmonious Vision: Studies in Milton's Poetry*, enl. ed. (Baltimore, 1970), pp. 88, 90.

12. "Dalila's Return: The Importance of Pardon," *College English*, XXVI (1965), 616.

13. "Dalila's Role," p. 134.

14. *Milton's Debt to Greek Tragedy in "Samson Agonistes"* (Baltimore, 1937), pp. 130, 131.

15. "Dalila's Role," p. 127.

16. See Dayton Haskin, "Divorce as a Path to Union with God in *Samson Agonistes*," *ELH*, XXXVIII (1971), 373–74.

17. "The Dramatic Structure of *Samson Agonistes*," *PMLA*, XXXV (1920), 381.

18. *The Harmonious Vision*, p. 89.

19. *Milton's God* (London, 1961), pp. 221, 223–24.

20. "Relativism in *Samson Agonistes*," *Studies in Philology*, LXVII (1970), 89, 91.

21. Ibid., p. 96.

22. Ibid., pp. 94–95.

23. Introduction to *Samson Agonistes*, p. 534.

24. "Language and the Seal of Silence," pp. 185, 187.

THREE MUSES AND A POET:
A PERSPECTIVE
ON MILTON'S EPIC THOUGHT

E. R. Gregory

I N HIS *Considerations on Milton's Early Reading*, Charles Dunster wrote that "while neither Calliope, nor Clio, could aspire to
the divine sublimity of Urania, the Heavenly Muse in reality united,
with her own native dignity, the sweetness of the one and the powers
of the other."[1] The historical materials do not support Dunster,
suggesting that the relation of Milton's Urania to her sisters was one
of opposition rather than amalgamation. His statement nevertheless
contains an interesting possibility that Miltonists have overlooked—that Milton's use of Urania cannot be understood separately
from the use he made of the other two.

The task posed is difficult, for the muses in Milton involve a
complex tradition that disintegrated long ago. Ernst Robert Curtius
notes that "unlike the Olympians, the Muses had no well-marked
personalities. . . . Their image was vague even in ancient Greece.
From the earliest times there were conflicting traditions as to their
number, lineage, dwelling-place, and function."[2] The confusion
multiplied with the references, so that a late-Renaissance poet like
Milton had at his fingertips a vast array of riches, but jumbled up and
badly in need of sorting.

When the tradition disintegrated, the riches disappeared with
the confusion. The process, which began within forty years of
Milton's death, can be traced in writers from Shaftesbury to
Coleridge.[3] Its conclusion was the muses' embalmment in works
like Bulfinch's *Age of Fable*, where they have remained ever since.
Today's reference works almost all give the same definitions: "Calliope is Muse of the heroic epic, Clio of history . . . Urania of
astronomy."[4]

If we must have definitions, a better set for Milton would be the
following: Calliope, prime and general representative of poetry;
Clio, muse of history as the Renaissance understood it and consequently of fame, glory, and heroic poetry; Urania, muse of divine

35

poetry. This, like the preceding set of definitions, turns the living figures of Milton's art into abstractions. Still, when we observe the results of so distinguished a Miltonist as Douglas Bush assigning to Clio Calliope's function as "prime and general representative of poetry," we have to concede the necessity of definitions. If we use them cautiously, they can illuminate the passages where Milton refers to these muses and the development of his epic thought as well. With regard to the latter, they support those critics who feel that *Paradise Lost* and *Paradise Regain'd* represent not only a clean break with epic tradition in general but also with the epic that he himself originally contemplated writing.

The plan of this article is as follows: (1) to analyze the three interpretations that have been made of Milton's use of Clio: (a) as "prime and general representative of poetry"; (b) as "guardian of lustration"; and (c) as muse of history; (2) to examine in detail Clio as the Renaissance understood her; (3) to examine the pairing of Clio and Urania and what it meant; and (4) to demonstrate the appropriateness of the Urania discussed in this article as a figure in the prologues of *Paradise Lost*. Scholars interested in the aspect of deity addressed by Milton in the prologues will find little of interest here. It can be demonstrated syntactically that two figures are present in the prologues; and once this is done, I shall concentrate on how the muse figure, Urania, epitomizes Milton's authorial concerns as "antiepic" writer.

I. INTERPRETATIONS OF MILTON'S CLIO

In *Elegia quarta* Milton pays tribute to his tutor, Thomas Young, in the following lines: "I first surveyed the Aonian retreats through his guiding, / and the sacred lawns of the twin-peaked mountain, / and the Pierian water I drank, and by favor of Clio, / I thrice moistened my happy lips with pure Castalian wine."[5] In *Ad Patrem* he sums up for his father all the wealth that he possesses as insignificant save that which "golden Clio" has given him: "But notwithstanding, this page exhibits mine, / and I have reckoned up on this paper whatever I possess of abilities, / which to me are insignificant, save those which golden Clio has given, / those which to me slumbers have begotten in the remote cave / and the laurel groves of the sacred wood, Parnassian shadows" (12–16). In *Mansus*, finally, after praising the Marquis of Manso as an "eloquent rival" of Herodotus, Milton salutes him: "Therefore, in the name of Clio and great Apollo, / father Manso, I bid you be well through a long life, / a young pilgrim sent from an Hyperborean clime" (24–26).

"Prime and General Representative of Poetry"

The little that has been done on these passages Douglas Bush collects in his variorum commentary on the Latin poems.[6] If he is correct, the allusions to Clio are simply not significant. Of the passage in *Ad Patrem* he writes that "the context shows that Milton is only naming Clio, in a traditional way, as the prime and general representative of poetry; she had acquired that function because from Hesiod (*Theog.* 77) onward, she commonly came first in lists of the Muses" (p. 241). He makes much the same statement in his notes on *Elegia quarta*, where he cites his evidence: the passage from Hesiod, G. Linocre's *Musarum Libellum*, and some texts of mnemonic verses once attributed to Virgil (p. 84).

In all fairness, Bush's evidence is solid in that the materials he cites were widespread. The passage in the *Theogony* was the *fons et origo* of information about the muses; Linocre's *Musarum Libellum* was often reprinted with Natalis Comes' *Mythologiae,* one of the most popular reference works of the Renaissance; the mnemonic verses were undoubtedly the most widely disseminated piece of information about the muses that the Renaissance possessed.[7] It is true, then, that Clio often, though not invariably, came first in lists of the muses; true even that she and Calliope vied for honors as greatest of the muses. When a general representative was desired, however, Calliope was usually chosen. It was she whom Renaissance dictionaries identified as "the goddesse of Poetrie," she whom Platonic tradition identified as the "totality" of her sisters' efforts. In Thomas Cooper's *Bibliotheca Eliotae,* and later his *Thesaurus,* we find for example the following entry on her: "One of the nine Muses, which excelled all the other in sweetness of voyce. Of some she is taken for the goddess of Rhetoryke: of other for the goddesse of Poetrie."[8] Cooper's entry "E.K.," whoever he was, more or less followed in glossing Calliope's name for *The Shepheardes Calender:* "one of the nine Muses: to whome they assigne the honor of all Poetical Inuention, and the firste glorye of the Heroicall verse. other say, that shee is the Goddesse of Rhetorick: but by Virgile it is manifeste, that they mystake the thyng."[9] He then quotes from the mnemonic verses, which assign rhetoric to Polymnia.

The widespread tradition that linked the muses with the spheres and their music also reinforced Calliope's claim as most representative muse. In Book X of the *Republic,* Plato had stated that each of the heavenly spheres had an attendant siren: "on the upper surface of each circle is a siren, who goes round with them, hymning a single tone or note. The eight together form one harmony."[10] These sirens antiquity sometimes identified with the muses; but since there were nine muses (at least according to the dominant tradition) and only eight spheres, what was to be done with the ninth muse? By the end of antiquity she was generally conceived as representing the harmony that the other eight produced and identified as Calliope. In the late fourth or early fifth century, Macrobius made the whole matter quite clear in his *Commentary on the Dream of Scipio:*

Moreover, cosmogonists have chosen to consider the nine Muses as the tuneful song of the eight spheres and the one predominant harmony that comes from all of them. In the *Theogony*, Hesiod . . . to show that the ninth was the greatest, resulting from the harmony of all sounds together, . . . added: "Calliope, too, who is preeminent among all." The very name shows that the ninth muse was noted for the sweetness of her voice, for Calliope means "best voice." In order to indicate more plainly that her song was the one coming from all the others, he applied to her a word suggesting totality in calling her "preeminent among all."[11]

The tradition that Macrobius has clarified for us persisted during the Renaissance. Comes' *Mythologiae* reproduced the same information (bk. VII, chap. xv), while Macrobius himself was widely read. Erasmus recommended him for study in *De Ratione Studii*.[12] "E.K." alluded to him in the general argument of *The Shepheardes Calender* and may indeed, as W. L. Renwick has written, have "had his Macrobius by him as he wrote."[13] George Sandys listed him among the writers to whom he was indebted in preparing the commentaries that accompanied his translation of Ovid and referred to him specifically in discussing the muses and their spheres, Calliope being "the melody which results from the rest."[14] Singly and together these works reinforced each other. In his *New Discovery of the Old Art of Teaching School*, Charles Hoole listed Sandys' *Ovid* along with Comes and other works as appropriate for inclusion in a school library.[15] We are discussing, then, a widespread tradition, not an isolated author or two.

That Milton was directly familiar with the Platonic passage, we know from the second prolusion.[16] By his day, however, there were generally considered to be nine spheres instead of eight; and this is the number he associates with the sirens or muses in *Arcades*, lines 62–64. Still, when we consider the popularity of writers like Comes and Sandys, we should not be surprised if Milton used Calliope as the most representative of the muses. Although he does not refer to her by name in any of his finished work, a preliminary version of *Lycidas* in the Trinity MS reads:

> what could the golden hayrd Calliope
> for her inchaunting son
> when shee beheld (the gods farre sighted bee)
> his goarie scalpe rowle downe the Thracian lee.

It is instructive to compare this with his final revision:

> What could the Muse her self that *Orpheus* bore,
> The Muse her self for her inchanting son
> Whom universal nature did lament,
> When by the rout that made the hideous roar
> His goary visage down the stream was sent,
> Down the swift *Hebrus* to the *Lesbian* shoar.   (58–63)

His substitution of the general for the specific suggests a view of Calliope as representative, a view that her role as mother of Orpheus the archetypal poet sustains. The sense of the passage, that is, dictates that we identify "the Muse" as the one most nearly capable of patronizing all poetry. With an important caveat, to be examined later, this identification explains Milton's same use of her, again unnamed in *Paradise Lost:* "nor could the Muse defend / Her Son" (VII, 37–38). Which muse? Surely the context suggests that the most representative one is intended.

"Guardian of Lustration"

John T. Shawcross first advanced this interpretation a number of years ago and has repeated it in both his editions of Milton's poetry.[17] From the *Theogony* he noted a reference to the muses as "bestowers of talents"; from Plutarch's *De Pythiae Oraculis*, Simonides' labeling of Clio as "holy guardian of lustration at the muses' shrine at the mountain spring."[18] As guardian of the purification that metaphorically bestowed the muses' gifts, "Clio in her later role as muse of history became the guardian of man's individual history, that is, the guardian of what a man was given and what he was to become because of those talents." Clio's gifts, then, enabled Milton to write poetry at an early age (*Elegia quarta*) and indeed constituted the sum total of his "abilities and capabilities" (*Ad Patrem*).

In his annotations to the minor poems, John Carey referred both to Simonides' fragment and to Shawcross's interpretation, implying a difference of opinion. Shawcross, writes Carey, "thinks Clio . . . 'the personification of man's individual history', but cites no classical precedent. It seems more likely that she is named as guardian of lustration."[19]

Bush rejects this as "abstruse," as in truncated form it is

(*Variorum Commentary*, pp. 85, 242). If we recall, however, that Renaissance historiography far more than modern emphasized the deeds of the individual, the view does not seem nearly so abstruse. In order to see its aptness we need only recall such definitions of history as Jacques Amyot's: "an orderly register of notable things said, done or happened in time past, to mainteyne the continuall remembrance of them, and to serve for the instruction of them to come."[20] Milton's own statement of purpose in his *History of Britain* parallels these words closely: "to relate well and orderly things worth the noting, so as may best instruct and benefit them that read" (YP, V, p. 4). So long as we are careful to remember that Clio was not the guardian of the history of Everyman, but of the few who did heroic deeds or set them down, this interpretation brings us closer to the heart of the matter than Bush's.

Muse of History

A majority of the critics, however, have identified Milton's Clio as the muse of history, though their explanations as to why the muse of history should appear in the passages quoted have not on the whole been very satisfactory. Of *Ad Patrem*, David Masson writes that Milton refers to Clio "inasmuch as what he is to say about his Father is strictly true,"[21] a statement that Walter MacKellar endorsed in his edition of the Latin poems.[22] A. S. P. Woodhouse states rather tentatively that "if the allusion is to historical reading, it reminds us of the enthusiasm for history expressed in Prolusion 7."[23] Milton's allusion, William Riley Parker maintains, refers "to the study of history ('Clio', 14) which Cambridge did not provide but is now possible."[24] Finally, Merritt Y. Hughes states: "If Milton meant anything in particular by referring to Clio, the Muse of history, it was the glory that he hoped to win for himself and his country by writing poetry based on the heroic past of England."[25]

I believe that Milton did indeed mean something in particular by referring to Clio and that the critics' failure properly to identify that something is their failure to come to terms with the Renaissance concept of history or to relate that concept to its most notable mythological embodiment. Certainly if we recall Amyot's or Milton's words, we shall not be surprised to discover that Clio was ubiquitously associated with fame and glory; yet of the statements in the preceding paragraph, only Hughes's even obliquely touches upon this association, and ironically he dropped it from his later edition of Milton's poetry.[26] Once we understand the association, we possess the key to Milton's use of Clio.

II. CLIO, MUSE OF HISTORY, FAME, AND GLORY

From his youth Milton was exposed to a large body of materials that specifically asserted Clio's connection with fame and glory. The reference works known to have been in the library at St. Paul's are unanimòus on the point. The general entry on the muses in Friar Ambrosius Calepinus' *Dictionarium Octo Linguarum* stated: "Primam enim à bonitate vocis dixêre Calliopen. Secundam Clio, à gloria & celebritate rerum gestarum, quas canit: quae eadem Historica dicitur."27 ("The first one, then, they call Calliope from the goodness of her voice. The second one, Clio, from the glory and fame of the warlike exploits of which she sings, which likewise are called history.") He thus draws a connection, as practically all Renaissance mythographers did, between Clio and the Greek word *kleos,* which means fame or glory. In his separate entry for her, Calepinus made another connection explicit: "κλίω, Vuna [*sic*] Musarum ex novem, apud Hesiodum in Theog. ἀπὸ τοῦ κλέους: id est, à gloria, quòd poëtis gloria ex carmine nascatur" ("*klio,* one of the nine muses, in Hesiod's *Theogony apo tou kleous:* that is, glory because glory is born to poets from their songs"). Carolus Stephanus, in the general entry on the muses in his *Dictionarium Historicum ac Poeticum,* used exactly the same words that Friar Calepinus had in his, while in his entry on Clio he repeated Calepinus and added: "Alii ἀπὸ τοῦ κλείειν, hoc est, à celebrando dictam putant, propterea quòd historiæ inuentrix esse putetur: cuius proprium est virorum fortium laudes celebrare, eorúmque gesta ad posteritatem transmittere."28 ("Others claim that the word comes from *apo tou kleiein,* that is, from *celebrando,* especially because she is said to be the inventress of history, of whom it is appropriate to celebrate the praises of brave men and transmit their deeds to posterity.") In his entry for Clio, Robertus Stephanus defined similarly: "Vna ex musis, à gloria & celebritate rerum gestarum quas canit: nomen habet a verbo Græco κλείω, quod est laudo. Vel à nomine Græco, κλεός, quod est gloria, fama."29 ("One of the muses, from the glory and celebration of the deeds she sings: she has her name from the Greek verb, *kleio,* that is, praise, or from the Greek noun, *kleos,* that is, glory, fame.")

Other well-known works of the period tell the same story. In Cesare Ripa's *Iconologia,* for example, we read: "Questa Musa è detta Clio, dalla voce Greca κλέα, che significa lodare, ò dall'altra κλέως, significante gloria, & celebratione delle cose, che ella canta, overo per la gloria, che hanno li Poeti presso gli uomini dotti, come dice Cornuto, come anco per la gloria, che ricevono gl'huomini, che sono celebrate da Poeti."30 ("This muse is called Clio, from the

Greek word *klea*, which means to praise, or from the other *kleōs*, signifying glory and the celebration of the things that she sings, or on account of the glory that the poets have among learned men, as Cornutus says, as also on account of the glory that men receive who are celebrated by the poets.")

Finally, in the tradition that associated the muses with the spheres, Clio's was Mars. The reason Sandys succinctly expressed: "*Clio* of Mars, for the thirst of glory" (p. 248).

As background material these quotations could be greatly augmented, but they suffice to illuminate Milton's thought on Clio, history, and epic writing. Almost unanimously they assert Clio's power to bestow fame and glory not only upon those whose deeds deserve them but also (for Milton most significantly) upon those who record the deeds. No doubt can exist that Milton long believed this, as his own writings show: "worthy deeds are not often destitute of worthy relaters: as by a certain Fate great Acts and great Eloquence have most commonly gon hand in hand, equally and honouring each other in the same Ages";[31] or "indeed from early youth I eagerly pursued studies which impelled me to celebrate, if not to perform the loftiest actions."[32] His celebration would be for the most part in poetry, and that branch of poetry which celebrated the loftiest actions was of course the epic, a genre that belonged at least as much to Calliope as to Clio. At this point, however, it should be clear that the recording of historical material in epic poetry had about it nothing of the eccentric and that associations with Clio were not lacking if the poet wished to develop them.

When Milton wrote *Elegia quarta*, he almost certainly had not decided to become an epic poet. What we need to keep in mind is that the Renaissance educational system stressed "good fame" as one of its rewards. The passage in *Elegia quarta* tells us that in some genuine sense Milton felt that his education began with Thomas Young. Through Young's guidance he first surveyed the Aonian retreats ("Primus ego Aonios illo præeunte recessus / Lustrabam"). The allusion to Clio strengthens the probability that Milton refers here to the commencement of his education. A passage from the sixth-century writer Fulgentius the Mythographer makes clear why and provides yet another link to fame. Identifying the muses as the stages of learning and knowledge, Fulgentius designated Clio as the first step: "First is Clio, standing for the first conception of learning, for *cleos* is the Greek for fame. . . . Since no one seeks knowledge except that by which he may advance the honor of his reputation,

Clio is named first, that is the conception of the search for knowledge."[33] Fulgentius' ideas were picked up by Boccaccio in his *De Genealogiae Deorum gentilium* (bk. XI, chap. ii), whence they passed into the general storehouse of Renaissance mythography. The passage above was reprinted, for example, in Linocre's *Musarum Libellus*, Hyginus' *Fabularum Liber*,[34] and Gyraldus' *De Musis Syntagma*.[35]

There is, then, an aptness in Milton's allusion to Clio. It was Young who introduced Milton to the glories of learning, and perhaps, as Shawcross suggests, to the writing of poetry.[36] It might or might not be some years before he acquired the confidence that he "might perhaps leave something so written to aftertimes as they should not willing let it die,"[37] but the desire to fit himself for such writing was probably already his, as he later indicated. It was a desire attached to concepts of history and serious poetry of which he would become increasingly aware with the passage of years.

At some point awareness turned to the commitment reflected in *Ad Patrem*, where Milton next alludes to Clio. He begins with an admission that his muse's work so far has not been very significant: "Now I long for the Pierian fountains / to whirl their watery paths through my breast and to roll / through my mouth the entire stream released from the twin peaks / so that my Muse, her trifling songs forgotten, might rise / on spirited wings in courtesy of my revered father." The posture that Milton assumes in these lines was *de rigueur* for the poet who felt he had served his apprenticeship and was ready to embark upon his major work. Following now consciously in the footsteps of Spenser and (at a greater distance) Virgil, Milton recognizes *Ad Patrem* as a digression, but a necessary one. His song to his father is a "poor attempt" to repay a debt that cannot in any case be repaid. Nevertheless he attempts to do so out of what he has: "But notwithstanding, this page exhibits mine, / and I have reckoned up on this paper whatever I possess of abilities, / which to me are insignificant, save those which golden Clio has given."

The page itself, then, should tell us what golden Clio has given, her gifts in turn defining her own nature more clearly. Since it contains a poem, her gifts must include poetry. The conventional attitude he began with, he maintains: his muse's trifling songs are best forgotten; *Ad Patrem* is a poor attempt; in conclusion, his earlier works are "juvenile songs and amusements" (115). On the other hand, lines 17–66 constitute a long statement on "the poet's task, divine song." The concept of poetry that he invokes—religious, prophetic, bardic—is not new to him. He had touched on it in *At a Vacation Exercise, Elegia sexta,* and *Il Penseroso,* for example, but the concreteness with which he attaches himself to it is new. This Clio's other gifts explain, especially the magnificent education that Thomas Young had instituted and that Milton after a brief address to his father (56–66) goes on to describe at length (67–91). As a result of this education, however inadequate his "juvenile songs and amusements" may have been, he is now convinced that he can do great things: "Therefore, now that I am a part of the learned company, however humble, / I shall sit among the ivy and the laurels of the victor."

Mansus, Epitaphium Damonis, and the listings in the Trinity MS indicate that the great things were to include an epic, and it is easy to establish what its general nature, if not its precise subject, was to be. In his *Poetics,* Scaliger had written that "epic poetry . . . describes the descent, life, and deeds of heroes."[38] Even the Christian version of this that Milton gave in the *Reason of Church-Government* had ample precedent, for he aligned himself with Tasso and others, especially Spenser, in speculating on "what K. or Knight before the conquest might be chosen in whom to lay the pattern of a Christian *Heroe*" (YP, I, pp. 813–14).

Epic theory and practice, in short, marked out clearly the path the aspiring poet was to follow. I stated that the epic belonged at least as much to Calliope as to Clio, though connections with Clio were not lacking if the poet wished to develop them. One might state the matter more strongly—that the Miltonic background mandated a careful consideration of Clio as epic muse. The copious citations that O. B. Hardison, Jr., has collected from Renaissance and earlier writers on the relation of epic, history, and fame, though not addressed specifically to the choice of a muse, are relevant.[39] More to the point is Spenser's choice of Clio as muse of *The Faerie Queene.* Spenserians have debated the matter at length, but the evidence —then current definitions of history, the etymologies of her name, its accord with his designation of Elizabeth as Gloriana and her capital as Cleopolis—all indicate Clio. Considering Spenser's reputation for idiosyncrasy, finally, it is noteworthy that numerous quotations can be culled from seventeenth-century writers to suggest that his choice of a muse at least was not regarded as unusual. Dr. Adam Littleton in his *Latine dictionary* of 1678, for example, gave the following definition for Clio: "One of the nine *Muses,* and she the first *Hes.* whence *Ovid* calls the rest her Sisters. She was the Mistress of History, and the Patroness of Heroick Poets."[40]

Mansus, the last poem in which Milton alludes to Clio, suggests that the epic projected in the late 1630s and early 1640s would have conformed to Scaliger's dictum and to Spenser's example, and that an important element was to be the reciprocal glory with which Clio was associated.

This glory accords nicely with the references to the poem's recipient, for the Marquis of Manso both derived glory from his association with Tasso and Marino and also, through his biographies of them, helped to preserve their glory. These biographies make him in Milton's estimation an "eloquent rival" to Herodotus himself. Not surprisingly, then, Milton salutes him "in the name of Clio and great Apollo." The following lines, however, contain allusions to Clio not generally recognized: "You, good man will not scorn a remote Muse, / who, hardly nourished under the frozen Bear, ignorant, / has recently ventured to fly to and fro through the Italian cities. / Furthermore I believe that in the dark shadows of night I have heard / the swans singing on our river / where the silvery Thames with pure urns / widely bathes her gleaming tresses in the abyss of the ocean" (27–33). The "remote muse" here is Milton himself, the word's denotation being "poet" as it is in *Elegia prima,* line 69, and *Lycidas,* line 29. It is not clear, however, why he has heard swans singing. The proverbial nature of the Thames's swans (at least in England) might be thought adequate explanation except for the Italian nationality of the poem's intended recipient. That considered, an allusion to Clio is more adequate, for it is certain that Clio and swans were frequently associated in Italian representations of the muses (see figures 1 and 2).[41] Milton has heard swans singing because they are associated with Clio, in whose name he has greeted the marquis; he has heard them singing in England because his homeland is not lacking in a heroic tradition in poetry: "the ancient Druid nation, experienced in the sacred rites of the gods, / used to sing the praises of heroes and their emulable deeds" (42–43). When in concluding Milton writes of the fame he hopes to achieve through a great epic about "our native kings . . . and likewise Arthur . . . or . . . the magnanimous heroes of the invincible table," the implication is that his work is part of an established tradition, the most fitting representative of which is the muse already invoked in a great poem about Arthur, the muse of history, fame, and glory—Clio.

III. CLIO AND URANIA

That epic, however, he never completed, and interestingly enough after the early 1640s Clio disappears from his poetry, never

Figure 1. *Clio*. Fresco, Umbrian School, early sixteenth century. Capitoline Gallery, Rome.

D · CLIO · XVIIII · ꟼ

Figure 2. *Clio*. Ferrarese engraving. British Museum.

to return. When he came to compose *Paradise Lost*, it was a very different epic he wrote and a very different muse, Urania, whom he invoked. Personal and public experience had made it impossible for him to reconcile Clio's values with those of Christianity as he increasingly understood them. This was indeed a major development in his thought, and the figures of Clio and Urania—coupled as they often were—may well have played a key role in clarifying that change to Milton and the expression it must now take.

The frontispiece of the 1645 edition of Milton's poems (figure 3) contains around the so-called Marshall portrait four muses —Melpomene, Erato, Urania, and Clio.[42] We do not know whether these iconographic embellishments were added at Milton's suggestion or whether Marshall simply pulled them out of a storehouse of appropriate figures. It is certain, however, that the pairing of Urania and Clio at the bottom of the frontispiece was not Marshall's invention. Long before, the Italian musicologist Gafurius had placed the two muses at opposite ends of the celestial octave depicted in the frontispiece to his own *Practica Musicae*, the highest note belonging to Urania, "who was frequently represented in an averted posture gazing at the stars, while the first and lowest note (Clio) was compared by Gafurius to 'the sigh of Proserpina', breaking (as he said) the silence of the earth"[43] (see figure 4). In the sixteenth century, an engraving of Marcantonio Raimondi after Raphael represents the muses of history and astronomy (figure 5). "Touched by the celestial music of the spheres, Urania has closed her book and appears to be seized with an ecstatic rapture, whereas Clio, bound to the earth, records the deeds to be remembered."[44] There is nothing novel, then, in Marshall's representation of Urania with her spheres, eyes turned upward toward the heavens, coupled with Clio writing in her book, eyes cast toward the ground.

As Milton looked at these figures, we can assume that he was familiar with a portion at least of the material that constituted their iconographic background, for some of it was quite common. Literature as well as iconography reflected it. Consider, for example, Urania's lines in Spenser's *Teares of the Muses*. Let the ordinary run of poets despise her if they will, she says,

> How euer yet they mee despise and spight,
> I feede on sweet contentment of my thought,
> And please my selfe with mine owne selfe-delight,
> In contemplation of things heauenlie wrought:
> So loathing earth, I looke vp to the sky,
> And being driuen hence I thether fly.   (523–28)

Figure 3. The Marshall "Portrait" of Milton, *Poems* (1645).
Lewis Collection, Texas Christian University.

Figure 4. Title page of Hyginus' *Astronomi de Mundi et Sphere* (Venice, 1502). Rare Book Room, University of Michigan, Ann Arbor.

Figure 5. *Clio and Urania*. Engraving by Marcantonio Raimondi, after Raphael.
Collection of Edgar Wind.

Urania's essence, whether portrayed in an averted posture or with
her eyes turned toward the heavens, was renunciation, a frank indifference to the things of this world.

Clio's values were those habitually labeled classic and pagan;
Urania's, Christian. In his earlier years, Milton may not have felt any
great tension between the two, for the Renaissance humanists had
effected a remarkable, if unstable, synthesis of the classic and Christian. When, therefore, Milton confessed to Diodati his longing for
"an immortality of fame," he probably felt his sentiment consonant
with his duties as a Christian, supportable if necessary by referral to
writers like Castiglione and Sir Thomas Elyot, who had urged the
value of glory and honor, and whose Christianity was not in
question.[45]

So too with his attraction to military topics: it was consistent not
only with epic tradition in general, but with the Christian writers
like Tasso and Spenser whom he most admired. In *The Faerie
Queene*, Red Cross Knight, with Contemplation as his guide, had
been confirmed in his impression that Cleopolis was nothing in
comparison with the new Hierusalem; but although Contemplation
warned him of the dangers inherent in earthly conquest, he nevertheless stated that Cleopolis was

> for earthly frame,
> The fairest peece, that eye beholden can:
> And well beseemes all knights of noble name,
> That couet in th'immortall booke of fame
> To be eternized, that same to haunt,
> And doen their seruice to that soueraigne Dame,
> That glorie does to them for guerdon graunt:
> For she is heauenly borne, and heauen may iustly vaunt.
>
> (I, x, 59–60)

The humanists, however, never obliterated the more austere
view that St. Augustine had expressed, that "contempt of glory is a
great vertue: because God beholdeth it, and not the iudgement of
man."[46] Horace's boast that he had "finished a monument more
lasting than bronze and loftier than the Pyramids' royal pile" acquired in writers like Dante a poignancy from the Christian's knowledge that earthly glory was the sum total of the pagan poet's
reward.[47] In Canto xxiv of the *Inferno*, Virgil warns Dante that

> "sitting on down,
> or under coverlet, men come not into fame;

without which whoso consumes his life, leaves
    such vestige of himself on earth, as smoke in
    air or foam in water."[48]

But as we all know, Virgil, however noble, is finally and irrevocably damned along with many others who, judged by classical standards, are worthy only of praise. The praise in fact they receive, but not salvation; and indeed of all the souls that Dante meets in the other world, only those in hell seem concerned about the memory, good or bad, that they have left behind. In Canto xi of the *Purgatorio*, Oderisi comments at length on the vanity of artistic pride that was his sin:

"O empty glory of human powers! How short
    the time its green endures upon the top, if it
    be not overtaken by rude ages!

Cimabue thought to hold the field in painting,
    and now Giotto hath the cry, so that the fame
    of the other is obscured.

Even so one Guido hath taken from the other
    the glory of our tongue; and perchance one
    is born who shall chase both from the nest.

Earthly fame is naught but a breath of wind,
    which now cometh hence and now thence,
    and changes name because it changes direction."   (91–102)

No need exists to fit all of Milton's statements on fame and glory to a Procrustean bed, but one can observe that the general direction of his thought was toward the Augustinian view. The most significant proof of this is the epics that he finally wrote. Notably unlike their predecessors, they are, as John M. Steadman has written, "Milton's condemnation of virtually the entire epic tradition, the final humiliation of the conventional heroic ideal."[49] If his final thoughts on the value of fame and glory are expressed with an unprecedented bluntness, a part of the explanation lies perhaps in the figures of Clio and Urania, who for him most notably summed up desire for and contempt of fame.

IV.   Urania, the "Heav'nly Muse"

Since the focus of this study is upon the Urania who in some sense at least belongs to "the muses nine," I shall pass over most of the speculation on the nature of the Deity referred to in the prologues and concentrate on two points: first, that two figures are

present in the prologues; second, that the nondeific figure there is
the Urania whom we have discussed.

The Two Figures

The presence of two figures can be demonstrated syntactically.
In the prologue to Book I of *Paradise Lost*, Milton invokes the
"Heav'nly Muse" in line 6, but he does not address the Spirit until
lines 17–18. Two features suggest that they are not the same:
Milton's use of a period at the end of line 16, and the word "chiefly"
in line 17. Although there are other places, like line 10, where a
period would have been grammatically appropriate, the one at the
end of line 16 is in fact the first in the poem.[50] This suggests that
Milton here is preparing to introduce a major new element. In
addition to the

> Heav'nly Muse, that on the secret top
> Of *Oreb*, or of *Sinai*, didst inspire
> That Shepherd, who first taught the chosen Seed,
> In the Beginning how the Heav'ns and Earth
> Rose out of *Chaos*,

he now—*and chiefly*—invokes that "Spirit, that dost prefer / Before
all Temples th' upright heart and pure." Or consider the following
lines from Book III:

> Thee I revisit now with bolder wing,
> Escap't the *Stygian* Pool, though long detain'd
> In that obscure sojourn, while in my flight
> Through utter and through middle darkness borne
> With other notes then to th'*Orphean* Lyre
> I sung of *Chaos* and *Eternal Night*,
> Taught by the heav'nly Muse to venture down
> The dark descent, and up to reascend,
> Though hard and rare.   (13–21)

"Thee" in line 13 has to refer to the "holy Light" that Milton has
invoked in the first twelve lines, but if "holy Light" and "the
heav'nly Muse" are the same, it is awkward that in addressing the
one, he refers to the other in the third person. If the two are the same,
it would be more logical for Milton to write "taught by you" in line
19 rather than "by the heav'nly Muse." The prologues of Book VII
and IX and the prologue to *Paradise Regain'd* provide no further
evidence for the identity of the two.

To be sure, Book VII of *Paradise Lost* suggests that Milton's muse is more than just a classical deity:

> Descend from Heav'n *Urania,* by that name
> If rightly thou art call'd, whose Voice divine
> Following, above th' *Olympian* Hill I soar,
> Above the flight of *Pegasean* wing.
> The meaning, not the Name I call: for thou
> Nor of the Muses nine, nor on the top
> Of old *Olympus* dwell'st, but Heav'nlie born,
> Before the Hills appeerd, or Fountain flow'd,
> Thou with Eternal wisdom didst converse,
> Wisdom thy Sister, and with her didst play
> In presence of th' Almightie Father, pleas'd
> With thy Celestial Song.   (1–12)

The lines, however, can be quite adequately explained in terms of Milton's consistent habit of using myth to suggest truth while stressing its inadequacy for such a task. Thus the architect of Pandaemonium had been famous as a builder even in heaven, though his skill did not save him from ejection with the rest of Satan's crew; and this, Milton tells us, the story of Mulciber reflects, albeit in a distorted way (I, 738–47). The fruits in Paradise, "burnisht with Golden Rind," remind us of "*Hesperian* Fables true, / If true, here only" (IV, 249–50). Disguised as a serpent, Satan sees Eve in a "spot more delicious then those Gardens feign'd / Or of reviv'd *Adonis,* or renownd / *Alcinous,* host of old *Laertes* Son" (IX, 439–41), and so on.

If there are two figures in the prologues, we may be sure that Milton had good reasons for including both of them. The appropriateness of God's presence is obvious enough, for Milton had written in *The Art of Logic:* "I suppose that no one doubts that the primal mover of every art is God, the author of all wisdom; in the past this truth has not escaped philosophers" (CM, XI, p. 11). It was natural then that Milton acknowledge God as the ultimate source of his poetry, and yet to do so was to leave much about his work unexplained—why, for example, God's inspiration had worked in him to create poetry rather than philosophical discourse; why it had produced the poems we have rather than ones cast in a more traditional epic mold. An intermediate figure was needed, then, as the agent through whom God's grace, *as it pertained to the poem being written,* could be conveyed. As such, the Urania we have discussed was eminently suitable in that she epitomized the major concerns that Milton felt as he dictated the poems.

Urania

That *Paradise Lost* and *Paradise Regain'd* are in the tradition of
explicitly Christian or divine poetry made Urania not only eminently suitable as that figure, but indeed practically inevitable. The
synthesis of classicism and Christianity that the Renaissance humanists had effected had been a remarkable achievement, but it was
never a stable one, for Christianity never lost its rigorously exclusive
tendencies. The Christian might grant that classical literature in
some ways pointed toward the ultimate truths of the Christian faith
and yet prefer their direct expression in the Holy Bible. His preference in fact often yielded to downright hostility; and this one finds in
rather surprising figures like John Colet, who certainly knew the
classics and yet admonished his audience to read only the Scriptures: "Those books alone ought to be read, in which there is a
salutary flavour of Christ—in which Christ is set forth for us to feast
upon. Those books in which Christ is not found are but a table of
devils. Do not become readers of philosophers, companions of
devils. In the choice and well-stored table of Holy Scripture all
things are contained that belong to the truth."[51]

One of the most striking manifestations of this sentiment was the
attempt to create an explicitly Christian literature in opposition to
the classical. For Milton, the most important figure in this attempt
probably was the Huguenot poet, Du Bartas. In his *Urania* (1574),
Du Bartas wrote of a youthful desire for fame and glory and of his
attempts to achieve them through writing on martial and amatory
themes. His career was redirected, he tells us, through a vision of
Urania, the muse of heavenly things, who pleaded with him to take
up the cause of religious poetry and pointed out to him the great store
of religious subjects that could be turned into great poetry by authors
who dedicated themselves to her service.[52]

Posterity has not taken a kindly view of Du Bartas' subsequent
efforts; but no doubt can exist that they were extremely popular in
England during the first half of the seventeenth century and that
Milton read them. Even so, Du Bartas was only one of a number of
writers who dedicated themselves to Urania. Lily B. Campbell has
drawn upon the large body of material that documents their efforts in
her study of "The Christian Muse";[53] and if her work should be
thought not exhaustive enough to help in expounding Milton's
meaning, it can be supplemented by Ernst Robert Curtius's stag-
geringly full studies of the muses, which trace the pagan-Christian
conflict in muse lore back to pagan antiquity itself.[54] To the literature

and iconography that connected Urania with the antiheroic posture that Milton embraced in both epics, we can add, then, an extensive and well-defined tradition that made her a most appropriate figure to invoke in two explicitly Christian poems like *Paradise Lost* and *Paradise Regain'd*.

I have suggested that Urania helps in the area of authorial concern or purpose. The most obvious fact about Milton's purpose in *Paradise Lost* and *Paradise Regain'd* is that he elected in them to reveal his meaning through art rather than theological or philosophical discourse. This explains the mysterious lines about Urania's playing with her sister "Wisdom" (*PL* VII, 7–12). To William B. Hunter and others, their phrasing has suggested Proverbs as the passage's ultimate source:

> The LORD possessed me in the beginning of his way, before his works of old.
>
> I was set up from everlasting, from the beginning, or ever the earth was.
>
> When *there were* no depths, I was brought forth; when *there were* no fountains abounding with water.
>
> Before the mountains were settled, before the hills was I brought forth. (viii, 22–25)

In *Christian Doctrine* Milton wrote "that the figure introduced as a speaker there is not the Son of God   [as had sometimes been maintained] but a poetical personification of Wisdom" (YP, VI, p. 304). In *Paradise Lost* Milton has turned the one figure of Proverbs into two. Hunter has plausibly explained his doing so as Milton's way of representing two of Christ's manifestations—Divine Beauty and Divine Wisdom—or as the result of Milton's "using 'sister' as a metaphor for self-identity: the Greek 'Heavenly Beauty' is the same being as the Hebrew 'Wisdom' in that they had been used to express a second deity in two different cultures."[55] Urania might better be identified, however, as a "poetical personification" of Divine Art. As such she is, of course, closely related to Wisdom. Indeed, if we look back at the sentence from *The Art of Logic* quoted earlier, we note that it easily translates itself into a metaphor, with God as the father, Art and Wisdom as sisters: "the primal mover of every art is God, the author of all wisdom." Furthermore it is most natural that the figure who now inspires Milton in his artistic efforts should have been present with God and Wisdom from the beginning, for the image of God as Artist was very old and had been popular during both antiquity and the Middle Ages. The dozens of references to God as Maker that Curtius cites in three packed pages are highly relevant to our understanding of this image,[56] and we can supplement them with as few or as many obscure or well-known authors as we wish. The orthodox and popular Du Bartas had filled his works with comparisons of God and human artists, in "The seauenth Day of the first Weeke," for example, where he compared God's feelings in finishing his creation with those of a "cunning Painter" (pp. 231–33). As we examine Urania further, she will tell us more about Milton's concerns; but at this point she has already revealed herself as a fit figure to inspire him as he reveals God's wisdom in the form of art, specifically religious poetry.

The prologue to Book I of *Paradise Lost* provides further evidence of the close relation between wisdom and religious poetry that Milton felt, and outlines the part of his purpose that he will more definitely define in Book IX—the writing of a Christian epic that will have nothing in common with its predecessors in the epic genre:

> Of Mans First Disobedience, and the Fruit
> Of that Forbidden Tree, whose mortal tast
> Brought Death into the World, and all our woe,
> With loss of *Eden*, till one greater Man
> Restore us, and regain the blissful Seat,
> Sing Heav'nly Muse, that on the secret top
> Of *Oreb*, or of *Sinai*, didst inspire
> That Shepherd, who first taught the chosen Seed,
> In the Beginning how the Heav'ns and Earth
> Rose out of *Chaos:* Or if *Sion* Hill
> Delight thee more, and *Siloa's* Brook that flow'd
> Fast by the Oracle of God; I thence
> Invoke thy aid to my adventrous Song,
> That with no middle flight intends to soar
> Above th' *Aonian* Mount, while it pursues
> Things unattempted yet in Prose or Rime.   (1–16)

The lines obviously embody one of the precepts of divine poetry as Lily B. Campbell defined it, "a curious balancing of pagan and Christian mythology"; and she herself notes in these lines "the usual opposition of Sion to Olympus, of the dove to Pegasus, of the Christian muse to the pagan muses."[57] To her list I would add that Urania's association with Siloa's brook, however we interpret that body of water, also invites comparison with a pagan parallel alluded to earlier, the mountain spring on Parnassus of which Clio had been the guardian (p. 39).

Of Clio in this role, Simonides had written:

> She, invoked in many a prayer,
> In robes unwrought with gold,
> For those that came to draw
> Raised from the ambrosial grot
> The fragrant beauteous water.

In quoting this, Plutarch observed that "the cult of the Muses as associates and guardians of the prophetic art" had been established by this very stream and that indeed some believed heroic verse to have been heard there for the first time.[58] At the literal fountainhead of pagan prophecy and heroic poetry, then, stood Clio; and Urania's association with Christian prophecy and poetry, indeed her geographical associations with "*Sion* Hill . . . and *Siloa's* Brook that flow'd / Fast by the Oracle of God" all take on greater meaning when measured against the shadowy figure of the now rejected muse.

Indicative of the high status that Milton gives his poetry is his choice of the word "shepherd" to designate Moses; for although it is accurate in that Moses had been a shepherd (Exodus, chapter iii), it is not so obvious a choice as "leader," "prophet," or "teacher." Its appropriateness becomes obvious when we recall the traditional identification of the shepherd and poet, an identification that Milton had notably exploited in *Lycidas*. The poet-shepherd association, further, works in both directions; for it not only associates Moses with poetry—again an association with a scriptural source (Exodus, chapter xv), though an unstressed one—but, more important, associates poetry with the greatest of the Old Testament teacher-prophets. If the muse of *Paradise Lost* is the same figure who inspired Moses, it is most fitting that she be labeled the sister of Wisdom; and we can expect the poem undertaken under her aegis to partake not at all of the frivolous or worldly.

This the remainder of the prologue confirms. Critics have often noted that the stated intention of the work—

> to soar
> Above th'*Aonian* Mount, while it pursues
> Things unattempted yet in Prose or Rime—

ironically echoes the opening lines of Ariosto's *Orlando Furioso:*

> Of Dames, of Knights, of armes, of loves delight,
> Of curtesies, of high attempts I speake,
>
> . . . .
>
> I will no lesse *Orlandos* acts declare
> (A tale in prose ne verse yet song or sayd).[59]

In the present study it is worth noting not only how perfectly Ariosto's work embodies the values discussed in the section on Clio, but how clearly its opening places it in the epic tradition. The gloss that accompanied Harington's translation noted this: "This beginning is taken by imitation from Virgil, the I of his Aeneads. Arma virumque cano." Milton then is emphasizing the dissimilarity of his work, not only from Ariosto, but from Virgil as well. He is in fact dismissing the entire epic tradition as built on martial deeds and suggesting that any poet who uses the models, however illustrious, that Ariosto had, cannot succeed as he hopes to.

In rejecting these models, he rejects Clio. It is barely possible, in fact, that the muse whom Milton dismisses as an empty dream in Book VII, lines 37–39, is Clio, not Calliope, since Clio was sometimes named as Orpheus' mother instead of Calliope.[60] Given his usage of Calliope in the Trinity MS, however, he more likely had her in mind. His slighting references to heroes and deeds of martial valor indicate Clio as his primary target, but his ire is more all-embracing. I stated (p. 39) that with an important caveat, Calliope could be considered the personification of all poetry. That caveat is "all earthly poetry." Because of the tradition that made her the muse of poetry in general, her dismissal as "an empty dream" underscores, even more than a direct reference to Clio would, the exclusive nature of the poetic concept that Milton invokes.

The exclusiveness of that concept is the theme of the prologue to Book IX. What Milton outlines in Book I, he now fills in with emphatic detail. Once again he compares his work with earlier epics, including the *Aeneid,* the *Iliad,* and the *Odyssey* (13–19), to stress his conviction that the Fall of Adam and Eve constitutes a more genuinely heroic subject than the action of these epics. Once chosen, his subject ensured the nightly visitation of his "Celestial Patroness," but this began only when he had rejected what can fairly be called the material of Clio—

> Races and Games,
> Or tilting Furniture, emblazon'd Shields,
> Impreses quaint, Caparisons and Steeds;
> Bases and tinsel Trappings, gorgious Knights
> At Joust and Torneament; then marshal'd Feast
> Serv'd up in Hall with Sewers and Seneshals—

all of which he dismisses as "Not that which justly gives Heroic name / To Person or to Poem" (33–41).

Without Urania's aid, all human poetry (Calliope) becomes hopelessly inadequate, especially the heroic poetry he had aspired to write under the aegis of Clio. With Urania's aid, all things poetic once again become possible; the Christian artist is able to do the work that God has set for him. Appropriately for a votary of Urania, he must give up his own inclinations. His times, the climate, old age—these may hinder him in the completion of his work "if all be mine, / Not Hers who brings it nightly to my Ear" (IX, 46–47). Such is the "Heav'nly Muse," Urania—Christian, renunciatory, and antithetically opposed to all that had previously been considered heroic in poetry.

Paradise Lost and *Paradise Regain'd* are remarkably Uranian in their values. Perhaps the most explicit evidence for this is Christ's long and unequivocal rejection of the glory that "is false glory, attributed / To things not glorious, men not worthy of fame" (*PR*, III, 69–70), but the passages that echo such rejection of the Clionian ideal are numerous—the prologue to Book IX, Michael's description of war and pronouncement on it (XI, 638–99), and Adam's pledge of obedience at the end of Book XII, for example. Elsewhere, as in his mock-heroic account of the War in Heaven, Milton registers his disapproval more subtly; but whether explicitly or implicitly expressed, his thought is easy to discern and inimical to Clio.

The view of Milton's epic thought—or, more precisely, "anti-epic" thought—that the preceding study has reflected is of course neither new nor unusual. In the last thirty-five years it has been reinforced by scholars and critics as diverse in their approaches as Charles Williams, C. S. Lewis, Arnold Stein, T. J. B. Spencer, John M. Steadman, and Stella Revard. Its most picturesque expression remains Dryden's comment that Milton would more nearly have merited consideration with the acknowledged masters of the epic—Homer, Virgil, and Tasso—"if the giant had not foiled the knight, and driven him out of his strong hold, to wander through the world with his lady errant."[61] Although the view has not gone unchallenged, this study, by helping to restore a portion of the Miltonic background that was fading even while Dryden lived, has provided a new perspective that essentially confirms his point and its twentieth-century explicators.

The University of Toledo

NOTES

This article is a much expanded and revised version of a paper read at the Wisconsin Milton Tercentenaries under the title "Milton and Clio, Muse of Fame and Glory." Sabbatical and research grants from the University of Toledo made possible its completion.

1. *Considerations on Milton's Early Reading* (London, 1800), p. 233.

2. *European Literature and the Latin Middle Ages*, trans. Willard R. Trask (1953; rpt. ed., New York, 1963), pp. 229–30.

3. Shaftesbury, "Letter concerning Enthusiasm" (London, 1708), pp. 7–8; Fielding, *Tom Jones*, bk. 8, chap. 1; Coleridge, *Biographia Literaria*, chap. 1.

4. *Oxford Classical Dictionary*, 2d ed. (Oxford, 1972), s.v. "muses."

5. Lines 29–32. Here as elsewhere I use the prose translations of John T. Shawcross (*The Complete Poetry of John Milton*, rev. ed. [Garden City, N.Y., 1971]). I have included original texts only in the following cases: where a crux is involved; where the original text is rare; or where an English translation other than my own does not exist.

6. *A Variorum Commentary on the Poems of John Milton* (New York, 1970), vol. I, pp. 84–85, 237–38, 241–42, 272. Since all further references are to volume I, only page numbers will be given.

7. On their ubiquity, see two notes of mine: "Spenser's Muse and the Dumaeus *Vergil*" (*Spenser Newsletter*, V [Spring–Summer 1974], 10); and "More About Spenser and 'De Musarum Inventis,' " *American Notes and Queries*, forthcoming. The tag for Clio from the verses appears in the background of figure 1. See note 41.

8. Third ed. (London, 1559). An augmentation of Sir Thomas Elyot's *Dictionary* of 1538, Cooper's work both as *Bibliotheca Eliotae* and after 1565 as *Thesaurus Linguae Romanae et Britannicae* was very popular. It was in the school library at St. Paul's. On the books at St. Paul's in the sixteenth and seventeenth centuries, see Robert B. Gardiner, *The Admission Registers of St. Paul's School* (London, 1884), app. I, "The School Library," pp. 452–53.

9. *The Minor Poems, The Works of Edmund Spenser: A Variorum Edition* (Baltimore, 1943), vol. I, p. 43. All subsequent quotations of Spenser are from this edition, hereafter cited as Var. Sp.

10. *The Dialogues of Plato*, trans. B. Jowett (1892; rpt. ed., New York, 1937), vol. I, p. 875.

11. Trans. William Harris Stahl, Records of Civilization, Sources and Studies, no. 48 (New York, 1952), p. 194.

12. William Harrison Woodward, *Desiderius Erasmus Concerning the Aim and Method of Education*, Classics in Education, no. 19 (1904; rpt. ed., New York, 1964), p. 167.

13. *Minor Poems*, Var. Sp., vol. I, p. 244.

14. Ed. Karl K. Hulley and Stanley T. Vandersall (Lincoln, Nebr., 1970), pp. 48, 248.

15. *A New Discovery of the Old Art of Teaching School, 1660* (Menston, Eng., 1969), p. 162.

16. *Complete Prose Works of John Milton*, ed. Don M. Wolfe et al. (New Haven, 1953), vol. I, p. 236, hereafter cited as YP. *Works of John Milton*, ed. Frank Allen Patterson et al. (New York, 1931–38) will be cited as CM.

17. "Clio," *N&Q*, CCVI (1961), 178–79; *Complete English Poetry* (Garden City, 1963), p. 26; and *Complete Poetry*, rev. ed. (Garden City, 1971), p. 46.

18. *Moralia*, Loeb ed. (Cambridge, Mass., and London, 1936), vol. V, pp. 302–03.

19. *The Poems of John Milton*, ed. John Carey and Alastair Fowler (1968; rpt. ed., New York, 1972), pp. 55–56, 149.

20. "Amiot to the Readers," *The Lives of the Noble Grecians and Romanes*, trans. Thomas North (Stratford-upon-Avon, 1928), vol. I, p. xiv.

21. *The Poetical Works of John Milton* (London, 1882), vol. III, p. 313.

22. *The Latin Poems of John Milton*, Cornell Studies in English, no. 15 (New Haven, 1930), pp. 307–08.

23. "Notes on Milton's Early Development," *UTQ*, XIII (1943), 90.

24. *Milton: A Biography* (Oxford, 1968), vol. II, p. 789.

25. *Paradise Regained, The Minor Poems, and Samson Agonistes* (New York, 1937), p. 274.

26. *Complete Poems and Major Prose* (New York, 1957), p. 83.

27. (Basel, 1584). The translations that follow are my own.

28. (Paris, 1553).

29. *Thesaurus Linguae Latinae*, 4 vols. in 2 (London, 1573).

30. Translated from the facsimile edition (New York, 1970), p. 346. The reference to Cornutus is to the following sentences in *De Natura Deorum:* "Cæterum Clio una è numero Musarum est, ἀπὸ τοῦ κλέους, id est à gloria sic dicta. Et quare? Quod docti gloriam consequantur, & etiam alios gloria illustrare possint" ([Basel, 1543], p. 18). ("For the rest, Clio is one from the number of the Muses, *apo tou kleous*, that is, so called from glory. And why? Because the learned pursue glory and also are able to make others illustrious with glory.")

31. *History of Britain*, YP, V, pp. 39–40.

32. *First Defense*, YP, IV, p. 305.

33. *Fulgentius the Mythographer*, trans. Leslie George Whitbread (Columbus, 1971), p. 56.

34. (Basel, 1570), p. 125.

35. *Opera omnia* (Leyden, 1696), vol. II, p. 563.

36. *Complete English Poetry*, p. 26; *Complete Poetry*, rev. ed., p. 46.

37. *Reason of Church-Government*, YP, I, p. 810.

38. Frederick Morgan Padelford, trans., *Select Translations from Scaliger's Poetics*, Yale Studies in English, no. 26 (New York, 1905), p. 54 (bk. III, chap. xcvi).

39. *The Enduring Monument* (Chapel Hill, N.C., 1962).

40. I document the Spenserians' quarrel and give other evidence for Clio as Spenser's muse in the brief articles cited in note 7.

41. Figure 1 is from a series of frescoes (Umbrian school, early sixteenth century) in the Capitoline Gallery, Rome. Figure 2, a Ferrarese engraving, is in the British Museum. Both appear in Raimond van Marle's *Iconographie de l'art profane au moyen age et à la renaissance*, vol. II, *Allégories et symboles* (The Hague, 1932), p. 270, fig. 300, and p. 267, fig. 297. They are reproduced with the permission of Martinus Nijhoff, the Capitoline Gallery, and the British Museum. Guy de Tervarent also discusses the swan as an attribute of Clio in *Attributs et symboles dans l'art profane, 1450–1600: dictionnaire d'un langage perdu*, 2 vols. in 1 (Geneva, 1958), vol. I, col. 139.

42. From a copy in the Lewis Collection, Texas Christian University.

43. Edgar Wind, *Pagan Mysteries of the Renaissance* (London, 1958), p. 113. I

have not thought it necessary to include a reproduction of Gafurius' frontispiece because it has frequently been reproduced. Wind includes a reproduction on p. 47 of *Pagan Mysteries,* and James Haar lists further reproductions and commentary (and includes yet another reproduction) in "The Frontispiece of Gafori's *Practica Musicae* (1496)," *Renaissance Quarterly,* XXVII (1974), 7–22. Figure 4 reproduces the title page of Hyginus' *Astronomi de Mundi et Sphere . . .* (Venice, 1502), from a copy in the Rare Book Room, University of Michigan, Ann Arbor. In it, we can see not only the averted Urania to which Wind refers, but also the familiar pairing of the two muses. Though labeled Astronomia, the figure on the left suggests Clio with her down-turned eyes and open book.

44. Wind, *Pagan Mysteries,* p. 127. *Pagan Mysteries* also includes a reproduction of this engraving (fig. 38) from Wind's private collection. I reproduce it here through the courtesy of his widow and literary executor, Margaret Wind.

45. *Book of the Courtier,* trans. Sir Thomas Hoby, Everyman ed. (London, Toronto, New York, 1928), p. 276; *The Boke named the Gouernour,* Everyman ed. (London and New York, 1907), p. 104.

46. *Of the Citie of God,* trans. J. H. (n.p., 1610), p. 225.

47. *Odes and Epodes,* Loeb ed. (Cambridge, Mass., and London, 1927), p. 279 (bk. III, ode xxx).

48. Lines 47–51, Temple Classics ed. (London and New York, 1932), p. 265.

49. *Milton and the Renaissance Hero* (Oxford, 1967), p. 1.

50. This is the punctuation as it appears in the MS in the Pierpont Morgan library. See *The Manuscript of Milton's Paradise Lost Book I,* ed. Helen Darbishire (Oxford, 1931), for photographic facsimiles and comparison of MS with a copy of the first edition (pp. 2–3).

51. "Lectures on Corinthians," quoted in J. H. Lupton, *A Life of John Colet, D.D.* (London, 1887), p. 76.

52. For the English translation of Joshua Sylvester that Milton probably read, see *Bartas His Devine Weekes and Workes, 1605* (Gainesville, Fla., 1965), pp. 528–42.

53. *Huntington Library Bulletin,* no. 8 (October 1935), pp. 29–70. She uses much of the same material in her *Divine Poetry and Drama in Sixteenth-Century England* (Berkeley and Los Angeles, 1959), particularly in chap. 9, "Du Bartas and King James and the Christian Muse," pp. 74–83.

54. "Die Musen im Mittelalter," *ZRPh,* LIX (1939), 129–88, and LXIII (1943), 256–68. These earlier studies are much more exhaustive than his chapter on the muses in *European Literature.*

55. *Bright Essence* (Salt Lake City, 1971), p. 153.

56. *European Literature,* pp. 544–46.

57. "The Christian Muse," pp. 45, 69.

58. Vol. V, pp. 302–03.

59. Trans. Sir John Harington, ed. Robert McNulty (Oxford, 1972), p. 19.

60. In his *Classical Mythology in Literature, Art, and Music,* Philip Mayerson notes that Polyhymnia and Clio were sometimes named as Orpheus' mother, as well as Calliope (Waltham, Mass., 1971), p. 270.

61. "Discourse on Epick Poetry," in *The Critical and Miscellaneous Prose Works,* ed. Edmond Malone (London, 1800), vol. III, p. 442.

BEELZEBUB AND ADAM AND "THE WORST THAT CAN BE"

Mark Crispin Miller

D ESPITE HELL'S grand atmosphere and Milton's bold images of half-glorious, unspeakable menace in Books I and II of *Paradise Lost*, Satan's underlings seem too quickly mollified by his high words, too easily swayed for "godlike shapes and forms / Excelling human, princely dignities, / And powers that erst in heaven sat on thrones."[1] Satan is the poem's one truly terrifying figure, the only inmate who has a mind to match hell's "floods and whirlwinds of tempestuous fire." The others are only so many noisy followers, formidable-seeming but too dull to be dangerous. Even Beelzebub, whom the poet calls Satan's "bold compeer" and "One next himself in power, and next in crime," is actually a much weaker force of evil than Satan and far too gullible to be taken seriously. He may come to run the proceedings in Pandemonium with all the adroitness and command of a Northumberland, but such administrative polish is not in itself satanic, because it is Satan's instrument and therefore dependent on the greater evil.

Beelzebub parodies Satan's resolve by striving to emulate it. His mind is not as "fixed" as Satan's; through his feeble echoes of Satan's rhetoric rings a clear whine of terror. After skirting the issue of the fall with snatches of his chief's propaganda, he presents the primary problem in hell, the problem of hell itself. After Satan struggles to get his rhetorical engine running after the "sad overthrow," Beelzebub brings up the very thing which that rhetoric has been working to conceal,[2] what Satan in *Paradise Regained* calls "the worst that can be" (III, 223).

Satan concludes his first supine oration with a long, powerful, and meticulously worded manifesto. Beelzebub then sets about violating the careful speech with his clumsy imitation:

> O Prince, O Chief of many thronèd Powers,
> That led th'embattled Seraphim to war
> Under thy conduct, and in dreadful deeds
> Fearless, endangered heav'n's perpetual King,

And put to proof his high supremacy,
Whether upheld by strength, or chance, or fate.

(*PL* I, 128–33)

The self-effacing tone of this scraping apostrophe gives the lie to the rhetorical fiction of equality that lent Satan's speech some of its false majesty. Satan has just wound up his first public resolution with its conspicuous plurals: "*We* may with more successful hope resolve / To wage by force or guile eternal war / Irreconcilable to *our* grand Foe" (I, 120–22); but Beelzebub has missed this egalitarian strain. He is too shaken and too dim to adopt any but the broadest of Satan's rhetorical patterns. The subtleties are lost in the translation downwards. His laudatory address is undone by its own banality and repetitiousness. Placed where it is, the phrase "Under thy conduct" takes on the emphasis of a further bit of praise, but the effect of additional celebration is illusory, for "Under thy conduct" is only another way to say "led": Beelzebub's opening lines dash Satan's egalitarian rhetoric, say nothing more than "You led us," and then degenerate into meaningless yet very telling flourishes of homage. By choosing to honor Satan's "dreadful deeds / Fearless" (as opposed, for instance, to his advice or endurance), Beelzebub manages to underscore their very puniness and futility. The present situation, a prostrate dialogue "In adamantine chains and penal fire," provides sufficient comment on these "deeds," but Beelzebub must make his own praise explicitly nonsensical. Having called Satan "Prince" and "Chief," Beelzebub refers to God, whom Satan has just established as their "grand Foe," as the "King" of Heaven. Not only does Beelzebub evoke the irrefutable hierarchy that Satan talks and talks to obscure, but he stumbles upon that King's invincibility, and the inflated apostrophe collapses. It is unlikely that the mad angel at his side has "endangered heav'n's perpetual King" (even if we consider the medieval political meaning of "perpetual," verb and adjective are in conflict), nor can the evident fact of God's "high supremacy" be "put to proof." In the apostrophe's concluding lines Beelzebub gathers up lame laudatory terms only to wreck them against the inadvertent expressions of truth in "heav'n's perpetual King" and "high supremacy."

Having thus concluded some praise that Satan can surely do without, Beelzebub comes to the beginning of his speech proper, which leaps, like Satan's first ten lines,[3] into hell, but with a tactless overemphasis on the details of their plight that ought to make Satan cringe (inwardly, of course). A superficial reading of Beelzebub's apostrophe might leave one with an impression of wan, sincere homage; if so, the ensuing statement cancels out even that little bit of bravado:

> Too well I see and rue the dire event,
> That with sad overthrow and foul defeat
> Hath lost us heav'n, and all this mighty host
> In horrible destruction laid thus low,
> As far as gods and heav'nly essences
> Can perish: for the mind and spirit remains
> Invincible, and vigor soon returns,
> Though all our glory extinct, and happy state
> Here swallowed up in endless misery.   (I, 134–42)

Here is the heart of Beelzebub's real concern and the reason he cannot make such a strong case for the bright side of things. Satan's rhetoric, with its abstract "study of revenge, immortal hate, / And courage never to submit or yield," has left the suffering Beelzebub far behind. Although not as impressive as Satan, Beelzebub is, in a very limited way, more perceptive: he can face and discuss hell while lying in it. Except for the hasty parenthetical qualification ("As far as gods and heav'nly essences / Can perish") and the glib shred of self-assurance ("for the mind and spirit remains / Invincible, and vigor soon returns") lifted from Satan's speech ("since by fate the strength of gods / And this empyreal substance cannot fail" [I, 116–17]), Beelzebub's report of what he sees is as uncompromising (although in a frightened, not contemptuous way) as Death's hard volley of questions at Chaos's gate (II, 685–89). The "bold compeer" is in mental and physical agony. What he cares most about, what ravages his limp verbal heroics, is the possibility of "endless misery," the worst that can be.

Beelzebub then projects ahead from the "horrible destruction" he sees around him, letting the truth slip out without any restraint other than one more parenthetical rationalization, quick lip service to satanic "principles." "Heav'n's perpetual King" becomes "our Conqueror," and "foul defeat," irrelevant battle rhetoric, expands into something far more hideous:

> But what if he our Conqueror (whom I now
> Of force believe almighty, since no less
> Than such could have o'erpow'red such force as ours)
> Have left us this our spirit and strength entire
> Strongly to suffer and support our pains,
> That we may so suffice his vengeful ire,

Or do him mightier service as his thralls
By right of war, whate'er his business be,
Here in the heart of hell to work in fire,
Or do his errands in the gloomy deep?
What can it then avail though yet we feel
Strength undiminished, or eternal being
To undergo eternal punishment?   (I, 143–55)

His understandable suspicion comes to dominate his words. The possibility of "endless misery" subsumes the little military terms that inform Satan's speeches. The focus of Beelzebub's language expands as his imagination works on the dreadful contingency; his feeble assertions and aphorisms give way to anguished questions that are half inquiry, half shocked intuitive rambling.

Beelzebub here prefigures Adam, who also asks "But what if . . . ?" when he too rolls in fallenness and hell: "Yet one doubt / Pursues me still, lest all I cannot die" (X, 782 ff.). But Adam lies outside Satan's hell and has been assured grace, whereas Beelzebub is a malleable pupil whose mentor is the source of fallenness. All Satan need do to silence Beelzebub's annoyingly well-founded suppositions is come back at them with a stern sequence of apothegms, blasting away his partner's queries with an aphoristic over-kill, then deftly change the subject: "But see the angry Victor hath recalled . . . " (I, 169). His words in response are "speedy," dazzlingly fast lest their senselessness become obvious, but also quick to shut off those terrible questions.

Even after Satan's rapid maxims and promises "that bore / Semblance of worth, not substance" have apparently ensured Beelzebub's loyal complacency, the gap grows between these two alleged near equals. Each time Beelzebub speaks, his comic blunders reveal how far from "fixed" his simple mind really is, thereby subverting Satan's rhetorical foundations a little more. Satan evokes the fiction of equality with redoubled emphasis in his observations on "our faithful friends, / Th'associates and copartners of our loss" (I, 264–65). Beelzebub's fawning reply once again exposes and unwittingly derides this fiction and brings up what Satan has been desperately avoiding:

"Leader of those armies bright,
Which but th'Omnipotent none could have foiled,
If once they hear that voice, their liveliest pledge
Of hope in fears and dangers, heard so oft
In worst extremes, and on the perilous edge

> Of battle when it raged, in all assaults
> Their surest signal, they will soon resume
> New courage and revive, though now they lie
> Groveling and prostrate on yon lake of fire,
> As we erewhile, astounded and amazed;
> No wonder, fall'n such a pernicious highth!"   (I, 272–82)

Beelzebub goes on just a little too long, although even his opening address is, as usual, inadequate as a satanic expression, in effect affirming what is already apparent, that "th'Omnipotent" has "foiled" this "Leader." Again Beelzebub plummets into hell, moving from his idealized vision of the past in heaven to the grimmer, more recent situation. He maunders on with an old soldier's nostalgia, blithely recalling what Satan did not do as if it had been something heroic. This in turn hints at the stupidity of the others: "that voice" certainly in no way prevented their "horrible destruction," but was a "pledge of hope," "Their surest signal" in the midst of "fears and dangers," "worst extremes," "the perilous edge / Of battle," and "all assaults," hardships that overwhelmed the satanic forces because of, not despite, "that voice." Beelzebub again crowds out his own praise by calling up too many reminders of what was encountered, as if in spite of his earnest partisanship he cannot entirely clear his mind of awful memories. But the truly appalling fact is that Beelzebub is correct: the others *will* "soon resume / New courage and revive" at the sound of the voice that originally confused them. Beelzebub tries to apply stock heroics—the charismatic leader and his loyal, rough-and-ready troops—to the situation and subverts his own notions of loyalty and charisma. His reminiscence over the recent past in hell is much too graphic, proof of the defeat, and charged with the same vividness that enlivens the poet's opening description of hell. Beelzebub has wandered back to the truth, which Satan's every word and gesture have proclaimed a forbidden subject.

Beelzebub's predicament is fraught with ghastly comedy. He stumbles between his leader's tacit insistence that nothing can stop them and the tormenting obviousness of their destruction, accidentally telling the truth by emulating inadequately its greatest opponent. As if to justify the fact that they were "astounded and amazed" (actually trying to justify his untimely admission of this fact), Beelzebub points to the fall, a reality more fundamentally disturbing than his image of the fallen. Like a vaudeville character who knocks his boss's wig askew, then removes and replaces it with exaggerated care, Beelzebub makes the situation look worse by trying to smooth it over.[4] Satan hurries off as if to prevent Beelzebub's further dilations, which would only expose more fully their real hopelessness: "He scarce had ceased when the superior Fiend / Was moving toward the shore" (I, 283–84).

This colloquy constitutes a kind of example which Adam, after his fall, must reject with as much certainty as Beelzebub comes to evince in the role of Satan's persuasive lieutenant. The postlapsarian Adam indulges in speculative evasion, then corrects himself, thereby foiling the devils with an uncluttered acknowledgment of the truth, which must begin with a hard look at the horrifying reality of hell. In his long soliloquy in Book X (720–844), Adam takes just such a look; he reenacts the angels' fall and suggests in his sufferings the damned human soul. He moves from hellish self-involvement to selfless contrition, from suicidal escapism to a sense of blameworthiness, then from a shattering vision of the abyss to a vision, ultimately, of new life.

Adam's soliloquy entertains metaphysical concerns with unprecedented intensity, only to resolve the many questions by abandoning them and the frame of mind that plays with them. While the soliloquy seems at times satanic in its self-centeredness and bursts of self-serving speculation, there is within it an ingenuousness unknown in hell. Even its most deluded moments are open-ended and retractable, as the reasonings of the fallen angels, "in wand'ring mazes lost," are not. Adam's questions crave answers; he blunders around the truth as Beelzebub had until he settles with it at the soliloquy's end, like Samson when we first encounter him, despairing and due to be saved. This salvation follows a purgatorial reenactment of the fallen state that begins the poem as if typologically.

The visual details of Adam's newly fallen state at once bring back to the mind's eye the image of Satan chained and burning: "in gloomiest shade" (X, 716) recalls hell's "darkness visible" (I, 63); "in a troubled sea of passion tossed" (X, 718) recalls Satan "rolling in the fiery gulf" (I, 52); "On the ground / Outstretched he lay" (X, 850–51) is reminiscent of the Devil, "his other parts besides / Prone on the flood" (I, 194–95). As Satan burns within, looking at a reflection of himself in hell, so Adam watches "The growing miseries" of Eden, "but worse felt within" (X, 713–16). This external similarity tells us only part of the story: as Adam speaks, his essential difference from Satan becomes increasingly obvious.

At first, Adam quickly comes to grips with what he thinks is the worst part of his punishment. After the first shock of absolute change for the worse runs the range of his expression (X, 720–25), he seems to understand easily all the ramifications of his plight; he gives an impression of selfless sorrowing for his descendants ("Yet well, if here would end / The misery, I deserved it, and would bear / My own deservings"), but then abruptly undercuts this apparent comprehension of his own blameworthiness and corruption with this jarring, self-centered complaint:

> for what can I increase
> Or multiply, but curses on my head?
> Who of all ages to succeed, but feeling
> The evil on him brought by me, will curse
> My head?   (731–35)

For all his seeming recognition of the nature and justness of his punishment, the mountains have labored and brought forth a mouse. Furthermore, a closer reading makes even that supposed selflessness and self-blame questionable. Adam fails to see that "the misery" has hardly begun, so far is it from ending. His use of the past tense in "deserved" is suspicious, as if he no longer deserves "the misery," or as if "it" is merely what he feels at present: that "the misery" is only eviction and demotion, nothing inhering in himself. But, most significantly, death is merely a vague verbal evil; the possibility of some endless postmortal torment is as yet unperceived.

It is the loss of Paradise compounded by posterity's ill will and harsh judgment that seems insupportable: "O fleeting joys / Of Paradise, dear bought with lasting woes!" This feeble idea of "lasting woes" builds suspense within the soliloquy, for we know that the issue first raised by Beelzebub on the lake of fire has still not been faced. This issue approaches the poem from afar, gaining frightening presence as it takes shape within Adam's mind. Like the fallen angels before him, Adam responds to this growing knowledge by constructing complex defenses, rich in forensic evasiveness, on the basis of his heretical question of the propriety of God's having created him at all: thus exalting the importance of his will and questioning God's goodness, he tries to restrict himself to a rational, impersonal context in which he cannot really believe.[5] Here again he suggests Beelzebub, his litigious terms recalling the fallen angel's bewildered, materialistic "whate'er his business be" (I, 150). As the world falls into decay around him, his forced legalisms sound

as unnatural as Satan's egocentric sophistry sounds in hell; but his
heart, filling with prevenient grace, is not satanic: the postlapsarian
world, and therefore the sense of death, can impinge upon his
consciousness despite the fluency of his rhetoric. Unlike Satan, he
can cry out in spontaneous anguish, and does so when something
less definite thàn "terms" and more horrible than "curses" takes
form within his busy mind:

> To the loss of that,
> Sufficient penalty, why hast thou added
> The sense of endless woes? Inexplicable
> Thy justice seems; yet to say truth, too late
> I thus contést.   (X, 752–56)

Here is Beelzebub's suspicion breaking through Adam's measured
administrator's diction. After the clipped terseness of "Sufficient
penalty," "why hast thou added / The sense of endless woes?" is a
surprising outburst, quickly subdued as Satan is quick to hush
Beelzebub's questions. Adam notices yet cannot bear the *sense* of
torment, but persists in battling this dimly intuited unease with his
lively, insufficient intellect. "Inexplicable" and "seems" work at
odds, indicating a satanic imposition of the rationalizing faculty
upon intuitive feeling. And as proof of his failure to apprehend the
suprarational nature of the problem, he goes on searching for
explanations, leaving behind his first intimation that his ingenious
intellect is now irrelevant; in short, he continues to play Satan to the
Beelzebub within.

   The possibility of "deathless death" finds explicit utterance
after Adam acknowledges his guilt in a perfunctory way and then
longs to get his punishment over with: after melding with
"earth / Insensible" he would be free from "cruel expectation" (X,
782). At this point, were the monologue read dramatically (as it ought
to be), there would be a thoughtful pause. Then Beelzebub's "But
what if . . . ?" finds its way in among Adam's arguments, as does
Moloch's question-begging "More destroyed than thus / We should
be quite abolished and expire" (II, 92–93). Adam struggles on with
satanic persistence against the "thought / Horrid," heaping assumption on assumption: "It was but breath / Of life that sinned" (X,
789–90); "Be it, man is not so" (795); "That were to make / Strange
contradiction" (798–99); "That were to extend / His sentence beyond dust and nature's law" (804–05). But his race from the truth is
impaired by grace and the exhaustion (presumably effected by
grace) of his speculative faculty and the rhetorical engine working in

its behalf. There is a final gray flourish of abstraction: "all causes else according still / To the reception of their matter act, / Not to th'extent of their own sphere" (806–08).

And with this Thomistic mouthful Adam has indulged in satanic rhetoric for the last time, settling into the abyss that Satan cannot see:

> But say
> That death be not one stroke, as I supposed,
> Bereaving sense, but endless misery
> From this day onward, which I feel begun
> Both in me and without me, and so last
> To perpetuity. (X, 809–14)

He takes up the issue dropped in hell, denying a whole train of assumptions with the ease of a man freed from the restrictive influence of language: his use of "supposed" is apocalyptic, casting out all the impure verbal fictions wherein Satan's power lies. Supposition is abandoned; he accepts the *sense* of woe ("which I *feel* begun") as a part of his punishment. The syntax of the rejection and the "But . . . but . . ." structure hold the revelation in reserve, until the very phrase Beelzebub used amid the terrors of hell, "endless misery" (I, 142), springs into the sentence with shocking force. But Beelzebub's phrase was not allowed to reverberate (it ended his sentence), whereas Adam prolongs the explosion with the kind of highly charged tautologies admired by Wordsworth: *"endless misery / From this day onward,* which I feel . . . / . . . *last to perpetuity."*[6]

Adam no longer pities himself for being the victim of the petty "fierce reflux" of posterity's nasty remarks, but now pities his descendants, of whose woe he is the cause and father. This compassion proves Adam's escape from satanic likeness as fully as his "reasonings" had expressed the likeness itself. The descendants to come recall those "condemned / For ever now to have their lot in pain, / Millions of Spirits for his fault amerced / Of heav'n" (I, 607–10), those other angels doomed because of Satan's tongue. Adam's sympathy is so strong that even without his descendants before him he feels compassion and the yearning toward self-sacrifice that will find fulfillment in the Son: "Fair patrimony / That I must leave ye, sons; O were I able / To waste it all myself, and leave ye none!" (X, 818–20). Satan, however, surveys his blasted legions and then melts into a public sort of emotion, perhaps sincere, perhaps histrionic—or, more likely, a disingenuous blend. His eyes "cast / Signs of remorse and passion to behold / The fellows of his crime" (I, 604–06), who are in hell because of him, and he repeatedly weeps before he can speak; but even what is most sincere in this spectacle of grief is perverted by Satan's ensuing address. While Adam rues and would undo what killed his progeny, Satan goes on reaffirming his fatal objectives, slyly excusing himself from blame, recommitting his temptations.[7]

Adam finally expects the worst that can be and feels that he deserves it. His soliloquy evades, then accepts this possibility, circling it with reasonings until coming to grips with it. Satan, too, is aware of the imminent worsening of his hell, but his admission of this awareness is startling in its brevity and small effect on his actions: "And in the lowest deep a lower deep / Still threat'ning to devour me opens wide, / To which the hell I suffer seems a heav'n" (IV, 76–78). This is the insight that finishes Adam's soliloquy, but for Satan it catalyzes the rhetorical working-away that at last obscures it. Only Satan could raise the possibility and still persist;[8] Adam is immobilized by the knowledge until Eve's return and contrition move him back to love and thence to prayer.

Paradoxically, it is at the moment when he finally ceases to resemble Satan that Adam acknowledges the similarity, which we realize is obsolete, between himself and the Fiend: "To Satan only like, both crime and doom" (X, 841). At this moment he is tormented by self-hate, hostile to Eve, eager for death; but his despair, although technically sinful, transcends Satan's blind pursuit of destruction. Here in the deteriorating garden, Adam, however miserable, can distinguish between what is and what he says and begin to make them one. And through this new ability to distinguish, Adam can see and accept his hell and his place in it, differing still further from Satan in this horrified acceptance: "O Conscience, into what abyss of fears / And horrors hast thou driv'n me; out of which / I find no way, from deep to deeper plunged!" (842–44).

Later in the poem, after Adam has come to terms with his punishment, his conspicuously unsatanic humility and hope are everywhere apparent. When Michael tells him to ascend the high hill that he may learn those virtues which will let him "lead / Safest thy life, and best prepared endure / Thy mortal passage when it comes" (XI, 364–66), Adam's noble, tentative reply reveals him chastened and subdued by grace and by his vision of hell:

> "Ascend, I follow thee, safe guide, the path
> Thou lead'st me, and to the hand of Heav'n submit,
> However chast'ning, to the evil turn

> My obvious breast, arming to overcome
> By suffering, and earn rest from labor won,
> If so I may attain."   (371–76)

He replies with the gratitude about which he had lectured Eve before the fall, and with a directness and simplicity unprecedented in his career as a student of God and the world. He is at once resolute and unpretentious, vigorously eager to be taught, yet unlike his former self for whom the desire to be educated was a kind of acquisitiveness. His tone is forceful, his request humble: the paradox of strong acceptance, easy and familiar to the soldier of Christ, stands against all that took place in the poem's first two books. "My obvious breast," like "my defenseless head" (X, 815), is not only an expression of vulnerability, but a confession of the humility of ignorance, of the need rather than the desire to be tutored. His request to be led by Michael overcomes Death's foul, slavering vow of complicity (X, 265–71). Now that the babbling devils have been exorcised, this new conception of self and this readiness to do good are at once result and proof of Adam's clarified vision.

The University of Pennsylvania

NOTES

I would like to thank Professors Arnold Stein and Stanley Fish for their guidance and advice in the preparation of this article.

    1. I, 358–60. All references to Milton's poetry are to *The Complete Poetical Works of John Milton,* ed. Douglas Bush (Boston, 1965).
    2. Satan's rhetorical imitation of escape is the subject of Jack Foley's " 'Sin, not Time': Satan's First Speech in 'Paradise Lost,' " *ELH,* 37 (1970), 37–56.
    3. Satan's first ten lines break down into three movements: an exclamation on lost angelic beauty (presumably Beelzebub's, but Satan is probably thinking of himself), a less coherent encomium on the less happy enterprise, and finally an agonized, seemingly inadvertent confession of dismay.
    4. This recalls the blunder of Patenson, Thomas More's fool, who remarked, of "a gentleman with an unusually large nose . . . 'By my blood—this gentleman has one whale of a nose!' . . . Realizing that he had erred, Patenson tried to put himself in the right again by saying, 'I lied in my throat when I said this gentleman's nose was so large. On my word as a gentleman, it is quite a small nose.' " When that failed to alleviate the general embarrassment, "he went to the head of the table and said, 'Well, I just want to say one thing: this gentleman has no nose at all' " (Ellis Heywood, *Il Moro: Ellis Heywood's Dialogue in Memory of Thomas More,* ed. and tr. Roger Lee Deakins [Cambridge, Mass., 1972], p. 20).

Perhaps this similarity between fool and angel is more than accidental. The court fool exposed folly by reenacting it, making broad and blatant the subtle errors of his masters. Beelzebub's folly derives from Satan's seemingly serious behavior, and so subverts Satan's grand display, revealing moral transgressions with inadvertent parody.

5. Cf. Stanley Fish, *Surprised by Sin* (Berkeley, 1967), pp. 282–85.

6. See the *Note to "The Thorn,"* from *Lyrical Ballads, with Other Poems* (London, 1800), vol. 1, p. 213: "now every man must know that an attempt is rarely made to communicate impassioned feelings without something of an accompanying consciousness of the inadequateness of our powers, or the deficiencies of language. During such efforts there will be a craving in the mind, and as long as it is unsatisfied the Speaker will cling to the same words, or words of the same character."

7. "For me, be witness all the host of heav'n, / If counsels different, or danger shunned / By me, have lost our hopes" (I, 635–37).

8. Different from Adam's and Satan's expressions of the worst that can be is Belial's (II, 170–86), the most poetically vivid and yet the shallowest: all a forensic evocation, nothing but talk for a specious debate.

A NEW LOOK AT MILTON'S PARADISE

George Yost

FINDING THE physical features of Milton's Paradise in the area
of the world to which he assigns it has given difficulty. At least
one scholar has suggested that Milton's concession in *Paradise Lost*
to the Maker's intention to leave certain knowledge unrevealed
might well cover the site of Paradise. This search for Milton's Paradise today echoes an intense search in his day for the historical
reality of the biblical Paradise, a search that ranged over the whole
earth and included especially Mesopotamia, Syria, the Holy Land,
and Armenia. Most writers, including Raleigh, favored Mesopotamia, and people in general agreed. This article will be confined
to the background in ancient historical records of the geographical
and topographical description that Milton chose for his Paradise,
with an adducing of fresh materials and the reasons why I believe
Milton chose them.

There has been no great problem about the general location of
Milton's Eden, which contains Paradise. He tells us in Book IV:

> *Eden* stretch'd her Line
> From *Auran* Eastward to the Royal Tow'rs
> Of Great *Seleucia,* built by *Grecian* Kings,
> Or where the Sons of *Eden* long before
> Dwelt in *Telassar.*   (*PL* IV, 210–14)[1]

With due allowance for a little vagueness about the location of these
cities, we may say that Eden stretches from the Euphrates, where
Auranitis is located, eastward to the Tigris, which flows by Seleucia
and, apparently, Telassar (if Milton has not, indeed, identified Telassar with Seleucia).[2] In his recent book Joseph Duncan argues well
for an extension of Milton's Eden somewhat beyond the Tigris,[3] but,
in any event, most of it is placed in ancient Mesopotamia (now Iraq),
above the point where the Tigris and Euphrates join. Milton goes
further and narrows down the location of Paradise within Eden:

> For blissful Paradise
> Of God the Garden was, by him in the East
> Of *Eden* planted.   (*PL* IV, 208–10)

Paradise, then, is in southeast Mesopotamia near the Tigris River.

The difficulty begins now. Milton describes Paradise as a high mountain, or really a plateau, with heavily wooded sides (*PL* IV, 131–53; VIII, 302–06). Its Eastern Gate is "a Rock / Of Alabaster pil'd up to the Clouds" (*PL* IV, 542–48). Except in its northern portion, far from the juncture of the Tigris and Euphrates, Mesopotamia is woodless and so flat that the Euphrates often wanders from its borders. Common conjecture based on Genesis and biblical interpretation in Milton's time had it that Paradise was on a mountain, that a river ran south through Eden into or beneath this mountain, and that this river rising as a fountain watered the garden.[4] Milton has not only not disappointed the common expectation but has added so much character to his description as to make certain for those familiar with his mind that he is not making up from whole cloth.

The consensus of scholars has been that Milton has imported into Mesopotamia and synthesized descriptions of earthly paradises located elsewhere.[5] Following the hint given by Milton's comparison of four such places with his Paradise (*PL* IV, 268–84), they have him taking his description from Enna (Sicily), Daphne (on the Orontes in Syria), Nysa (a river island in modern Tunisia), and Mount Amara (in Abyssinia).[6]

There are three objections to accepting these four as Milton's originals. The first is that in comparing them with his Paradise he does so to their disadvantage: they "might [not] with this Paradise / Of *Eden* strive" (*PL* IV, 268, 274–75). The second objection he particularly applies to Mount Amara, but it is relevant to all four: they are "wide remote / From this Assyrian Garden" (*PL* IV, 284–85). The third objection is that in comparing his Paradise with the others he is keeping the others separate from his Paradise. It would be much more satisfactory to find Milton's description of Paradise in writings and maps accessible to him of the Mesopotamian ("Assyrian") area, which includes not only Assria but Babylonia and Chaldea.

A good place to begin is with the river of Milton's Paradise:

> Southward through *Eden* went a River large
> Nor chang'd his course, but through the shaggy hill
> Pass'd underneath ingulft, for God had thrown
> That Mountain as his Garden mould high rais'd
> Upon the rapid current, which through veins
> Of porous Earth with kindly thirst up-drawn,

> Rose a fresh Fountain, and with many a rill
> Water'd the Garden; thence united fell
> Down the steep glade, and met the nether Flood.
>
> (*PL* IV, 223–31)

With the comment that sin had changed the geography, Milton in Book IX identifies the river as the Tigris:

> There was a place,
> Now not, though Sin, not Time, first wrought the change,
> Where *Tigris* at the foot of Paradise
> Into a Gulf shot under ground, till part
> Rose up a Fountain by the Tree of Life.   (*PL* IX, 69–73)

Here is Milton's Tigris in Pliny: "The stream itself in its comparatively sluggish part is named Diglitus, but where its flow accelerates, it begins to be called Tigris, owing to its swiftness. . . . It flows into Lake Aretissa. . . . After traversing the Lake it comes against Mount Taurus, it plunges into a cave, glides underground, and bursts out again on the other side of the mountain. . . . Then it crosses a second lake called Thespites."[7]

Pliny's stream "called Tigris, owing to its swiftness" becomes Milton's Tigris, "a river large" of "rapid current." After traversing Lake Aretissa, Pliny's Tigris "comes against Mount Taurus" and goes under it; Milton's Tigris "through the shaggy hill / Pass'd underneath ingulf'd," or "at the foot of Paradise / Into a Gulf shot under ground." The "Gulf" is Lake Aretissa—a name that, like Diglitus, Mount Taurus, and Thespites, Milton chose to omit, probably in order not to overload his cosmic story with local names, especially since Mount Taurus will not do for Paradise plateau. Pliny's "second lake called Thespites" is Milton's "nether Flood" on the other side of Paradise. Milton's "fresh Fountain," "Fountain by the Tree of Life," demanded by tradition, will be covered below as part of Paradise itself. He is assembling his Paradise from three main components—all in the pocket of the Euphrates and Tigris— and we are now in Babylonia, which is southern Mesopotamia.[8]

If we look up the Tigris River in the atlases of Milton's time and earlier we get a different account. In the description he gives in his *Grand Atlas,* Blaeu translates, paraphrases, and condenses Pliny, with some changes in names of lakes, not neglecting the underground interlude and reappearance of the river, but his maps do not agree. Obviously following an independent tradition, he shows an uninterrupted Tigris with no mountains on its course.[9] Atlases of

Claudius Ptolemaeus show the Tigris flowing through (in one instance under) the divide between Mount Amanus, or Taurus, and Mount Nymphates, or Niphates.[10] The mountains are far to the north of Pliny's Babylonia—on the Armenian border of Mesopotamia. Ortelius, who professes a neutral position on the disputed location of Paradise (thus reminding us that the Milton problem is only part of the general problem), takes a neutral position as well on the course of the Tigris. As usual he makes a chain of mountains the northern boundary of Mesopotamia, but he places it far south on the course of the Tigris, after "Lake Thospites" (*sic*). The Tigris apparently flows through the mountains, not under them.[11] He has chorographically gone part way with Pliny. What Milton has done is this: he has taken his River Tigris in Paradise from Pliny's account, but is aware that the atlases almost without exception (possibly without exception in his experience) have the river flowing through rather than under the mountains, which are generally placed far to the north of Babylonia and his Paradise. From a concrete tradition coming down to his time, Pliny sets forth for Milton's descriptive purpose the antediluvian condition of the river, and the atlases give him its modern situation, without the paradisiacal topography: "There was a place, / Now not, though Sin, not Time, first wrought the change."

For the second component of Paradise we must first see it as Satan sees it. Approaching Paradise mountain in Book IV, he gets a full side view of it:

> Delicious Paradise,
> Now nearer, Crowns with her enclosure green,
> As with a rural mound the champaign head
> Of a steep wilderness, whose hairy sides
> With thicket overgrown, grotesque and wild,
> Access deni'd; and over head up grew
> Insuperable highth of loftiest shade,
> Cedar, and Pine, and Fir, and branching Palm,
> A Silvan Scene, and as the ranks ascend
> Shade above shade, a woody Theatre
> Of stateliest view. Yet higher than thir tops
> The verdurous wall of Paradise up sprung:
> Which to our general Sire gave prospect large
> Into his nether Empire neighboring round.
> And higher than that Wall a circling row
> Of goodliest Trees loaden with fairest Fruit.
>
> (*PL* IV, 132–47)

Nebuchadnezzar, King of Babylonia (605–562 B.C.)—

magnificent, called "my servant" by a Jehovah who used him to
punish the Jews for their iniquities (Jeremiah xxv, 8–11; xxvii, 6;
xliii, 8)—carried the Jews in captivity to Babylonia; and he also
carried to Babylon, the capital, as wife Amytis, or Amyhia, daughter
of Astyages of Media, whom he loved. It is written that after a time
she yearned for the wooded mountains of her native land.[12] The
royal man of dreams, whose dreams were always significant, had a
dream that was interpreted by his favorite analyst, the prophet Daniel, with, let us surmise, a glance toward the royal bedchamber. After
shattering an image, a stone "cut out by no human hand" "became a
great mountain and filled the whole earth." That stone and that
mountain, said Daniel, are the Kingdom of God (Daniel ii, 34–35,
44–45). Nebuchadnezzar's dream rose in material form as a wooded
mountain on the treeless flatland of Babylon—the Hanging Garden,
one of the seven wonders of the ancient world. Of the several
descriptions, that of Diodorus is best, and clearly the one Milton
drew upon for Paradise mountain:

> The park extended four plethra on each side, and since the approach to the
> garden sloped like a hillside and the several parts of the structure rose from
> one another tier on tier, the appearance of the whole resembled that of a
> theatre. When the ascending terraces had been built, there had been con-
> structed beneath them galleries which carried the entire weight of the
> planted garden and rose little by little one above the other along the ap-
> proach; and the uppermost gallery, which was fifty cubits high, bore the
> highest surface of the park, which was made level with the circuit wall of the
> battlements of the city.

Then follow details of the construction, and:

> On all this again earth had been piled to a depth sufficient for the roots of the
> largest trees; and the ground, when levelled off, was thickly planted with
> trees of every kind that, by their great size or any other charm, could give
> pleasure to the beholder. . . . and there was one gallery which contained
> openings leading from the topmost surface and machines for supplying the
> garden with water, the machines raising the water in great abundance from
> the river.[13]

Adding not much more than tree names, Milton follows
Diodorus closely. Three details of Diodorus—the sloping hillside,
the hollow galleries, and the planted trees—become Milton's "steep
wilderness," "grotesque" or grottoed, and "Sylvan Scene" of
"loftiest shade, / Cedar, and Pine, and Fir, and branching Palm." In
addition, Diodorus' "tier on tier" of "ascending terraces," which
"rose little by little one above the other along the approach" (to the

top), with Diodorus' trees upon them, become, with Milton's trees upon them, "ranks," or tiers, that "ascend / Shade above shade." Further, Diodorus' "circuit wall of the battlements of the city" becomes Milton's "verdurous wall of Paradise." Then Diodorus' "highest surface of the park, which was made level with the circuit wall," with Diodorus' trees growing on that surface and therefore projecting above the circuit wall, becomes Milton's "circling row / Of goodliest Trees," growing on a similar surface and, so, projecting "higher than that [verdurous] Wall." Diodorus' machine-raised water, which watered the Hanging Garden from the top down, joins tradition to become Milton's "Fountain" of Tigris that "rose up . . . by the Tree of Life" (*PL* IX, 71–73) and his "fresh Fountain" that "with many a rill / Water'd the Garden; thence united fell / Down the steep glade" (*PL* IV, 229–31). Milton's comparison of the whole to a "woody Theatre" echoes Diodorus' "the appearance of the whole resembled that of a theatre." Finally, Diodorus' use of the Greek word *paradeisos* for the whole garden—a term which may be taken to mean not only "park," but, as Giamatti points out (pp. 12–13), "Heaven" or "garden in Eden" in a biblical context—probably clinched Milton's resolution to adopt this description for his Paradise.

Other writers could remind Milton of the resemblance between the Hanging Garden and a wooded mountain: Josephus, whose work Milton consulted for another Babylonian structure, and Rufus.[14] Sebastian Münster, writing of the Hanging Garden in his *Cosmographiae Universalis* (1559) and basing his description on Diodorus, says "access was just as to a mountain," and adds a little later, "Whoever saw this garden thought he saw a forest on a mountain."[15]

Milton could accept the dream-inspired mountain, "Kingdom of God," of Nebuchadnezzar, Jehovah's servant, as equivalent to the handiwork of God by reason of the insight and creativity God may impart to the human imagination in dreams. He accepts a number of dreams elsewhere as such equivalents. When Adam desires a companion, he sees in a dream a lovely creature fashioned from his rib. He awakes and sees her "such as I saw her in my dream" (*PL* VIII, 450–82). Adam's first dream has special relevance here. Soon after he begins life, when he is still outside Paradise, he has a dream in which a being "of shape Divine"

> led me up
> A woody mountain; whose top was plain,
> A Circuit wide, enclos'd, with goodliest Trees

Planted, with Walks, and Bowers, that what I saw
Of Earth before scarce pleasant seem'd.

. . . .

                        whereat I wak'd, and found
Before mine Eyes all real, as the dream
Had lively shadow'd.   (*PL* VIII, 295, 302–06, 309–11)

Thus, Adam's dream of a wooded mountain paradise is translated into material Paradise, and it parallels Nebuchadnezzar's dream of a mountain that is translated into the material, wooded mountain paradise of the Hanging Garden. The prophet Daniel's naming the dream mountain of Nebuchadnezzar the Kingdom of God provides a link. Milton could not miss the Lord's interest in Nebuchadnezzar's dream: he had revealed to Daniel "in a vision of the night" not only the interpretation but, what would have been infinitely more difficult for an uninspired prophet to come by, the content of Nebuchadnezzar's dream, which the wily monarch had refused to divulge (Daniel ii, 3–19). In fact, Milton himself demonstrates in *Paradise Regained* his accepting as divinely inspired Nebuchadnezzar's dream of the shattering stone that became a mountain as well as Nebuchadnezzar's dream of a towering tree that we will soon see entering into Milton's Eastern Gate. In rejecting Satan's temptation of worldly power, Christ chooses both dreams as similes of his Kingdom to come:

> Know therefore when my kingdom comes to sit
> On *David's* throne, it shall be like a tree
> Spreading and overshadowing all the Earth,
> Or as a stone that shall to pieces dash
> All Monarchies besides throughout the world,
> And of my Kingdom there shall be no end.
>   (*PR* IV, 146–51)[16]

In providing Adam's dream and fulfillment in Paradise as a parallel, Milton is tacitly defending his choice of Nebuchadnezzar's dream-fulfilling mountain, the Hanging Garden, as descriptive of his Paradise. Man's dreaming imagination, whether Adam's or Nebuchadnezzar's, may issue in a paradisiacal mountain.

Milton argues in *Paradise Lost* a closer resemblance than is usually thought between the things of earth and those of heaven. Raphael makes a statement to Adam in the form of a question, "What if Earth / Be but the shadow of Heav'n, and things therein / Each to other like, more than on Earth is thought?" (*PL* V, 574–76).[17] And he later exemplifies with heavenly uplands; the hills of earth resemble those of heaven, says Raphael (*PL* VI, 639–44). A wooded mountain of Nebuchadnezzar's creation resembles the God-created mountains of earth and, in turn, those God has created in heaven.

Nebuchadnezzar's creation of the Hanging Garden was an independent imaginative act, but it had about it a certain Babylonian typicality. Only a few pages from his remarkable passage on the Tigris river, in a section containing some details on the founding of Seleucia and the "canalized Euphrates" that Milton has used elsewhere (*PL* IV, 212; *PR* III, 257), Pliny describes Babylon as a city of high walls within walls;[18] and as he does so one thinks of the rising, concentric walls of verdure on Milton's Paradise mountain. Milton has sometimes been criticized for a lack of pictorial imagination. I think rather that it went against his grain to create a scene out of whole cloth or the irrelevant, that his strong sense of authenticity demanded that Paradise be in the traditional form of a mountain and that it be Mesopotamian and typically Mesopotamian. A hundred and fifty years later Keats was to speak of the imagination with Milton in mind: "The Imagination may be compared to Adam's dream—he awoke and found it truth. . . . Adam's dream . . . seems to be a conviction that Imagination and its empyreal reflection is the same as human Life and its spiritual repetition."[19] For both poets the imagination draws on human life to parallel the creativity of God; and Milton has taken Nebuchadnezzar's creation as both typically Mesopotamian and authentically reflecting the divine. What has been said earlier applies not only to the second component of Milton's Paradise but to the next component as well.

The third component of Milton's Paradise is the Eastern Gate, which rises from one side of the mountainous plateau:

> It was a Rock
> Of Alabaster, pil'd up to the Clouds,
> Conspicuous far, winding with one ascent
> Accessible from Earth, one entrance high;
> The rest was craggy cliff, that overhung
> Still as it rose, impossible to climb.   (*PL* IV, 543–48)

Nebuchadnezzar was a builder, and he had other interests besides love gardens in the form of wooded mountains. He loved the grandiose, and his thronging dreams demanded a watch above the sultry dust of Babylon where his own Chaldean priests and magicians might consult the stars. Even his dreams soared: "The visions of my head as I lay in bed were these: I saw, and behold, a tree grew

and became strong, and its top reached to heaven; and it was visible
to the end of the whole earth" (Daniel iv, 10–11). This dream, which
would in *Paradise Regained* couple with the shattering stone of
Nebuchadnezzar's mountain dream to typify Christ's Kingdom to
come, emerged for Nebuchadnezzar, like the other dream, in physical form, and this also takes its place in Milton's Paradise. Jehovah's
servant Nebuchadnezzar lifted up his eyes to Jehovah—especially
after Shadrach, Meshach, and Abednego stepped forth from the fire
and he himself "was driven from among men and ate grass like an
ox" (Daniel, chapters iii, iv)—though it seems to have been in the
name of the god Bel that his great ziggurat, or temple tower,
Etemenanki, "foundation stone of heaven and earth," sprang from
among the buildings of Babylon. Its destination was heaven, and at
possibly three hundred feet it almost made heaven for Babylonia and
the gaping nations around.[20] Nebuchadnezzar cannot claim sole
credit. Long before, Esarhaddon inscribed his own claim as builder.
Nabopolassar, father of Nebuchadnezzar, began the rebuilding, and
Nebuchadnezzar adds, "To raise up the top of Etemenanki that it
may rival heaven, I laid to my hand."[21]

The ancient Jews saw this tower as the symbol of human
presumption and rejoiced that Jehovah had stopped its construction:
"Therefore its name was called Babel, because there the Lord confused the language of all the earth; and from there the Lord scattered
them abroad over the face of all the earth" (Genesis xi, 1–9).

The description of the ziggurat Etemenanki-Babel for antiquity
and for Milton's Eastern Gate is in the account of Herodotus:

In the one [division of the town] stood the palace of the kings, surrounded by
a wall of great strength and size; in the other was the sacred precinct of
Jupiter Belus, a square enclosure two furlongs each way, with gates of solid
brass; which was also remaining in my time. In the middle of the precinct
there was a tower of solid masonry, a furlong in length and breadth, upon
which was raised a second tower, and on that a third, and so on up to eight.
The ascent to the top is on the outside, by a path which winds round all the
towers. When one is about half-way up, one finds a resting place and seats,
where persons are wont to sit some time on their way to the summit. On the
topmost tower there is a spacious temple.[22]

Here is the Eastern Gate, very high and steep and "winding with one
ascent / Accessible from Earth, one entrance high." The "entrance
high" admits to the temple-observatory at the top of the ziggurat. As
Robert Koldewey, excavator of Babylon, points out, there is no evidence either in the excavations or in the words of Herodotus that the

successive towers became smaller as they went up.[23] When Milton says that the Eastern Gate is "conspicuous far," he quite likely is harking back to Nebuchadnezzar's dream tree that begot the temple-tower model for the Eastern Gate. It "was visible to the end of the whole earth." For the detail that except for the "one ascent" the Gate went beyond verticality and "overhung / Still as it rose, impossible to climb," Milton could make a flying visit to the Armenian area (one of the candidates for the biblical Paradise) just north of Mesopotamia, not greatly distant from the place on the telescoped map where Pliny has the Tigris flowing under Taurus. In this area Strabo has a sheer rock of immense height with a ridge or neck projecting in such a way as to make it unclimbable.[24]

Milton has a great deal to say in many places of Nebuchadnezzar, Babylon, and Babel, and he does not underestimate them.[25] Nebuchadnezzar's Babylon is "the wonder of all tongues" (*PR* III, 280). "And here let those / Who boast in mortal things, and wond'ring tell / Of *Babel* and the works of Memphian Kings," says Milton, comparing the two "greatest monuments of Fame" in human architecture (*PL* I, 692–95). Babel was impressive and worthy of significant treatment. Milton will not hesitate in *Paradise Regained* to have Christ typify his Kingdom to come by the substance of Nebuchadnezzar's dreams, and he has even less reason to abstain in *Paradise Lost* from the physical embodiment of those dreams as fortunately located and aptly formed models for his Paradise. Although he dutifully echoes in Book XII and elsewhere[26] the folk etymology in Genesis, chapter xi ("therefore its name was called Babel, because there the Lord confused the language of all the earth"), he could not but be aware that Babel is in no way related to the Hebrew *balal*, "to confuse." He had probably not studied the ancient Assyrian, whose *bab-ilu*, the "Gate of God," is the origin of both *Babel* and *Babylon*, but his conjecture that the varied languages "which the builders of Babel suddenly received" were "possibly derived from the first," "which Adam spoke in Eden,"[27] recognizes the great similarity among Semitic languages. He had studied Hebrew, Aramaic, and Syriac,[28] and knew that both *bab*, "gate," and *el*, "God," are common Semitic elements. His Eastern Gate, reaching into the heavens, is the Gate of God. Milton has planted Nebuchadnezzar's brick-and-bitumen Gate of God on Nebuchadnezzar's nearby, earthly Kingdom of God as Adam's dream of a paradisiacal mountain, and Nebuchadnezzar's dreams of a mountain and of a lofty tree take substantial form, via substantial intermediates for Nebuchadnezzar, as Paradise and its Eastern Gate.

The pinnacle of the Eastern Gate is the loftiest reach of earth, but in the vertiginous heights far above, "just o'er the blissful seat of Paradise," awaits another towering structure. As Satan lands on the outer sphere of the world,

> he decries
> Ascending by degrees magnificent
> Up to the wall of Heaven a Structure high,
> At top whereof, but far more rich appear'd
> The work as of a Kingly Palace Gate.   (*PL* III, 501–05)

"A Kingly Palace Gate!" To the upper reaches of Book III Milton has carried a reminiscence—really, an anticipation—of the Tower of Babel, Nebuchadnezzar's Gate of God, which will yearn heavenward in the next book, and he has forged an airy bond between them. But Adam's dream and Nebuchadnezzar's two dreams, having taken substantial form, are far below. A new dream of man parallels the creativity of God:

> The Stairs were such as whereon *Jacob* saw
> Angels ascending and descending, bands
> Of Guardians bright, when he from *Esau* fled
> To *Padan-Aram* in the field of *Luz*,
> Dreaming by night under the open Sky,
> And waking cri'd, *This is the Gate of Heaven.*
> (*PL* III, 510–15)

Nebuchadnezzar's earthly Gate of God, planted by Milton on Nebuchadnezzar's earthly Kingdom of God, points directly upward to Jacob's Gate of Heaven. On the morning following his dream, Jacob poured oil on the stone that had been his pillow and called the place Bethel, the House of God (Genesis xxviii, 19).

It was not simply Nebuchadnezzar's convenient mountain where a mountain was needed and none other available that induced Milton to make the Hanging Garden and Etemenanki the models for Paradise. And it was not simply the acceptability of man's dreams as paralleling the creativity of God that induced him to accept Nebuchadnezzar's dream mountain and artificial mountain for this purpose. Nor was it simply the acceptability of Nebuchadnezzar at this stage as a God-inspired dreamer. It was all of these and more. The appropriateness of the biblical designations Kingdom of God, Gate of God, Gate of Heaven, and House of God as applied to the concatenation of dreams and earthly realities made the whole espe-

cially attractive. His making heavenly reality of the dream of Jacob
and his giving Adam an anticipatory dream are overt marks of his
commitment to the translation of man's dreams into paradisiacal and
heavenly reality. These, his "Kingly Palace Gate" in the pen-
ultimate quotation above, his likening the hills of earth to those of
heaven, and his typifying Christ's Kingdom to come by
Nebuchadnezzar's dream tree and stone are places where his mental
processes rise to the surface. For the final creation, four human
dreams mount three towered stairs, plus an almost infinite space
through the spheres, and at last reach heaven.

Even the God-given creative dreams of man may carry admoni-
tions with them, and God in his own way and time visits punishment
for evil on those he has favored, as he so frequently punished the
ancient Jews. The other half of the double vision of humanity takes
over. As Giamatti says, summarizing a great deal of scholarship,
Milton "must describe perfection while, because of the story and
because we know the ending, preparing for sin" (p. 299). In the end,
sin destroyed all that was paradisiacal, the shadows of dreams and
their substance. Adam fell. Nebuchadnezzar—for all his kindness to
the Jews he carried into captivity and for all his serving the Lord in so
doing, as well as his bows in the direction of Jehovah—was adjudged
a symbol of tyranny.[29] The mountain of his dream, the Kingdom of
God, would, said Daniel, destroy not him but his posterity; his
visioned tree whose "top reached to heaven" was on its obverse side
his own ego, and when it was cut down in the dream and Daniel's
interpretation, he fell into madness (though later, like the tree, he
was regenerated, when his sins to that point were expiated). Babylon
crumbled; the Hanging Garden and the Tower of Babel were ruins
soon after Nebuchadnezzar's time.[30] Jacob was fleeing the consequences of having deceived Esau when he had his dream of the
heavenly stair. The stair was let down from heaven when Satan saw
it, but was "drawn up to Heav'n sometimes / Viewless" (*PL* III,
517–18). As a consequence of sin, the archangel Michael tells Adam,
Paradise will be destroyed by the Flood:

> Then shall this Mount
> Of Paradise by might of Waves be mov'd
> Out of his place, push'd by the horned flood,
> With all his verdure spoil'd, and Trees adrift
> Down the great River to the op'ning Gulf,
> And there take root an Island salt and bare,
> The haunt of Seals and Orcs, and Sea-mews' clang.
>
> (*PL* XI, 829–35)

This is the end of the garden, the gates, and the stairways to heaven; and Mesopotamia returns to its treeless flatland. But the construction of access ways goes on. After Satan's triumph on earth, Sin and Death build a bridge to earth, from hell.

Florida State University

NOTES

1. The edition of Milton used throughout is *John Milton: Complete Poems and Major Prose*, ed. Merritt Y. Hughes (New York, 1957).

2. A. H. Gilbert, *A Geographical Dictionary of Milton* (New Haven, 1919), pp. 40, 289.

3. *Milton's Earthly Paradise* (Minneapolis, 1972), p. 222. In an excellent chapter, "The Search for Paradise," pp. 188–233, Duncan covers the sites advanced for Paradise in Milton's time and earlier.

4. A. Williams, *The Common Expositor* (Chapel Hill, N.C., 1948), p. 97; Grant McColley, *"Paradise Lost," an Account of Its Growth and Major Origins* (Chicago, 1940), p. 146. A. Bartlett Giamatti, *The Earthly Paradise and the Renaissance Epic* (Princeton, 1966), pp. 53–54, finds the mountaintop location in both Christian and classical tradition.

5. Thomas Pakenham, "On the Site of the Earthly Paradise," *TLS*, February 15, 1957, p. 104, and March 8, 1957, p. 151.

6. Since Enna seems to offer little besides flowers, attention has concentrated on the last three. Daphne has a rich growth of trees and an underground river that emerges in a fountain—both features of Milton's Paradise. The "Nyseian Isle" is pictured in Diodorus as abounding in rich fruits and vegetables and grottoes. These correspond to parts of Milton's Paradise. (Gilbert, *Geographical Dictionary*, pp. 98, 214–16; G. W. Whiting, *Milton's Literary Milieu* [New York, 1964], pp. 66, 107; D. T. Starnes and Ernest W. Talbert, *Classical Myth and Legend in Renaissance Dictionaries* [Chapel Hill, N.C., 1955], p. 237; E. M. Clark, "Milton's Abyssinian Paradise," *University of Texas Studies in English*, XXIX [1950], 138–41; and D. T. Starnes, "The Hesperian Gardens in Milton," *University of Texas Studies in English*, XXXI [1952], 46–50.) Purchas's account of Mount Amara, which Milton used for his description of it, could contribute to both Milton's Paradise proper and his Eastern Gate if we move details about between Paradise proper and the Eastern Gate. It has a hill on top of a hill, a path up to the top, and a spring watering the garden and forming a lake. It overhangs at the top, and it abounds with trees and fruits, which are named (Gilbert, pp. 19–20; Clark, pp. 144–46). Among mountain paradises in several authors, Duncan (*Milton's Earthly Paradise*, pp. 223–24), prefers Mount Amara for Milton's Paradise. Three recent writers have advanced claims for genre descriptions without naming specific locales, or at least locales smaller than a country. John R. Knott, Jr. ("Symbolic Landscape in *Paradise Lost*," *Milton Studies*, II, ed. James D. Simmonds [Pittsburgh, 1970], p. 47), says Milton's "Eden appears as a Christianized Arcadia." (This chapter was reprinted in his *Milton's Pastoral Vision: An Approach to Paradise Lost* [Chicago, 1971], chap. 2.) Charlotte F. Otten, " 'My Native Element': Milton's Para-

dise and English Gardens," *Milton Studies,* V, ed. James D. Simmonds (Pittsburgh, 1973), pp. 249–67, sees in Milton's Paradise the various elements of the English "Paradise" gardens of his day. Similarly, G. Stanley Koehler, "Milton and the Art of Landscape," *Milton Studies,* VIII, ed. James D. Simmonds (Pittsburgh, 1975), pp. 3–40, says Milton is describing on one level the English countryside and on another the elaborately developed seventeenth-century landscape.

7. Pliny, *Natural History,* trans. H. Rackham, Loeb Library ed. (Cambridge, Mass., 1942), vol. II, pp. 433–34.

8. Evidently Milton has followed Pliny and not Strabo, who locates Taurus far to the north in accordance with the usual practice and has the Tigris doing about as Pliny has it beginning at Lake Thespites ("Thopitis" in Strabo) (*The Geography of Strabo,* trans. Horace Leonard Jones and J. R. S. Sterrett, Loeb Library ed. [New York, 1917–44], vol. VII, p. 229). There is only ground above buried Tigris, no mountain.

9. Johan Blaeu, *Le Grand Atlas ou Cosmographie Blaviane* (Amsterdam, 1663; facsim. ed., Amsterdam, 1967–), XI, 2, 1a, 5a.

10. Claudius Ptolemaeus, *Geographia,* ed. Sebastian Münster (Basle, 1540; facsim. ed. with intro. by R. A. Skelton, Amsterdam, 1966), p. 19a; *Geography of Claudius Ptolemy,* trans. Edward L. Stevenson (New York, 1932), "Tertia Asiae Tabula."

11. Abrahami Ortelii, *Theatre Orbis Terrarum Parergon; Sive Veteris Geographiae Tabulae* (Antwerp, 1624), pp. 1, ia. via.

12. Diodorus Siculus, *The Library of History,* trans. C. H. Oldfather, Loeb Library ed. (Cambridge, Mass., 1946), vol. I, pp. 385–86, bk. II, 10; Flavius Josephus, *Against Apion,* trans. H. St. J. Thackeray and Ralph Marcus, Loeb Library ed. (Cambridge, Mass., 1926–65), vol. I, pp. 217–19, bk. I, 138–41; Quintus Curtius Rufus, *History of Alexander,* trans. John C. Rolfe, Loeb Library ed. (Cambridge, Mass., 1946), vol. I, pp. 337–39, bk. V, i, 31–35.

13. Diodorus, *Library of History,* vol. I, pp. 385–86, bk. II, 10.

14. Josephus, *Jewish Antiquities,* trans. H. St. J. Thackeray and Ralph Marcus, Loeb Library ed. (Cambridge, Mass., 1926–65), vol. VI, pp. 281–83, bk. X, 223–26; Rufus, *History of Alexander,* vol. I, pp. 337–39, bk. V, i, 31–35.

15. (Basle, 1559), bk. VI, pp. 1027–28.

16. Hughes, *Complete Poems and Major Prose,* p. 519 n.: "Christ appropriates Nebuchadnezzar's vision of a tree which 'reached unto heaven, and the sign thereof to the end of all the earth' (Dan. iv, 11). He reads his own destiny in Daniel's [actually, Nebuchadnezzar's] vision of a stone which smote the image of worldly power and 'became a great mountain and filled the whole earth' (Dan. ii, 35)."

17. Cf. Raphael: "Thus measuring things in Heav'n by things on Earth / At thy request" (*PL* VI, 893–94).

18. Pliny, *Natural History,* vol. II, pp. 429–30.

19. To Benjamin Bailey, November 22, 1817, *The Letters of John Keats 1814–1821,* ed. Hyder Edward Rollins (Cambridge, Mass., 1958), vol. I, p. 185.

20. Robert Koldewey, *The Excavations at Babylon,* trans. Agnes S. Johns (London, 1914), pp. 193–97.

21. Ibid., pp. 186, 195.

22. *The History of Herodotus,* ed. Manuel Komroff, trans. George Rawlinson (New York, 1928), pp. 66–68.

23. Koldewey, *Excavations,* p. 194.

A New Look at Milton's Paradise   91

24. Strabo, *Geography*, vol. V, pp. 429–31. Duncan, *Milton's Earthly Paradise*, p. 212, presents the support in the middle of the seventeenth century for Armenia as the site of the biblical Paradise.

25. In his account of Babel in *PL* XII, 33–62, Milton follows Genesis except for his addition of the notion current in his time (Starnes and Talbert, *Classical Myth and Legend*, pp. 264–66) and set in motion by Josephus (*Jewish Antiquities*, vol. IV, pp. 55–57, bk. I, 113–21) that Nimrod, not Esarhaddon, first built the tower. But Milton has no difficulty making Nebuchadnezzar king of Babel after its first construction (*PR* III, 280–83; *Doctrine and Discipline of Divorce, Tetrachordon*, and *Eikonoklastes*, in *The Works of John Milton*, ed. Frank Allen Patterson, et al. [New York, 1931–38], vol. III, pt. 2, p. 424; vol. IV, p. 119; vol. V, p. 306, hereafter cited as CM).

26. *PL* XII, 62, 343; *Of Education*, CM, IV, p. 277.

27. *The Art of Logic*, CM, XI, p. 221.

28. Harris Francis Fletcher, *Milton's Semitic Studies* (Chicago, 1926), pp. 67 ff., 79–81.

29. *Animadversions, Eikonoklastes, The First Defence, and Christian Doctrine*, CM, III, pt. 1, pp. 140–41; V, pp. 124, 215; VII, pp. 179–81, 229; XV, p. 75.

30. Diodorus, *Library of History*, vol. I, pp. 381–83, bk. II, 9:4–9; *Of Reformation*, CM, III, pt. 1, pp. 6–7.

EPISTEMOLOGY AND
THE TUTELARY WORD
IN *PARADISE LOST*

Robert L. Entzminger

I N PARADISE LOST, Creation derives from the Word, and its
verbal source continues to inform the metaphors used to describe it. Raphael calls the universe "the Book of God" (VIII, 67),[1]
and Adam also ascribes verbal characteristics to natural phenomena.
Of the stars, he observes that "Spaces incomprehensible . . . Thir
distance argues" (VIII, 20–21), and his first self-reflective act is
described in terms which emphasize that he is himself a part of the
Book of Nature that he reads: "Myself I then perus'd" (VIII, 267).
God (VIII, 316–17), Raphael (VII, 591), and Adam (VIII, 360) all
refer to God's role in Creation as his authorship; and as if bearing
witness to its origins, nature at times becomes quite communicative,
its sympathy with the human couple characteristically expressed as a
verbal response to their actions. Celebrating their nuptials,

> the Earth
> Gave sign of gratulation, and each Hill;
> Joyous the Birds; fresh Gales and gentle Airs
> Whisper'd it to the Woods, and from thir wings
> Flung Rose, flung Odors from the spicy Shrub,
> Disporting, till the amorous Bird of Night
> Sung Spousal, and bid haste the Ev'ning Star
> On his Hill top, to light the bridal Lamp.   (VIII, 513–20)

At Eve's fall, "Nature from her seat / Sighing through all her Works
gave signs of woe" (IX, 782–83), and as Adam sinned, "Nature gave a
second groan, / Sky low'r'd, and muttering Thunder, some sad
drops / Wept" (IX, 1001–03). While these usages are figurative
commonplaces, their denotations indicate the signatory properties
that nature and language share. Like phenomenal signs, words convey knowledge in one of two ways: either they are indicative, pointing to a reality not yet known, or they are commemorative, evoking a
prior experience.[2] Thus, words do not constitute reality; at best, they
point to or evoke experience which verifies the aptitude of the sign.

93

In Augustinian/Calvinist epistemology, God is the ultimate goal of the quest for knowledge, and he is communicated through signs both indicatively and commemoratively.[3] God reveals himself in Creation and in Scripture as parallel ways of accommodating himself to man's limited powers of perception, and these external revelations are in part indicative, leading man to an ever fuller experience of his Creator. Accommodation is in the first instance condescension: God initiates his revelation to man in the external world. But signs are always inadequate to their *significata,* and the disparity is greatest when the reference is to God. Thus, the corollary to condescension is reticence. Even the angels cannot know God in his essence, but only as he chooses to manifest himself. Similarly, man knows of God no more than is useful, with the result that he is always seeking yet never (or only rarely, under special and transitory circumstances) achieving total harmony with God.

But the signs of God have also a commemorative aspect. Even fallen man has, from birth, the same "sense of divinity" that leads Adam initially to infer a Creator from the Creation.[4] Through the action of grace, this intuition is reinforced by Christ, the Interior Teacher, who confirms from within the reality to which the external signs of God point. Acting commemoratively, the signs evoke this internal confirmation, but they can never produce it or create it. And for Augustine and Calvin, this operation of the indwelling Christ is the crucial aspect of all learning. Edward Dowey has examined Calvin's application of Augustine's concept to the Scriptures:

True enough, the Bible has intrinsic validity. But this does not constitute its authority or even one source of its authority. The authority derives solely from the inner witness of God himself through which the intrinsic validity or inherent truth of the sacred oracles is recognized and confirmed.[5]

The sign theory of epistemology, then, places a great burden on the memory. This faculty is first engaged by the signs functioning commemoratively, evoking and in turn being confirmed by the Interior Teacher in a kind of dialectic between internal and external revelation. Further, subsequent knowledge of God subsumes yet never really transcends earlier experience, and so education is cumulative, ever augmenting like Creation itself.

In Adam's discourse with Raphael, particularly in Book VIII, the nature of signs, their relation to God and to human psychology, is most apparent. But the subject is crucial to Milton's entire poetic effort. Unlike the Adam of Book VIII, Milton's readers are fallen, and this condition implies a radical diminution of prelapsarian man's facility with signs. Reducing his powers of perception, however, only makes his dependence upon signs more complete, for even less than Adam is fallen man able to sustain a direct encounter with divinity. As a gloss on the now problematic Book of Nature, he has Scripture, and as another means of illumination Milton provides his own text, aiming to "justify the ways of God to men" (I, 26). Adam displays both a growing facility with signs and a recognition of their limitations, and in a parallel development he shows an alteration in his use of language, from his apt naming of the animals to his fruitless search for a name worthy of the Creator. Finally, at the Fall his language becomes perverse, and the terms of its redemption illuminate the nature of the bard's inspiration and the poetry it produces.

I

Because, as Calvin had said, God is within man as well as external to him, "the knowledge of ourselves not only arouses us to seek God, but also, as it were, leads us by the hand to find him."[6] Adam at first perceives the Creation, but his facility with signs leads him to appreciate their, and his, limitations, and this development in self-knowledge also brings him to a fuller apprehension of God. The first time he sees the sky, he springs erect "By quick instinctive motion" (VIII, 259), intuitively distinguishing himself from the other animals in posture as his capacity to speak distinguishes him in constitution. His first recollections are of sensory experience, but he soon comes to reflect on himself, and he poses the ontological problem, "But who I was, or where, or from what cause" (VIII, 270), to a universe that cannot help him. Unlike Satan, who argues that he is "self-begot, self-rais'd" (V, 860) because he is unable to recall an existence prior to himself, Adam surveys the cosmos and acknowledges his own contingency:

> Ye Hills and Dales, ye Rivers, Woods, and Plains
> And ye that live and move, fair Creatures, tell,
> Tell, if ye saw, how came I thus, how here?
> Not of myself; by some great Maker then,
> In goodness and in power preëminent.   (VIII, 275–79)

But even though it is a sign of divinity, nature, as William Madsen has said in discussing this passage, "is witness to its inability to reveal the will of God."[7]

If Adam's reading of the signs of God in Creation brings him to acknowledge his contingency, so his verbal precocity leads him to acknowledge the limitations upon his ability to rise above the signs without divine aid. His knowledge of external nature manifests itself in his ability to name what he sees. Jackson Cope has noted, "The hexamerist commentators had long insisted that Adam's naming of the animals was a special function of his insight into their essential natures."[8] Adam supports this thesis, though he is careful to give credit to God for his clarity: "I nam'd them, as they pass'd, and understood / Thir Nature, with such knowledge God endu'd / My sudden apprehension" (VIII, 352–54). But his powers of language falter when he first meets his Creator, and as God supplements nature with a direct revelation, so in introducing himself when Adam cannot provide a suitable name, he extends human language beyond its normal limitations. The lesson, however, is primarily one in self-knowledge. If, as God explains (VIII, 343–45), the naming of the animals seals Adam's lordship over the rest of Creation, then his fruitless search for a name when he encounters God indicates his own subordination to the beings higher on the Great Chain.

Adam's subsequent dialogue with his Maker elaborates the relation of language to self-knowledge, and of self-knowledge to the knowledge of God. As the Logos grows to an increased awareness of the terms of his Sonship through the colloquy in Book III, so Adam gains Eve only when he is capable of articulating what his need for a mate signifies. God has condescended to speak with Adam in response to the queries he directs to Creation concerning the Creator, but in his reticence, withholding from Adam his intention to provide a mate, he allows Adam to discover for himself the differences between man and God.[9] In reply to God's feigned puzzlement at his discontent, Adam reminds him,

> Thou in thyself art perfet, and in thee
> Is no deficience found; not so is Man,
> But in degree, the cause of his desire
> By conversation with his like to help,
> Or solace his defects.   (VIII, 415–19)

Providing the occasion for this process of self-discovery, God prepares Adam to accept Eve as a reminder of his own incompleteness, so that he will not fail to remember what Satan, arguing himself his own creator, willfully forgets.

Both Adam and Eve are intrinsically valuable, and their value is enhanced by the reciprocal love they share, yet each is also a sign to the other of his mate's identity. Because each needs the other to fulfill his own role, both are aware of their incompletion as individuals. Raphael suggests the possibility that their relationship, as well as their appreciation of all Creation, may continue to develop without end:

> Love refines
> The thoughts, and heart enlarges, hath his seat
> In Reason, and is judicious, is the scale
> By which to heav'nly Love thou may'st ascend,
> Not sunk in carnal pleasure, for which cause
> Among the Beasts no Mate for thee was found.
>
> (VIII, 589–94)

Thus, the particularly human nature of Adam's need for a mate is a reminder of his human responsibility to exercise his reason, controlling his fascination with Eve and directing it to spiritual ends in a straightforward Neoplatonic progression from earthly to divine love. Eve, on the other hand, has Adam's more dignified presence to remind her of his sovereignty in this process of exaltation.

But their development is not as linear as Raphael's description of love's refinement suggests. The free and joyous play of the exploring prelapsarian mind must occasionally reach an educative cul-de-sac. Some critics have taken these Edenic false starts as an indication that Adam and Eve are fatally flawed from the outset. Certainly the reader, aware of the story, can detect in the couple characteristic tendencies which, when yielded to, will prove disastrous. But for Adam and Eve they are no more ominous than the tumble of the speaker in Marvell's "The Garden," whose most serious lapse is that "Ensnared with flowers, I fall on grass." What keeps their exploration within bounds is the persistent, tutoring voice of God and his agent Raphael, whose response to the propensity of the human mind to educate itself is to explicate the signs which are most crucial or most unyielding to human attempts to probe their mystery.[10]

Typically, as with Adam's initial encounter with his Creator, this elucidating voice evokes self-reflection which ends in acknowledgment of human contingency and God's sovereignty. Once explained, the Tree of Knowledge becomes a reminder of Adam's subordination just as Eve is a reminder of his incompletion. These signs are provided before he has the opportunity to deviate from the divine plan, to take their meaning amiss. But in his later experiences, and in Eve's, human development is manifested in pursuits which require divine direction. Eve's "narcissism" is the first of these incidents. Citing Peter Sterry as an authority, Lee Jacobus defends Eve's fascination with her own image as an attempt, laudable in aim if faulty in method, at self-knowledge.[11] If Jacobus is right, it seems

further significant that it is a divine voice, a direct revelation, which
leads her from an image inadequate to communicate her identity,
and that the voice urges her with an apostrophe which describes the
purpose of her creation: "Mother of human Race" (IV, 475). But it is
Adam, replacing the epithet with the synonymous name "Eve," who
persuades her to accept the role and the subordination it entails.
Though her reflection is attractive, Eve admits, her marriage has
shown her "How beauty is excell'd by manly grace / And wisdom,
which alone is truly fair" (IV, 490–91).

To Raphael, the lesson Eve offers here is one Adam seems in
danger of forgetting. Though the process of articulating his need for a
mate should define his response to her, in fact her person seems
nearly as arresting to him as her image had been to the less well-
informed Eve. His doting praise elicits from the angel a stern
admonition to remember the hierarchy of values implicit in his
narration of Eve's creation:

> be not diffident
> Of Wisdom, she deserts thee not, if thou
> Dismiss not her, when most thou need'st her nigh,
> By attributing overmuch to things
> Less excellent, as thou thyself perceiv'st.   (VIII, 562–66)

Adam responds, assuring Raphael that despite his confession he
knows enough to "Approve the best, and follow what I approve"
(VIII, 611). And if subsequent events show him abandoning that
pursuit, still there is no reason here to doubt Adam's steadfastness.

The educational process that Adam undergoes in prelapsarian
Eden reveals him to be in a state of "improvable perfection." His
experience with the signs of divinity in nature allows him to grow in
self-knowledge and in knowledge of God. While pursuing this
course, he must necessarily probe less rewarding ways in order to be
surer of the right one when he is led to discover it for himself. Adam
is as free to make false starts as he is to fall, but the former freedom, as
it increases his knowledge of self and God, is actually a safeguard,
though of course not an absolute bar, against the latter. In this way
Milton avoids the problem of embarrassingly primitive innocence,
on the one hand, and a static but dull completeness, on the other, in
his depiction of prelapsarian humanity.

II

The pressure Adam's probing mind exerts in exploring the
world about him, supplemented as it is with divine guidance, leads

to knowledge. But each advance is premised on what has gone before, and typically every sign that functions indicatively, leading Adam to new experience, has also a commemorative dimension, evoking and enriching his prior discoveries about himself and God. Thus, even when he is unable to resolve a problem that presents itself in external nature, the attempt leads him to appreciate more fully his own place and his relationship to Creation and Creator. This is the case when, in his discussion with Raphael about astronomy, he infers worth, not from beauty, as he has with Eve, but from size and luminosity. Raphael's gentle reproof serves to correct this tendency to oversimplify. Even though Adam's facility with signs and Raphael's superhuman knowledge both falter before the problem of the universe's precise shape, the angel's admonition to "be lowly wise" (VIII, 173) is a positive lesson, for if it does not provide Adam with the answer he seeks, it nonetheless reminds him of the address to all the signs of God appropriate to human epistemology, a review his doting on Eve shows he needs.

Because of the clear relationship of Adam's unfallen uxoriousness to his later sin, his false start regarding his identity and his mate's has been generally accepted as relevant to the drama of the poem, even when it has raised questions about Milton's doctrinal consistency. The earlier discussion of astronomy, however, has drawn more serious criticism. Howard Schultz excuses it, noting that for the seventeenth century, "in contrast to self-knowledge, astronomy became a favorite symbol of idle curiosity."[12] In "Vanity (I)," for example, Herbert uses the astronomer's probing as an instance of man's distraction from God: "Poor man, thou searchest round / To find out death, but missest life at hand." But to an age which values disinterested scientific inquiry with fewer reservations, lowly wisdom sounds suspiciously like blissful ignorance. Arthur Lovejoy has urged the impropriety of the passage, objecting that the angel's equivocal reply to Adam reveals Milton's illiberalism to the poem's detriment:

For the dialogue between Raphael and Adam, in so far as it relates to seventeenth-century astronomy, obviously had no natural place in an epic of the Fall of Man; it was not a part of the 'plot' of the poem nor of the dramatic characterization of the human protagonist. The subject was violently introduced—'dragged in'—because Milton had in mind his contemporary readers and wished to bring them to accept a theorem of his own. . . .

Milton's position, in short, is pragmatic, in the most vulgar sense of that ambiguous term, the sense in which it designated an obscurantist utilitarianism hostile to all disinterested intellectual curiosity and to all inquiry into unsolved problems about the physical world.[13]

But in terms of Adam's education, the passage on astronomy is parallel to the dialogue about Eve. In both cases, Adam seems about to lose himself in external Creation when, properly regarded, all of nature, including Eve, is a reminder of his own place in the divine scheme; and Raphael's purpose is less to circumscribe the range of man's inquiry than to recall to Adam what sort of knowledge is most valuable and how it is acquired.

Even for fallen man, knowledge begins with the senses. After the Fall, this epistemological prerequisite is fraught with danger, as Satan demonstrates when, in preferring Eden to heaven, he chooses the corporeal sign over the spiritual reality to which it points. But for Adam, provided only that they are subject to restraint, the senses are a medium through whose transmission knowledge is virtually equated with delight. In conversation with the angel, Adam enjoys the sensuosity of the words as well as their meaning, hearing Raphael "With wonder, but delight" (VIII, 11). Only in the rapture that attends direct revelation from God is Adam completely exempt from recourse to sensory perception, and he collapses as a result of the strain this kind of learning places on him:

> My earthly by his Heav'nly overpower'd,
> Which it had long stood under, strain'd to the highth
> In that celestial Colloquy sublime,
> As with an object that excels the sense,
> Dazzl'd and spent, sunk down, and sought repair.
>
> (VIII, 453–57)

Adam's speculations about astronomy remove him from this important first source of knowledge without the warrant of ecstatic communion. Noting that the immense distances involved make certainty impossible, Raphael points out to Adam that he is proceeding on the basis of inadequate data:

> God to remove his ways from human sense,
> Plac'd Heav'n from Earth so far, that earthly sight,
> If it presume, might err in things too high,
> And no advantage gain.   (VIII, 119–22)

And despite Lovejoy's charges, Adam's overhasty leap from a few observable phenomena to a theory that will save those appearances is a violation of the scientific methodology Milton is said to be scorning. If contemporary issues are at all relevant, the choice seems to be not so much between Ptolemy and Copernicus as between the empirical, Baconian method of inquiry and the speculative, Cartesian one.[14] Raphael, speaking for Bacon as well as for Milton and God, seems to get the better of the argument.

But the issues of seventeenth-century science, while vital to history and no doubt engaging to Milton, are peripheral to the major current of the poem. What is significant is the belief Milton shared with Bacon, which is manifested in the latter's inductive methodology, that to man truth is partial and is to be pieced together only gradually. Bacon's religious avowals notwithstanding, he was mainly concerned with the application of perception and reason in the realm of natural philosophy, and his mammoth projects give evidence that he believed man capable of completing the puzzle. Milton, on the other hand, addresses the Creation chiefly as a means to know God, and his emphasis on man's fallenness makes him skeptical that the *novum organum* is capable of being completed in any meaningful way prior to the Second Coming.

The same sort of leap Adam fails to negotiate here Eve will later attempt, but with disastrous results. Without Adam, her reminder of the limitations of being human, Eve accepts Satan's argument to taste the fruit. In effect, he convinces her on the one hand that it is just an apple, without significatory value, and on the other that it has magical properties which will allow her to bypass the process whereby the human ascends to the divine only by stages. Geoffrey Hartman notes of Eve's yielding to temptation,

For her the forbidden fruit is like a drug, a hallucinogen that holds out the promise of jumping several rungs in the Scale of Nature, even of transcending from human to divine. . . . There is a small margin between vision and ecstasy, which is the educable margin; and Eve fails to respect it. She tries to go straight up, and falls.[15]

Adam's fall is more damning, in part because he does it willfully, in part because he has Eve there as a tacit reminder that he should know better. But he ignores the truths about himself he had acknowledged when he requested a companion. They are both unfinished, in the process of attaining their potential, and hence they must accept the guidance of their Creator. Yet he takes Eve, as he has said earlier, to be "in herself complete" (VIII, 548), and as a result he precipitates the poem's climactic episode.

Adam's fall, like Eve's, is partly an epistemological lapse. The delight Eve provides for Adam begins to overcome his reason, and he is limited at the Fall to the sensory and passionate faculties as he

has been limited in the dialogue on astronomy to the purely intellectual. But as both Raphael and Eve demonstrate, the dualism
which separates delight from reason and spirit is false. Earlier,
Adam's precocity has led him to criticize nature's apparent prodi-
gality in apportioning the universe. She has, Adam observes, appointed bodies of greater magnitude "merely to officiate
light / Round this opacous Earth" (VIII, 22–23). Raphael's reply
suggests Adam's theories result from a twofold failing: his speculations separate truth from delight, and he refers what he observes
not to God but to himself. Adam's impatience with empiricism,
discussed above, is an aspect of the former mistake, and Eve's departure anticipates the angel's judgment at a dramatic level. Eve,
Milton's narrator tells us, is as capable of purely speculative discourse as Adam is, but she prefers to receive her lessons from her
husband, who will "intermix / Grateful digressions, and solve high
dispute / With conjugal Caresses" (VIII, 54–56).

Adam's second failing follows from the first. As he is temporarily
limited to his intellect in trying to dissect what he should simply
appreciate, so he is unable to rise above reason to apprehend what
intellect cannot fathom. He assumes that he is, like the human figure
in da Vinci's squared circle, the measure of all things, or, at the very
least, that his reason is sufficient to discover the precise nature of the
universal scheme. But Raphael must provide him with a gloss on the
Book of Nature more adequate than the one he is able to imagine.
The angel approves Adam's inquisitiveness, but he makes clear that
no value attaches to magnitude for its own sake: "Great / Or Bright
infers not Excellence" (VIII, 90–91). As phenomena, the heavenly
bodies are important to man only insofar as they serve his life, and as
signs only as they lead the observer to God. Whatever their other
purposes may be, Adam is in no position to detect them. Viewing the
universe, man must admire its beauty, recognize his own contingency, and celebrate the Creator. In Raphael's words,

> And for the Heav'n's wide Circuit, let it speak
> The Maker's high magnificence, who built
> So spacious, and his Line strecht out so far;
> That Man may know he dwells not in his own;
> An Edifice too large for him to fill,
> Lodg'd in a small partition, and the rest
> Ordain'd for uses to his Lord best known.   (VIII, 100–06)

Raphael, then, does not place arbitrary limits on human inquiry.
Rather, he reforms Adam's attitude toward inquiry. God's book

communicates God, points to him, but the meaning cannot be grasped by any one faculty. For Milton as for Calvin, knowledge of God engages the whole personality,[16] and Adam's address to Creation should approximate that of Erasmus' pious Epicurean, who advises:

> The godly man beholds with reverent, innocent eyes, and with surpassing inward delight, the works of his Lord and Father, marveling at every one, finding fault with none but giving thanks for all, since he considers them all to be created for man's sake. And so in individual things he reveres the Creator's omnipotence, wisdom, and goodness, of which he discerns traces in created objects.[17]

Thus, Eve's withdrawing when Adam and Raphael begin to discuss astronomy is not Milton's way of belittling the feminine mentality. Instead, it represents in dramatic terms the same lesson Raphael has tried to make clear: Creation is to be both enjoyed and understood as a sign of God; to examine it critically is to forget man's place in it.

But Raphael's reasons for advising Adam to "be lowly wise" leave Lovejoy skeptical. To him, Raphael's ignorance or indifference at the answer to the question is another trick of Milton's insufferable God: "It is even suggested that the stellar system may have been so constructed as to be an insoluble enigma to astronomers in order that the Creator may chuckle over their blunders."[18] To one who approaches Creation in the attitude Raphael and Erasmus enjoin, however, Lovejoy's objection would not occur. Even though God is the referent for all inquiry, one should not expect that the process implies a goal man can reach. God condescends to man, revealing himself partially in Creation, and man is expected to answer this accommodating movement with spiritual striving. But the corollary to condescension is reticence, which makes the process of exaltation unending.

Yet the process is pleasurable, offering rewards of delight which are not separable from the goal the process contemplates. Lovejoy's use of the term *enigma* is revealing in this context. In Ciceronian rhetoric, *aenigma* refers in general to a way of approaching a difficult subject through similitude. To a Christian, God is the ultimate difficult subject, and with Augustine the Christian *rhetor*, the rhetorical concept acquired new importance. As Marcia Colish has said, "While literal signification is a suitable way to express fairly straightforward realities, metaphorical signification is far better suited to express realities that are themselves intrinsically obscure and difficult to understand."[19] For Augustine, however, metaphoric language is appropriate even where discursive language is adequate. Discussing a passage from Canticles that he has just allegorized, he admits:

But why it seems sweeter to me than if no such similitude were offered in the divine books, since the thing perceived is the same, is difficult to say and is a problem for another discussion. For the present, however, no one doubts that things are perceived more readily through similitudes and that what is sought with difficulty is discovered with more pleasure.[20]

Extrapolating from Scripture to the Book of Nature, Adam's only text, the cosmic enigma that annoys Lovejoy is really presented as an opportunity for growth and pleasure. The simile is a recurrent technique for Milton, who uses it often as a way to indicate the ineffable. The device is one of overtopping, leading us from a reality with which we are familiar to one for which our world is only a shadowy type. To accommodate his readers, whose medium is more fully time than space, Milton draws his examples from history. But Adam has no history in this sense, and so Raphael uses space as the bard uses time. Adam's problem with astronomy, then, functions as a cosmic epic simile, carrying Adam from his relatively simple theory to a reality beyond the capacity of even prelapsarian ratiocination. In his precocity he offers a Ptolemaic model, only to have Raphael suggest the more elaborate Copernican theory and finally to offer a further complication, the possibility of multiple creations. Given this progress toward an *O altitudo*, Adam's subsequent humility is both proper and understandable.

III

Adam's speech evinces what Jun Harada has called "the monolithic honest quality of Edenic language,"[21] and his facility with God's signs suggests that he is able to understand, at least with the help of divine guidance, the absolute signatory system Raphael calls the "Book of God." But as a result of godly reticence, the shortcomings of perception his humanity imposes upon him are always met and resolved with a further complication, one available not to reason but only to celebration and obedience. To take account of this complexity in simplicity that defines Creation, Milton has recourse to a language more subtle than the one Harada attributes to Adam. It involves a kind of punning, in which dual meaning is mutually supportive, in contrast to the tension arising from, say, Donne's sexual-religious puns. Anne Ferry calls the device "sacred metaphor" and describes its effect in this way:

We are made to feel that this world, and everything with which God filled it in the six days of creation, has the reality and meaning of divine truth in itself as well as metaphorical value for the abstract or inward meaning of the epic argument.[22]

Like the bard, Adam uses this kind of trope, but before the Fall his usage seems unselfconscious. Adam is intuitively a monist, but in having him speak in this way, Milton can create the effect Ferry describes, for the reader knows monism only as an alternative to the dualism the metaphor overcomes. The *felix culpa*, then, which is the theme and focus of *Paradise Lost*, is reduplicated in Milton's styles: Adam's "pure" language assumes, in the few hours between the Fall and the Judgment scene, "the hypocritically ambiguous quality of our fallen language,"[23] but through the intercession of the Word, language is redeemed as a medium to overcome the Fall, converting the response to ambiguity from frustration to awareness of possibility.

The progress of language from unfallen through fallen to redeemed is traceable most clearly in Adam's relationship with Eve, which has been defined from the first in verbal terms. Confessing man's incompletion, Adam says he needs a companion "By conversation with his like to help, / Or solace his defects" (VIII, 418–19), and his response to God's gift, characteristically, is to give her a name:

> I now see
> Bone of my Bone, Flesh of my Flesh, my Self
> Before me; Woman is her Name, of Man
> Extracted.   (VIII, 494–97)

Similarly, when he learns later what she has done, Adam says he cannot "forgo / Thy sweet Converse and Love" (IX, 908–09), and he repeats the naming process he has described to Raphael. As "conversation" suggests all the kinds of proper, loving intercourse between man and woman, so fornication is a traditional metaphor for the mind's attachment to false ideas or to incomplete goods. About magic, for instance, Augustine observes to God, "A soul that pants for such figments of the imagination is surely committing fornication against you, is putting its trust in falsity and feeding upon the winds."[24] Edenic conversation subsequently turns to sexual incontinence and to verbal abuse, and Adam begins his most vitriolic tirade against Eve with the abusive and inappropriate apostrophe "thou Serpent" (X, 867).

Their regeneration is likewise traceable in their language. Repentant, they decide to confess, a verbal process stimulated by God's "Prevenient Grace" (XI, 3) and relayed to the Father through the Logos:

> Now therefore bend thine ear
> To supplication, hear his sighs though mute;
> Unskilful with what words to pray, let mee
> Interpret for him.   (XI, 30–33)

Partly restored through prayer, Adam recalls God's promise "that thy Seed shall bruise our Foe" (XI, 155), and he promptly renames Eve:

> Hail to thee,
> *Eve* rightly call'd, Mother of all Mankind,
> Mother of all things living, since by thee
> Man is to live, and all things live for Man.   (XI, 158–61)

Ultimately, it is Michael's words that teach them how to regain Paradise and in what way Eve's motherhood will provide the means to vanquish Satan. But Adam's regeneration, of which his renaming Eve is an index, does not eradicate the Fall, and recovered speech is likewise not Edenic language. In Paradise, words have no real etymology, just as Adam has no real history, and so even when speaking "sacred metaphor," Adam's use of language is unselfconscious, unaware of the dualism which makes the expressed unity all the more striking to Milton's readers. After the Fall, words, like man, acquire a history, making them ambiguous. Thus, though Adam replaces "Serpent" with "Eve," he cannot forget the complex associations with the serpent that his wife now evokes.[25] If he infers "Serpent" from "Eve," he must recall both the Fall and the promised victory. And so redeemed language exploits the ambiguities the Fall interjects into human existence, turning tragic implications to hopeful ones.[26]

Calvin held that God's revelation in Creation remains constant; fallen man is simply unable to draw from it conclusions adequate for his salvation. Milton, on the other hand, asserts that nature falls along with Adam and Eve. Thus, "the Book of knowledge fair" (III, 47) is obscured both objectively, with reference to the perceived sign, and subjectively, with reference to the perceiver. The practical results of Milton's view, however, are much the same as Calvin's. For both, fallen man requires, more urgently than Adam, supplementary revelation. Further, redeemed inward vision, like unfallen physical vision, is at least partly constitutive of the paradise that is available to it. Adam owes his perceptual and verbal clarity, his capacity to see and tell accurately, to providential sustenance, but while he is unfallen, he possesses his acumen by right. After the Fall, he and his heirs must depend more explicitly and more tenuously on divine aid.

The narrator of *Paradise Lost* is one of Adam's progeny, and his blindness is a sign of his first father's disobedience. The bard begins Book III with an invocation, asking that

> Celestial Light
> Shine inward, and the mind through all her powers
> Irradiate, there plant eyes, all mist from thence
> Purge and disperse, that I may see and tell
> Of things invisible to mortal sight.   (III, 51–55)

Milton's own loss of sight has prompted some critics to treat the entire passage as an embarrassing autobiographical digression, but Ferry has shown its metaphoric significance to be integral. The bard's quest for a style answerable to his yet unattempted task leads him to recall the "*Orphean* Lyre" (III, 17) that he had temporarily abandoned in his survey of hell, and he credits God with the prophetic powers that secure him a place in the tradition of blind seers.[27] All this tends to exalt Milton's narrative persona, allowing him to sustain a level of oracular delivery which the reader can accept more easily because it is impersonal. Yet the bard never totally transcends the humanity he shares with his audience. If we are neither literally blind nor frequenters of Sion, nonetheless, according to orthodox Protestant theology, our sight is dimmed by the Fall, and our only hope for even partial recovery lies in the operation of the Christ within. Invoking his "heav'nly Muse" (III, 19) to compensate for his blindness, then, the bard asks for inward eyes "that I may see and tell / Of things invisible to mortal sight" (III, 54–55).

Even more than Raphael, who calls attention to the inadequacy of even prelapsarian discourse to convey divine reality (V, 563–76), the bard must use a medium which, rendered problematic by the Fall, is incapable of communicating its subject directly. As God's Creation is ultimately verbal and signatory, so is Milton's poem. John Steadman has observed of *Paradise Lost:*

For its author it was essentially an "imitation" of reality. It was, as he conceived it, less an object in itself than a reference to an object. Far from existing in and for itself, it pointed to an ideal order outside and beyond itself. Implicit in its very nature was its epistemological character, its reference to external—and eternal—truth.[28]

To Steadman's adjectives we should add "internal," implying cognition which depends on recovery as well as discovery. The most crucial aspect of religious knowledge is the awakening of the memory. Raphael's mandate is simply to bring Adam to know himself and thus his value and his contingency. Responding to the angel's discourse, Adam's recollection of his "birth" and education, progressing from an intuitive "sense of divinity" to an encounter with the true God, accomplishes that end and makes his sin indefensible. Similarly, grace subsequent to the Fall is first manifested in Adam as the restoration of memory, for he begins to overcome despair only when he remembers the prophecy in which the hope of mankind resides. But as Adam cannot forget his sin even when he is redeemed for it, neither are Milton's readers asked to recover Paradise on the same terms our first parents held it. Rather, the sinuosity and ambiguity of the language, the overtopping use of similes, evokes a sense that the Fall is ultimately fortunate, and the acceptance of that paradox forms the basis for the recovery of an internal Eden "happier far" (XII, 587).

Virginia Polytechnic Institute and State University

NOTES

1. Quotations from Milton's poetry are from *John Milton: Complete Poems and Major Prose*, ed. Merritt Y. Hughes (New York, 1957), and will be cited parenthetically by book and line number in the text.

2. The sign theory of language is given seminal treatment in Augustine's *De magistro*. The terms "indicative" and "commemorative" are borrowed from Marcia L. Colish, *The Mirror of Language: A Study in the Medieval Theory of Knowledge* (New Haven, 1968).

3. Calvin's reliance on Augustine in this matter is implicit in much of his writing. Particularly relevant to this article is Calvin's conviction that "the commonest phenomena of the world are not self-explanatory, and we must rise above them to their Author." See Edward A. Dowey, Jr., *The Knowledge of God in Calvin's Theology* (New York, 1952), p. 75.

4. The sense of divinity is one internal sign of God common to everyone. The other is conscience, the moral sense. See ibid., p. 50.

5. Ibid., p. 108.

6. *Institutes of the Christian Religion*, trans. Ford Lewis Battles (London, 1960), I, i, 1; vol. 1, p. 37.

7. William G. Madsen, *From Shadowy Types to Truth: Studies in Milton's Symbolism* (New Haven, 1968), p. 142.

8. Jackson I. Cope, *The Metaphoric Structure of Paradise Lost* (Baltimore, 1962), p. 36.

9. See John E. Parish's treatment of these conversations with God in "Milton and an Anthropomorphic God," *Studies in Philology*, LVI (1959), 619–25.

10. On God's willingness to explain his signs, Calvin commented, "Whenever God gave a sign to the holy patriarchs it was inseparably linked to doctrine without which our senses would have been stunned in looking at the bare sign" (*Institutes*, IV, xiv, 4; vol. 2, p. 1279).

11. Lee A. Jacobus, "Self-Knowledge in *Paradise Lost:* Conscience and Contemplation," *Milton Studies*, III, ed. James D. Simmonds (Pittsburgh, 1971), pp. 108–16.

12. *Milton and Forbidden Knowledge* (New York, 1955), p. 5.

13. Arthur O. Lovejoy, "Milton's Dialogue on Astronomy," in *Reason and the Imagination: Studies in the History of Ideas 1600–1800*, ed. J. A. Mazzeo (New York, 1962), pp. 141–42.

14. For the affinity between Bacon and the Puritans, see R. F. Jones, "The Background of the Attack on Science in the Age of Pope," in *Pope and His Contemporaries: Essays Presented to George Sherburn* (Oxford, 1949), pp. 96–113.

15. "Adam on the Grass with Balsamum," *ELH*, XXXVI (1969), 180.

16. See Dowey, *Knowledge of God*, pp. 24–31.

17. "The Epicurean," in *The Colloquies of Erasmus*, trans. Craig R. Thompson (Chicago, 1965), p. 548.

18. Lovejoy, "Milton's Dialogue," p. 140.

19. Colish, *Mirror of Language*, p. 79.

20. *On Christian Doctrine*, trans. D. W. Robertson, Jr. (Indianapolis, 1958), p. 38.

21. "Self and Language in the Fall," *Milton Studies*, V, ed. James D. Simmonds (Pittsburgh, 1973), p. 222.

22. Anne Davidson Ferry, *Milton's Epic Voice: The Narrator in "Paradise Lost"* (Cambridge, Mass., 1963), p. 108.

23. Harada, "Self and Language," p. 222.

24. *Confessions*, trans. Rex Warner (New York, 1963), p. 71.

25. See D. C. Allen, "Milton and the Name of Eve," *MLN*, LXXIV (1959). Allen cites the etymology of Clement of Alexandria to show that, in the Hebrew, "if the name of Eve is aspirated it is the same as the feminine of serpent" (p. 682).

26. See Geoffrey Hartman, "Milton's Counterplot," *ELH*, XXV (1958), 1–12, in which Hartman suggests that Milton's similes often have this effect.

27. See Ferry, *Milton's Epic Voice*, chap. 1, "Tone—The Bird and the Blind Bard," pp. 20–43.

28. John M. Steadman, III, "Mimesis and Idea: *Paradise Lost* and the Seventeenth-Century World-View," *Emory University Quarterly*, XX (1964), 79.

"COLD CONSOLATION":
THE ART OF MILTON'S LAST SONNET

Kurt Heinzelman

> To whom then will ye liken God? or what likeness will ye
> compare unto him?   —Isaiah xl, 18

A DESCRIPTION of the rhetorical elements in Milton's *Sonnet XXIII* reveals the poet's singular use of the simile. The poem begins with an extensive four-line comparison in which "my late espoused Saint" is seen in the explicit likeness of Alcestis. She is like a figure in a play, a character from classical story. Following the initial simile, the sonnet inaugurates a series of resemblances, all of which depend upon the word *as* having the rhetorical force of *like as:* (a) "mine as whom" in line 5; (b) "such as yet once more" in line 7; (c) "pure as her mind" in line 9; and (d) "so clear as in no face" in line 12.[1] The significance of these similes engages literary interpretation in two ways. The poet tries, simultaneously, to imagine his late espoused Saint as being like Alcestis and the Alcestis story as being like the Christian myth.[2] As we interpret Milton's poem the speaker interprets his own Christian gloss of another literary figure, Euripides' Alcestis.[3] One reason, then, for the poem's elusiveness is that both we and the speaker are involved in the act of literary interpretation, and the speaker interprets poetically by reading that initial likeness through a series of other likenesses.

Although the comparison of one thing to another is the simplest exertion of imaginative energy, it also can be one of the most elusive, since things resemble other things only selectively. Similes do not equate disparate objects; they merely point to like qualities. If Milton's wife is explicitly like the Alcestis who was rescued from death, it is unclear how much she is like the Alcestis who died for the sake of her husband. Yet Alcestis' act of self-sacrifice, of dying for another's sake, may be presumably a primal gesture of Christian selflessness. I say presumably, because how we understand the selectivity of simile-making involves choosing which aspects of a

111

likeness to emphasize. If this constitutes the reader's judgmental burden, it is also the speaker's labor, for he is himself characterized in the very similes he chooses to employ. If "my late espoused Saint" is like Alcestis, is there not an implicit resemblance between the two husbands, Admetus and Milton? Also, if Alcestis is brought to her husband by Heracles, is not the vision of the Saint attained in the poem through the Heracles-like effort of the poet's similes? The speaker, therefore, bears an implicit resemblance to both Admetus and Heracles, even as we readers bear in our interpretive labors a burden similar to the speaker's: the burden of interpreting the vision's significance.

In rehearsing the basics of simile-making I am looking forward to the later description of the Saint who is "pure as her mind." In this later resemblance she is compared to herself. Through the Heraclean poem "my late espoused Saint" is realized, not as resurrected body, but only as an image—a likeness of Alcestis, a likeness of herself. The next logical step would be to identify her as herself. This, I shall argue, is precisely what the speaker would like to do, and this is precisely what he cannot do for the simple reason that he does not know which self she is. Is she a saint in the likeness of his wife? Or is she his wife in the likeness of a soul in heaven? The crisis of reaching this question occasions the emotional utterance of line 13: "But O, as to embrace me she inclin'd." The question is, Which self offers that embrace? Which woman? Is she a woman or a heavenly spirit? Or is the embrace itself a simile, a poetic conception of that final embrace which is eternity?

In the two most recent attempts to find "a truly satisfactory interpretive solution" to the sonnet, both John Ulreich and John Colaccio view that "embrace" as the critical dilemma of the poem.[4] Ulreich sees "the basic pattern of experience in the poem" to be the Orphic myth (the "archetype of love and loss"): "Milton's identification with Orpheus defines the emotional content of the poem."[5] In the "embrace" of line 13 this myth is slightly altered so that the Saint seeks to embrace the man, not vice versa as in the Orpheus story. For Ulreich this means that "her love becomes more significant than his lost desire," and "because his love is charitable rather than merely erotic, because it is the expression of faith, the poet is able to reach beyond the despair which ends Orpheus's experience."[6] That reaching beyond, which I should like to call the poem's "indirection," also concerns Colaccio, but he reads the embrace in exactly the opposite way. According to him, the speaker's "failure to recognize [his Saint's] new life in Christ and her Christlike mission of grace causes him to interpret her gesture as she 'enclin'd' . . . on the conjugal level on which he interpreted her 'delight.' "[7] In other words, because the speaker's love is here erotic (or at least implicated by "delight"), the speaker fails "to recognize the saint as revelatory of man's promised 'day of grace.' "[8]

These markedly different readings proceed from each critic's understanding of how much typological significance he thinks the speaker of the poem is himself aware of. I believe that a more specific examination of the speaker's own choice of similes, the central rhetorical element in the poem, will reveal a clearer definition of the imagination in action.[9] The "indirection" of the poem is inherent in the nature of those similes. In this light the key to understanding the speaker's response to the embrace is the word that he uses to describe it—the word *as*, which throughout the poem has meant *likeas*. In order to show how the action intended by the word *as* in line 13 recapitulates, revises, and at last brings all the previous similes in the poem to a crisis, we must take care not to confuse resemblances, a warning of particular gravity when human speech attempts, as it does in this sonnet, to describe heavenly things.

Although a consideration of the far-reaching implications of Christian accommodated speech is beyond the scope of this study,[10] it might be helpful to keep in mind the inherent paradox of Christian imagination. Isaiah's questions, which I have taken for an epigraph, make the crucial point. It is not possible to liken anyone to God; therefore, the only means of understanding divine things is through partial images. Likenesses are both inadequate and decorous in respect to human apprehension of God. In her brilliant study of the poet in *Paradise Lost*, Anne Ferry explains how Milton solved that paradox by inventing the persona of the "blind bard" who is able to speak through inspired "sacred metaphor" of things invisible to mortal sight. Ferry identifies the perversion of such speaking with Satan, who "turns images which are properly similes into metaphors, and by these false identifications destroys the true sacred metaphors."[11] In *Sonnet XXIII* there is no inspired, bardic persona. The speaker's heroism will be his avoidance of satanic aspiration through his realizing that likenesses are not shared identities, that what is properly a simile cannot be turned into metaphor. At the point where he might attempt an outright identification of his late espoused Saint, who has appeared throughout the sonnet in both the likeness of a wife and the likeness of a heavenly soul, he wakes to the necessary limitation of humanly comparative speech. Thus, the

poem illustrates both the achievement and limitation of seeing comparatively, through likenesses, as the paradox of human imagination.
If the poem ends in a kind of failure, it is not aesthetic failure;[12]
rather, the sonnet succeeds in articulating the failings to which all
human desire and human speech are heir. Properly imagined, this
need not be seen as failure at all, but as a measure of human heroism.
Since Milton's speaker does not transgress those limitations inherent in human endeavors (in this case, the making of a poem), his
willed choice to abide within that context of human loss affirms, by
indirection, the greater life promised by God. The poem displays the
difficulty of articulating that indirection.

The poem's imaginative act occurs in the context of what "methought I saw." Seeing is seen *as* an exercise in thought. Since the
sonnet explores the imaginative possibilities of thought seen as
sight, we must apprehend Milton's use of the formulization, "methought I saw," in its deliberate, literal sense. If we feel, as some of
us must, an extraordinary poignancy in remembering Milton's actual
physical blindness, we should not forget the extraordinary assertion
of poetic vision which the opening words of the poem evoke and
which the rest of the poem never obscures. In our scholarly surmises
about the identity of "my late espoused Saint" in the first line, we
should not overlook that the sonnet's attention in the remaining
thirteen lines is directed toward the act of identification itself. What
will be identified is the saintliness of that "Saint," a saintliness
described through the images of the poem itself. The narcissistic
temptation to embrace his own graven image constitutes the
speaker's trial in the poem's last line. Indeed, the speaker's careful
understanding of the limits or "restraint" of his own visionary
thought explains the poem's evenhanded, almost solemn tone and
its remarkable serenity even in the most poignant moments.

The first four lines sound a note of expectant certainty in the
speaker's pronouncement of the first simile: "Methought I saw my
late espoused Saint / Brought to me like *Alcestis* from the grave."
Then he unhurriedly elaborates the simile and not, as one might
expect, his own experience: "Whom *Jove's* great Son to her glad
Husband gave, / Rescu'd from death by force though pale and faint."
Or rather, the resemblance-making power of the poet *is* the experience of the poem, which effects a rescue from death of a humanly
understandable image of life, however pale and faint, through the
force of its poetic language. The studied syntax of line 3, the pauses
which frame the phrase "by force" in line 4, mark the deliberate
speaking tone which is echoed in the closing lines of the poem

where the speaker's personal emotion becomes, for the moment, manifest: "But O, as to embrace me she inclin'd, / I wak'd, she fled, and day brought back my night." Even in the last line the voice pauses after every other word as if meditating the loss it experiences even while speaking it. Night is brought *back* in an almost rehearsed or presentational way as if it were not an unexpected return. That sense of deliberate, formal presentation pervades the compositional attitude of the whole poem. "My late espoused Saint" is "brought to me," as Heracles "gave" Alcestis to her husband, as night is "brought back" by day. The poem provides the thoughtful representation of this presentation of likenesses; its distinction between compared likenesses, between literal presence and figurative apprehension, consciously concerns the speaker throughout the poem.

Similarly, Milton had called upon the mediational force of thought in *Sonnet XXII* to act as a helpmeet against the loss of his own sight and the possible loss of power. The poem as thought mediates the very sense of loss which makes such mediation necessary. Milton says he will not "argue" "against heav'n's hand or will" (6–7), and then, repeating Cyriak Skinner's question ("What supports me, dost thou ask?"), he builds upon that poetic repetition an affirmation of heaven's supporting hand and will:

> What supports me, dost thou ask?
> The conscience, Friend, to have lost them overplied
> In liberty's defense, my noble task,
> Of which all Europe talks from side to side.
> This thought might lead me through the world's vain mask
> Content though blind, had I no better guide.   (9–14)

The metaphor of "this thought['s]" self-support relinquishes itself to a startling (in a poem about blindness) visual image of a man being led by the hand through the world. Heaven's hand, the "better guide" of Providence, "leads" here in a resolutely physical imagining of "what supports me." The sonnet's persuasiveness further depends upon the indirectness of its argument. His will to "argue not," his proud assertion of his "noble task," is balanced through his singular disdain for ire or self-pity. So when he reaches the seemingly conditional phrase, "had I no better guide," the reader is stunned into realizing that he has had no *better* guide than "this thought" all along, and that the speaker is not only "content" but is not even "blind," since he is guided by the eyes of God. Properly imagined, "this thought" has been a mode of self-support which leads one, almost unconsciously, to the greater support which is the thought of Divine Providence.

The ineffable mystery of divine things—heaven, the soul, saintliness—predicates the need for speaking so indirectly. Ultimately, blindness in *Sonnet XXIII* is the blindness of the human condition itself when face to face with a likeness to divinity that would require someone more than man to make it identical with divinity. The humanly conceived resemblances occur within the restraint of seeing, seen as thought, and within the bounds of human, poetic invention. Aquinas pointedly warns against the danger of self-illusion:

> The occasion of all these errors was that in their thoughts about divine things [men] had recourse to their imagination, which can reflect none but corporeal likenesses. Wherefore it behoves us to put the imagination aside when we meditate on things incorporeal.[13]

Because Milton is aware of this imaginative limit, his poem may assert what imaginative powers are proper to poetic utterance. Because the poem declares both the magnificence and the limitations of its "fancied sight" (10), it comprehends what Adam learned about human aspiration, "what this Vessel can contain" (*PL* XII, 559). In defining what this vessel of poetic language can contain, the sonnet realizes a certain measure of human sufficiency in proclaiming all that the vessel *does* contain. A religious sense of hopeful sufficiency will mediate the drastic divisions implicit in the poem between day and night, mind and body, image and substance, purification and taint, the living and the dead, husbands and wives—those dichotomies which inform an unmediated, fallen world.

What "methought I saw" affirms the image-making powers of the poet's own thought, but by the end his purpose will be indirectly consumed, as in *Sonnet XXII*, by an infinitely greater thought. Between the emotion and the response falls the shadow of an elaborate allusion to the Alcestis story that suggests a greater significance in Milton's choice than is usually understood. Heracles' rescue of Alcestis "by force" from the jaws of death and his subsequent presentation of her to "her glad Husband" resembles primarily the bringing of "my late espoused Saint" before the thoughtful vision of the sonnet's speaker. The specific "force" which has brought this image before him is his willed apperception of her. In line 5 she is called "mine," belonging to the speaker. The Heraclean force of the speaker's willed simile constitutes one way in which she is "mine"—as his created image.

But as his "espoused" she has belonged to him in other ways as well: namely, in the biblical way that all wives are to their husbands "like of his like, his Image multiplied" (*PL* VIII, 424). The speaker is also a husband like Admetus. The history of husbands shows how Eve was brought to Adam as "Thy likeness, thy fit help, thy other self, / Thy wish, exactly to thy heart's desire" (*PL* VIII, 450–51). Actually, Adam's first glimpse of Eve in *Paradise Lost* also occurs in a vision:

> Mine eye he clos'd, but op'n left the Cell
> Of Fancy my internal sight, by which
> Abstract as in a trance *methought I saw,*
> Though sleeping, where I lay, and saw the shape
> Still glorious before whom awake I stood.
>
> (*PL* VIII, 460–64; italics added)

This "internal sight" gives way to a true identification of Eve as "Bone of my Bone, Flesh of my Flesh, my Self / Before me" (*PL* VIII, 495–96). Woman belongs to prelapsarian man as his "other self" and as his very self. But death and all our woe, which entered the world with the loss of Eden, have also severed what may be humanly attained on earth from what is "exactly to thy heart's desire." Death literally stands between dream and waking vision. In this sonnet the Christian husband attempts to imagine his late espoused wife as she appears in the new likeness of a heavenly Saint—my heavenly self before me.

In Eden what Adam thought he saw is instantly translated into reality, "before whom awake I stood." In the Alcestis myth Heracles stands against death in order to return Alcestis to the living. In this sonnet the Heraclean poem retrieves and consecrates the husband-poet's image of his wife as a saint now espoused to heaven. But neither Alcestis nor Milton's wife returns as her earthly husband's likeness; that is, both are "veil'd" in the likeness of themselves when they were wives. In a moment of terrified surprise Admetus (in Euripides' play) questions the meaning of this change:

> Gods, what shall I think! Amazement beyond hope, as I
> look on this woman, this wife. Is she really mine,
> or some sweet mockery for God to stun me with?[14]

Is she really mine? For the Miltonic speaker her image can be a "fit help," but only if it is apprehended *as* a likeness. It is explicitly in her poetically imagined likeness to herself that she is "mine." She belongs, for the moment of this poem, not to heaven but to the speaker's comparison of her as being like his late espoused wife, like

Alcestis. She is lent to him in this brief reprieve of fourteen lines just as Alcestis is lent to her husband for the period between her premature death for his sake and the moment of her actual death. It is a period of poetic grace, admirable perhaps, but not to be confused with or to supplant the infinitely finer, ineffable grace of God, who promises "full sight" in heaven "without restraint." That is the Christian gloss of Euripides' last chorus:

> Many are the forms of what is unknown.
> Much that the gods achieve is surprise.
> What we look for does not come to pass;
> God finds a way for what none foresaw.   (1159–62)

In the context of imagining things unknown, the conversation in which Heracles hands over Alcestis to Admetus is significant:

> *Heracles:*   Do you have her?
> *Admetus:*   Yes, I have her.
> *Heracles:*   Keep her, then.   (1119)

Possession is tentative. Keeping is the problem. It is implied throughout Euripides' play and explicit in the Christian premises of the sonnet. The question of keeping is the dilemma of the word *mine.* In its emphatic position at the beginning of the poem's fifth line the word acts as a kind of thematic hinge between the first and second quatrains. It is also a thematic thread back into Euripides' story. As the Saint bears the poetically revealed likeness which belongs to the speaker's imagining powers of willed thought, so Admetus tries to imagine an image which he can keep of his wife's memory after she is gone:

> Am I not to lead a mourning life
> when I have lost a wife like you? I shall make an end
> of revelry and entertainment in my house.
>
>   .   .   .   .
>
> I shall have the skilled hand of an artificer
> make me an image of you to set in my room,
> pay my devotions to it, hold it in my arms
> and speak your name, and clasp it close against my heart,
> and think I hold my wife again, though I do not,
> cold consolation, I know it, and yet even so
> I might drown the weight of sorrow. You could come
> to see me in my dreams and comfort me. For they
> who love find a time's sweetness in the visions of the night.
>   (341–43, 348–56)

By lifelike images Admetus imagines he can keep the only thing which is truly his, a comfort. The made image is "mine," the husband's and the poet's, although it only speaks of loss. And that is "cold consolation, I know it." Recognizing that this illusion, this "image of yŏu," remains an illusion, however rhapsodically desired, spares the speaker at least from being self-deluded about what skilled art can do in the face of actual loss. What is "mine" in Milton's sonnet is both the resemblance of his wife which his skilled art has made and the awareness that this may be all it is, "a time's sweetness in the visions of the night," perhaps "a sweet mockery."

The concerns of the sonnet's first four lines have been those of giving, bringing, and keeping. The fifth line explicates another likeness and another concern, the question of saving: "Mine as whom washt from spot of child-bed taint, / Purification in the old Law did save." The old law in Leviticus xii, 2–8, describes the process of cleansing the impure body in order to realize the soul's true creatureliness as an image of God. In the old law of Greek mythology Alcestis, too, must undergo a period of purification. Heracles says to Admetus, "You are not allowed to hear her speak to you until / her obligations to the gods who live below / are washed away. Until the third morning comes" (1144–46). But neither the washing in the Greek law nor the purification described in the Old Testament can account for the *saving* that Milton's Christian sonnet affirms. In Christian history the third day following death is specifically the day of the Savior when he rose into "full sight of Heaven without restraint" and assured mankind that they could "trust to have" that same full sight themselves. Only when Milton's sonnet is seen to be a Christian interpretation of *both* the old law of Leviticus and the old law governing Alcestis does the choice of the word *save* pertain to *both* the high hopes which human utterance can "trust to have" and the disappointing resemblances with which it must now be content: "And such, as yet once more I trust to have / Full sight of her in Heaven without restraint." Being saved is the inevitable, projected meaning of these lines whose literal sense is that of "cold consolation," articulated in the feeling of "restraint" in line 8 and in the echo of *Lycidas* at line 7, "such as *yet once more*." The speaker is not yet saved, although the vision of his saved wife promises that it will happen yet once more.

The mortal speaker has attained here, with scrupulous honesty, a vision of immortal attainment. Both the human achievement (of the poem's vision) and the projected achievement (of Christian Life, of

which Alcestis' self-sacrifice is exemplary) are affirmed at once, and
in doing so the poem will confirm the only proper kind of human
hope. In the poetic art that would like to have the Saint resurrected
outright, not merely as a *figure* of holiness, her face remains
"veil'd"; yet at the same time the imagination does invest her with a
measure of sanctity, albeit confined to the vestitures of resemblance:

> And such, as yet once more I trust to have
> Full sight of her in Heaven without restraint,
> Came vested all in white, pure as her mind:
> Her face was veil'd, yet to my fancied sight,
> Love, sweetness, goodness, in her person shin'd
> So clear, as in no face with more delight.

The inner purity of her "mind" is what "shin'd" outwardly. The
rhymes aspire to an illusion of identity between inner purity and
outer light; and that illusion is nearly confirmed by the phrase "in
her person," where the preposition suggests a shining which is both
immanent and emanating from her person. Such illusions of whole-
ness are accomplished through rhyme: "to my fancied sight" she
betokens "more delight." But this rhyme precisely identifies the
limits and aspirations of poetic language. The speaker might well
have desired "more delight" than this imagined sight of a woman
can provide. Prefiguring "more delight" which he can trust himself
to have in heaven, she remains to him only a figure, an image, even
though she shines "so clear." The momentary suspension of the
phrase, "so clear," as it enjambs lines 11 and 12, testifies to this
yearning; yet the constraints to poetic utterance undercut longing
that goes beyond a mortal's share. He refers, significantly, to the
Saint's "person," a word which connotes either an essence or an
insubstantiality, the figure of her but not her *self*. His vision of her
depends upon her likeness to Alcestis, but Alcestis is herself only a
figure in a story, although she bears at the same time a moral likeness
to one (Christ) who is beyond comparison. When the speaker desires
most intently to identify his whole delight, to see his Saint and his
wife completely, she remains either a mere figure (like a persona, a
"person" in a play) or an unembodied abstraction ("love, sweetness,
goodness").

In line 12 the tortuous syntax of the poem comes to rest, marking
the point at which the actualizing power of poetic language must
admit its limitation to be the nature of human expression itself: "So
clear, as in no face with more delight." If her shining person inspires
a yearning for "more delight," it also summons up the rather sinister

implication of that "veil'd" face: indeed, behind the veil there may be "no face" (as Admetus wondered if "she is really mine / or some sweet mockery for God to stun me with"). At the least, her divinely shining person is in danger of occluding all possible delight in merely mortal faces. If we choose to imagine the speaker as actually blind, then the further significance of the line is to remind him how utterly he has lost sight of all human faces. For him indeed no face shines with more delight than he can imagine. In any case, the privative phrase, "no face," stands at the exact center of line 12 and haunts the speaker's final attempt to comprehend the woman's full saintliness without the loss of human delight. In being pressed to see her either as a saint or as a woman he will be forced to relinquish even the initial delight which he found in her as an image. Is she really mine?

That question has never been a source of doubt for the Miltonic speaker as it was for Admetus. She has been only lent to his thought from the start. The poem's position has always been *intermediate*, reading the projected Christian meaning through the classical myth as imagined by Euripides while envisioning my late espoused Saint through her resemblances to an actual woman and to the typologically significant one, Alcestis. So balanced in its comparisons, so tactfully aware of the deception of resemblances, the poem seems to attain an almost Virgilian pathos in its (Christian) acknowledgment of *pietas* and *caritas*. Perhaps this is why the closing image of the poem reminds one of the lost and fleeing women, Creusa and Dido, in the *Aeneid*. But the likenesses of the first twelve lines are brought to a crisis in line 13 beyond which the delicate balance of comparison cannot be sustained. That crisis brings the first (and only) emotional outcry in the poem, and it is occasioned by the very word that had been to this point the focal point of the balance. Throughout the poem the word *as* has been a signal word for the making of similes, but in line 13 it suddenly takes on a wholly different meaning: "But O, as to embrace me she inclin'd, / I wak'd, she fled, and day brought back my night." *As* here does not mean *likeas* but *as if*, as if she were actually going to embrace him. But a physical embrace by a spirit can be only a figure of speech, not an actuality. This is the limitation of his vision and of poetic language in respect to spiritual things. Simultaneously, *as* suggests causal effect (*as this, then that*) and initiates the restitution of temporal progression which occurs in the last line. Both of these new senses of *as* come together at once in her gesture of embrace. Since the speaker cannot be actually embraced by her essence *as* a woman or *as* a saint, he must admit her insubstantiality *as* an image: he chooses to awake, to see this poem *as* what it has always almost seemed to be—a dream, the likeness of reality. The vision becomes a dream only as he wakes. If he did not wake, the last line would have to say, "And in her embracing me, I did attain full sight of her in heaven without restraint." In waking at the prospect of such an embrace the speaker concedes the proper limits of the human will beyond which, in Adam's words, it is "folly to aspire" (*PL* XII, 560). Admetus-like "cold consolation" must remain just that, a cold paradox, in which the poet's words, "sight" and "delight," although they are identical in sound, are not identical in meaning—as they are in heaven. Since seeing has been seen as thought, the speaker, however "inclin'd" himself to be embraced, must awake into the necessary limits of thought beyond which such sights cannot be thought in solely human terms, not even as dreams. Instantly, then, the temporal restraints return, "and day brought back my night." As I have tried to show, the speaker's conscious awareness of "restraint" has conditioned the emotional and thematic thrust of the poem from the start.

In an earlier poem, *On Time*, Milton tried to articulate the heavenly grace that devours the temporally bound, merely individual self in order to restore the greater human identity with God which occurs in eternity. He is speaking to Time:

> For when as each thing bad thou hast entomb'd,
> And, last of all, thy greedy self consum'd,
> Then long Eternity shall greet our bliss
> With an individual kiss.   (9–12)

"Individual" may mean indivisible, but it also means perfectly articulated, completely unalloyed, fully found, in the singular embrace of God, "t'whose happy-making sight alone" (18) Time, Death, and Chance, those figurations of happenstance, are seen as soundly defeated. The proffered "embrace" of *Sonnet XXIII* is this "individual kiss" of eternity. The speaker's "late espoused Saint" can offer it because she is already individuated by eternity, whereas the speaker must refuse her offer as not commensurate with his still mortal state. The quotidian light of day brings back the blinding night of the still mortal self.

Despite the syntactical nearness of "me" and "she" in line 14 ("as to embrace *me she* inclin'd"), a nearness which is emphasized by the emotional longings of the word "inclin'd," the discrete identities of mortal speaker and imagined saint cannot be joined. The thoughtful, poetically conceived likenesses of the poem cannot pass over the temporal progression which is implicit in the very word which inclines toward metaphorical identity, the word *as*. The only site where that embrace could take place is in eternity, but the language of the poem almost unknowingly (through the suggestion of causal effect in line 13) insists upon a return into time. "Full sight" in heaven means a direct and absolute identification with God which a mortal (any mortal, actually blind or merely blinded by the human estate) may understand only figuratively, by comparing it to kinds of partial, human sight. By refusing the embrace the speaker returns to that temporal world of divisions. But the refusal is not emotional cowardice; it is a measure of the speaker's mortal heroism, what Adam calls "my fill / Of knowledge, what this Vessel can contain." He cannot be embraced by eternity now, because his knowledge of eternity is contained in his own merely human, comparative understanding of it through the poem. And eternity is not comparative on human terms: it is "individual." He must wake to that. And he does.

The loss described in the poem's last six words is not, therefore, utter loss: "and day brought back my night." As day and night seem indistinguishable in their obscuring powers they may suggest the vanity itself of this world. Day and night are indeed indifferent; they are strangely like each other but utterly unlike "full sight" in heaven. *Utterly unlike:* that is the almost unconscious, indirect affirmation of God I referred to earlier in this article. Whereas in line 8 "full sight" was thought to be a merely hoped-for ultimatum, in line 14 such attainment is *proved* to be possible by the very darkness that both night and day bring. The vision proves itself true by being so much more vivid and distinct than what follows it.[15] In not being deceived by his own part in the making of that vision, the speaker is able to suggest, by indirection, what in the vision was *not* his making, what was "full sight" in spite of the partialities of his resemblances. This explains, then, the resigned but not defeated rhythm and tone of the last lines as he tacitly meditates upon the triumphant waking *from* this loss even while he speaks of waking *to* it. What makes Milton's last line so beautifully moving is that it recognizes this necessary loss of human delight by directly acknowledging human limitation, and yet it points indirectly toward "more delight" which is absolute individualization in the indivisible "happy-making sight of [God] alone," where we are all changed in a moment, in the twinkling of an eye. A poem so concerned with the making of similes thus depends for its final meaning on the utterly unlike or the transcendence of similitude. Shining "in no face with more delight" is the light of heaven, the metaphor that speaks identity.

Meantime, men must abide the temporal balance described by St. Paul, whose vision of restraint in respect to marriage is an analogue for Christian temperance in respect to God. Such Pauline poise depends upon the same kind of deliberate, fully imagined thoughtfulness that Milton's sonnet displays. It depends upon figuratively seeing *as,* as if such seeing can be understood as merely an interlude:

Art thou bound unto a wife? seek not to be loosed. Art thou loosed from a wife? seek not a wife. . . . But this I say, brethren, the time is short; it remaineth, that both they that have wives be *as though* they had none; and they that weep, *as though* they wept not; and they that rejoice, *as though* they rejoiced not; . . . for the fashion of this world passeth away. (1 Corinthians vii, 27, 29–30, 31; italics added)

St. Paul's metaphor, mediated by Milton's poem, provides the Christian sense of the chorus's final assertion in *Alcestis:* "God finds a way for what none foresaw. / Such was the end of this story" (1162–63).

I have hoped to show that in *Sonnet XXIII* Milton found his way by careful indirection, by not seeing what could not be seen, by seeing through Alcestis an analogue of Christian salvation. Through his singular use of similes, which by definition imply contrasts even as they name likenesses, Milton was able to manage the inferences behind his similes so that, in effect, he could imagine unspeakable heaven by explicitly not likening it too much.

University of Massachusetts, Amherst

NOTES

1. All references to Milton's poetry are to *John Milton, Complete Poems and Major Prose,* ed. Merritt Y. Hughes (New York, 1957). I should like to thank Kathleen M. Swaim for her help in bringing the complexities of Milton's rhetoric and the densities of my own into a clearer light.

2. The Renaissance understood that " 'story' as such is history" (Rosemond Tuve, *Elizabethan & Metaphysical Imagery* [Chicago, 1947], p. 246) and that Christian myth is the one true history. This use of myth in respect to Milton's poetry is, of course, the premise and thesis of Isabel Gamble MacCaffrey, *"Paradise Lost" as "Myth"* (Cambridge, Mass., 1959).

3. That Milton's reference is to Euripides' *Alcestis* was noted long ago by Thomas Warton, who is cited, along with a summary of other major critical positions,

in *A Variorum Commentary on The Poems of John Milton,* ed. A. S. P. Woodhouse and Douglas Bush (New York, 1972), vol. II, pt. 2, pp. 486–501.

4. J. C. Ulreich, "Typological Symbolism in Milton's Sonnet XXIII," *Milton Quarterly,* VIII (1974), 7–10; J. J. Colaccio, " 'A Death Like Sleep': The Christology of Milton's Twenty-Third Sonnet," *Milton Studies,* VI, ed. James D. Simmonds (Pittsburgh, 1974), pp. 181–97.

5. Ulreich, "Typological Symbolism," p. 9.

6. Ibid., p. 10.

7. Colaccio, " 'A Death Like Sleep,' " p. 193.

8. Ibid., p. 194.

9. Ulreich ("Typological Symbolism," p. 9) lucidly formulates the sonnet's concern with the imagination: "Considered archetypally, the sonnet describes the struggles of the human imagination to realize itself; indeed, the poem *is* such an imaginative act." Considered thematically, the poem's imaginative action is also the subject of Marilyn Williamson's "A Reading of Milton's Twenty-Third Sonnet," *Milton Studies,* IV, ed. James D. Simmonds (Pittsburgh, 1972), pp. 141–49. This reading does much to exorcise the poem of "sentimental, extrapoetic associations" (p. 148). By simply following the text, Williamson argues that the poem "may be read without reference to Mary Powell, Katherine Woodcock, or the poet's blindness" (p. 141). Williamson understands that the poem is a dramatization of its own imaginative predicament, but she is less convincing in telling how and why the predicament comes about. By failing to apprehend fully the rhetorical surface of the sonnet—its imaginative logic of similitudes, its interplay of resemblances—Williamson finds herself concluding that the poem has two "movements," one "rising" and one "falling" (147–48). This dynamic is not observed in the rhetoric of the poem but is appropriated from secondary critical descriptions, especially Leo Spitzer's analysis of the sonnet's "tripartite crescendo arrangement."

10. For a concise description of accommodation as it applies to Milton and to Protestant theology in general, see Roland M. Frye, *God, Man, and Satan* (Princeton, 1960), pp. 3–17.

11. Anne Davidson Ferry, *Milton's Epic Voice: The Narrator in "Paradise Lost"* (Cambridge, Mass., 1967), p. 142. See also her chapter on "Sacred Metaphor," pp. 88–115.

12. The aesthetic failure of the sonnet is argued by John Huntley, "Milton's 23rd Sonnet," *ELH,* XXXIV (1967), 468–81.

13. *Summa Contra Gentiles* I.xx., trans. Dominican Fathers (New York, Cincinnati, and Chicago, 1924). In *Christian Doctrine* (p. 905b) Milton imposed a necessary restraint upon thinking about God: "No one, however, can have right thoughts of God. . . . When we speak of knowing God, it must be understood with reference to the imperfect comprehension of man; for to know God as he really is, far transcends the powers of man's thought, much more of his perception."

14. Richmond Lattimore, trans., *The Complete Greek Tragedies: Euripides I* (Chicago, 1955), p. 51. All subsequent translations and line references are from this text.

15. The use of unlikenesses to demonstrate typological significance (as between the old and the new Adam) is explained by Barbara Kiefer Lewalski, *Milton's Brief Epic* (Providence, 1966), p. 176: "Adam was a rather special type in that his figural relation to Christ was defined chiefly through contrasts rather than, as is the usual emphasis, through resemblances, though of course in all typological symbolism both elements are present."

"ALCESTIS FROM THE GRAVE": IMAGE AND STRUCTURE IN *SONNET XXIII*

John Spencer Hill

I N 1951 LEO SPITZER suggested that, structurally, Milton's twenty-third sonnet has a "tripartite *crescendo* movement" which passes from pagan through Jewish tradition to an apotheosis in Christian tradition.[1] Spitzer's view of the sonnet's structure has been generally accepted and vigorously developed in recent years. Martin Mueller, for instance, believes the poem to be based on a "triptych Greece-Judaism-Christianity"; and Marilyn Williamson sees in the sonnet "a progressive definition of salvation" which moves "from physical salvation according to pagan legend to ritualistic salvation according to the Old Dispensation to true Christian salvation, in which the saint is the bride of the Lamb."[2] A similar triadic ascent from type to truth is proposed by John C. Ulreich: "Pagan, Hebraic, and Christian images are thus characterized respectively as physical (literal), moral (allegorical), and spiritual (symbolic); the poem works typologically to transform the emotionally charged pagan image into a fully significant Christian one."[3]

Although in agreement with those readers who have stressed the significance of the sonnet's tripartite structure, I believe that some of their observations require qualification and that certain others might be expanded and strengthened by additional evidence. There is, for example, much more that might be said about Milton's use of the Alcestis myth. It is customary, having cited Milton's debt to Euripides, to dismiss this allusion with little or no comment: "since it is pagan and contrary to fact," the Alcestis analogy "has given us little difficulty."[4] Rightly understood, however, Milton's handling of the myth is both rich and complex. The analogy established in the opening lines of the sonnet between the return of the "late espoused Saint" in a dream-vision and the restoration of Alcestis to "her glad Husband" is not abandoned after the first quatrain; rather, the influence of the analogy persists through the entire poem and is organic and not merely ornamental. The effect of the allusion

127

is cumulative; as the imagery of the sonnet moves from type to truth in allusive crescendo, the connotative value of the Alcestis image expands and deepens in association with Hebraic ritual and Christian truth.

I

It has long been recognized that the *Alcestis* of Euripides contributes a good deal to the imagery of *Sonnet XXIII*. The opening quatrain of Milton's poem

> Methought I saw my late espoused Saint
> Brought to me like *Alcestis* from the grave,
> Whom *Joves* great Son to her glad Husband gave,
> Rescu'd from death by force though pale and faint

is essentially a condensed restatement of the conclusion of the Euripidean version of the myth, in which Heracles forcibly wrests Alcestis from the control of Death and restores her to her "glad Husband," Admetus. A number of other parallels between the English sonnet and the Greek play have frequently been noted: like the restored heroine in Euripides, Milton's wife is silent; like her, she is veiled; and like her, she requires a period of ritualistic purification.

To these correspondences, all of which come from the end of the *Alcestis*, I would like to add a striking passage which occurs much earlier in the play and which, to my knowledge, has not so far been cited in connection with Milton's sonnet. The lines in question form part of a speech addressed by Admetus, well before the catastrophe, to his doomed wife:

> And through my dreams you'll come and go when day
> is done, and bring me bliss before you part:
> for it is sweet (long as such visions last)
> to see in dreams our loved ones from the past.
>
> But if I had the tune and tongue to sing
> like Thracian Orpheus (so I might charm
> with song Demeter's daughter and her king),
> I would have gone already and from harm
> and Hades won you back—not Pluto's cur,
> and not old Charon at the oar (whose right
> it is to guide the dead) would then deter
> me 'till I had restored your soul to light.
>   But since this cannot be, wait there for me
> to join you whensoe'er I die; prepare
> the house where we shall live eternally;

> and I shall charge our friends to place me there
> in that same cedar-box, stretched by your side:
> for even death cannot true love divide.[5]

There are several points of contact between these and Milton's lines, suggesting the possibility that Milton may have had this passage in mind as·he composed his sonnet. In the first place, both pieces concern themselves with the dream of a dead wife. Admetus anticipates the temporary restoration of Alcestis as a phantom who will gladden his dreams; in Milton's sonnet, which is a dream-vision, the hypothetical has become the actual, and the poet's wife appears as a restored Alcestis whose image is lost when the poet awakens. Second, as Admetus expects to be reunited with his wife after death, so too Milton trusts "once more . . . to have / Full sight of her in Heaven without restraint." And finally a third parallel, while explicit in the play, is only implicit in the sonnet—namely, Orphic myth. In the *Alcestis*, Admetus envies the lyric might of Orpheus which had charmed Eurydice away from the infernal powers;[6] in Milton's sonnet, the imagery in the concluding lines—"But O as to embrace me she enclin'd / I wak'd, she fled, and day brought back my night"—almost inevitably recalls the tragic tale of Orpheus and his "half-regained Eurydice" (*L'Allegro*, 149).[7]

The probability of there being a submerged allusion to Orpheus in the last two lines of *Sonnet XXIII* is considerably enhanced by several factors. First, as Milton would have known, the figures of Alcestis and Eurydice were frequently linked in Greek literature; such is the case not only in the lines quoted earlier from Euripides' *Alcestis,* but also in passages in Plato, Lucian, and Plutarch.[8] Second, Milton was throughout his life attracted by Orphic myth: the index to the Columbia edition lists fourteen references to the Thracian poet-priest and, as D. C. Allen notes, "Milton accents the legend of Orpheus in a way that suggests self-identification."[9] Third, interest in the sonnet's "tripartite *crescendo* movement" must not be allowed to obscure the fact that at the narrative level the poem records a loss rather than a restoration. In the empirical world of the poet's experience, the Alcestis-like apparition proves to be a false surmise and yields, as reality obtrudes on dream, to a Eurydice-like forfeiture. While the spiritual progression of the imagery traces an ascent from flesh to spirit, the narrative progression records a tragic countermovement which emphasizes in purely human terms the irreparable loss of the "late espoused Saint." The sonnet thus establishes a dialectical tension, building gradually through successive stages, between exoteric experience (narrative level) and esoteric understanding (symbolic level).

The tension established in the interaction of these two orders of reality is not resolved by the categorical rejection of one in favor of the other; indeed, no such simplistic resolution is possible, for both states are *real*. From the sonnet's opening line, Milton insists on the simultaneous apprehension of relative and absolute reality, of physical and spiritual truth: his wife is both dead ("late") and alive (a "Saint"). Throughout the poem Alcestis and Eurydice, as mythopoeic symbols of restoration and deprivation respectively, are held in suspended equilibrium, and the reader is neither invited nor permitted to choose between them. The epiphanic experience recorded in the sonnet combines loss with reunion, pathos with triumph; and, as in the final scene of *Paradise Lost* Adam and Eve in mingled hope and trepidation make their way toward the brave new world awaiting them beyond the gates of Eden, so too at the end of the sonnet Milton and the reader descend from vision to reality and are sent forth from the experience, "though sorrowing, yet in peace" (XI, 117).

In classical literature, Alcestis is invariably presented as a paradigm of wifely devotion and self-abnegation. She appears in this light in Euripides' play and in Plato's *Symposium*. Similar moral valuations are found in the writings of later mythographers such as Hyginus and Boccaccio; and, in English literature, the tradition is continued by both Chaucer and Spenser.[10]

Relative to Milton's sonnet, the most interesting of these later treatments of the Alcestis myth is that found in the Prologue to Chaucer's *Legend of Good Women*. In this poem, which is also a dream-vision, the narrator records an encounter between himself and the God of Love, who is accompanied by Queen Alcestis:

> Tho gan I loken endelong the mede,
> And saw hym come, and in his hond a quene
> Clothed in real habyt al of grene.
> A fret of goold she hadde next hyre her
> And upon that a whit corone she ber
> With many floures, and I shal nat lye;
> For al the world, ryght as the dayesye
> Ycorouned is with white leves lite,
> Swiche were the floures of her coroune white.[11]

For having defamed women in such compositions as *Troilus and Criseyde*, Chaucer is indicted by Cupid; however, before sentence can be pronounced on the apostate poet, Alcestis intervenes in his defense. She implores Cupid to be "somewhat tretable"—for, as she demonstrates in a catalogue of Chaucer's poems in praise of women, "The man hath served yow of this konnynge, / And forthered wel youre lawe with his makynge" (398–99). So eloquent is her *apologia* that Cupid relents and allows Alcestis to impose penance on the poet. The "milde quene" commands that for his misdeeds Chaucer shall atone by composing a legendary of Cupid's saints (469–75). It becomes apparent in the following lines that Chaucer is ignorant of the identity of his queenly intercessor, whereupon Cupid identifies her as "queene Alceste, / That turned was into a dayesye" (the transformation is Chaucer's invention) and briefly narrates the conventional myth of her self-sacrifice in the cause of true love. Knowledge of her identity, coupled with personal experience of her "grete goodnesse," leads the poet to exclaim:

> No wonder is though Jove hire stellifye,
> As telleth Agaton, for hyre goodnesse!
> Hire white coroun bereth of it witnesse.   (513–15)[12]

The number of parallels between Chaucer's treatment of Alcestis in the *Legend* and Milton's allusion to her in *Sonnet XXIII* make it improbable that these correspondences are entirely fortuitous. While both poets are conventional in treating Alcestis as an exemplary helpmate, several other parallels are not traditional aspects of the received myth. For example, in both Chaucer and Milton, Alcestis appears within the context of a dream-vision. Also, as Chaucer fails to recognize the "noble quene, / Corouned with whit" until Cupid reveals her identity, so Milton is initially uncertain of the precise nature of the apparition which visits him in sleep: "*Methought* I saw my late espoused Saint" (emphasis added).[13] Further, as the color most often associated with "Alceste" in the *Legend* is white, so the apparition in Milton's poem comes "vested all in white." Two other points of contact between the two works merit special notice. First, in the *Legend* Alcestis is a deified ideal who is literally apotheosized ("Jove hire stellifye": a Chaucerian innovation) and, in Milton's sonnet, the wife who appears to the poet "like *Alcestis* from the grave" is explicitly described as being a "Saint" with whom Milton trusts to be reunited "in Heaven." Second, it has long been recognized that Chaucer invests his Alcestis and Cupid with religious significance and that he applies theological concepts to the affairs of love: "It is therefore not surprising that Queen Alceste, the intercessor, should bear some resemblance in character and office to the Blessed Virgin. The God of Love, too, is not quite the ordinary Cupid, but has the character of a pitying lord."[14] Similarly, in *Sonnet XXIII,* which is a Christian poem, it needs to be remembered that it is a *saint* who appears to the poet "like *Alcestis* from the grave."

In the writings of the Italian Neoplatonists, the religious overtones of the myth implied in Chaucer are made quite explicit. In his *Commento sopra una canzona de amore,* for instance, Pico associates the death of Alcestis with the translation of the patriarchs Enoch and Abraham; and then, discussing the yearning of the mystic for union with Deity, he writes:

And from this we may understand with what mystery the story of Alcestis and Orpheus is endowed by Plato in the *Symposium.* . . . Alcestis achieved the perfection of love because she longed to go to the beloved through death; and dying through love, she was by the grace of the gods revived. . . . And Plato could not have suggested this more lightly or subtly than by the example he gave of Orpheus, of whom he says that, desiring to go and see his beloved Eurydice, he did not want to go there through death but, softened and refined by his music, sought a way of going there alive, and for this reason, says Plato, he could not reach the true Eurydice, but beheld only a shadow or spectre.[15]

Without attempting to unravel the tangled skein of Neoplatonic love theory (assuming that were possible), it is enough for present purposes to notice that Pico interprets the myth of Alcestis within the context of Judaeo Christian resurrection and of Christian mysticism, and that he brings the Alcestis legend and Orphic myth together in close thematic relationship.

To summarize briefly: since the Alcestis myth had been invested with theological significance by some Christian writers (Chaucer, Pico), and since there exists a long tradition linking Alcestis with Orphic myth (Euripides, Plato, Lucian, Plutarch, and Pico), there would seem to be adequate reason for believing that Milton's allusion to Alcestis is rich and complex, and for reassessing the implications of the analogy in terms of the sonnet's structure and intention. Toward at least a partial fulfillment of these aims, I offer the following reading of *Sonnet XXIII.*

II

The triadic structure of Milton's last sonnet furnishes, in miniature, another instance of a pattern which appears quite frequently in the later poetry. Similar allusive triptychs are discernible, for example, in the Proserpine-Eve-Mary progression centered in Books IV and V of *Paradise Lost,* and also in the Deucalion-Noah-Christ triad which provides a graded symbolic frame for the historical vision recorded in Books XI and XII; a further instance of the pattern exists in the Hercules-Samson-Christ figure in *Samson Agonistes.*[16] In each case, these structures move from type to truth in a series of three ascending stages: pagan (myth) to Hebraic (type) to Christian (antitype). And in each case, the three figures of the triptych are not wholly discrete or merely complementary, but cumulative; their significance is realized as process, the meaning of the first two types remaining potential rather than actual, partial rather than complete, until fulfilled in the antitype. Moreover, in none of the figural triads in *Paradise Lost* or *Samson Agonistes* is the classical allusion rejected as being "pagan and contrary to fact"; rather, it is in every instance developed through the imagery and expanded in such a way as to demonstrate its prefigurative significance. Since the Renaissance regarded Hercules, Proserpine, and Deucalion as shadowy emblems of Christian truths, it has not been difficult to see how Milton was able to treat them as organic components of the typological constructs in the various poems in which they appear. Orpheus, too, was confidently thought to prefigure Christian values. One of the major functions of the preceding section of this article has been to establish that Alcestis, while never as popular with the exegetes as Hercules or Orpheus, deserves a place in the roll of those classical heroes and heroines in whose histories medieval and Renaissance expositors discerned the dim foreshadowings of Christian truth. Once this point is granted, it becomes possible to demonstrate that Milton's allusion to Alcestis is an organic and pervasive image and to show in precisely what way *Sonnet XXIII* "works typologically to transform the emotionally charged pagan image into a fully significant Christian one."[17]

As noted above, the allusion to Alcestis in the opening quatrain is a condensed restatement of the Euripidean version of the myth in which Heracles rescues Alcestis and restores her to her husband. The lines thus introduce the themes of restoration and salvation. While the deliverance offered at this stage is pagan and physical only, the imagery anticipates the higher reality of an inward and spiritual grace. First, the mythic redemption of Alcestis foreshadows the Christian doctrine of the resurrection of the just and their translation to eternal bliss; and moreover, Alcestis' sacrificial death—she died that Admetus might live—extends still further her typological suggestiveness. Second, since Milton's century affirmed that "Our blessed Saviour is the true Hercules,"[18] the act whereby "*Joves* great

Son" restores Alcestis is equally clearly an analogue of Christian redemption, and Milton seems to stress the Hercules-Christ identification by insisting on the pagan hero's divine paternity. However, while there are obvious typological overtones in the Alcestis analogy, Milton is careful in the opening lines to place the allusion in its proper pagan context and to underscore the inherent limitations of pagan mythology as a foreshadowing of Christian truth: the restored Alcestis is "pale and faint," whereas Milton's wife *shines* with "Love, sweetness, goodness." The tentative character of the poet's vision ("Methought I saw") further qualifies the pre-figurative value of the analogy at this stage.

The stressed possessive "Mine," explicitly distinguishing the poet's wife from Alcestis, introduces the second movement and signals the progression, in theme and symbol, from pagan legend to Old Testament law. Typologically, the ascent brings us one step further toward the truth. The purification simile of the second quatrain is complex and has given critics considerable difficulty. For present purposes, however, it will suffice to notice two things. First, the purification image is a *simile:* "like Alcestis, the woman under the old Law is an analogue to the speaker's wife and not the wife herself."[19] The salvation offered by the Levitical rite of purification is ritualistic and imperfect, and is, in any case, unavailable to a Christian such as Milton's wife; she can no more be saved by cere-monial law than by the legendary might of Hercules, for under the Covenant of Grace men must "renounce / Their own both righteous and unrighteous deeds" (*PL* III, 291–92) and live transplanted in Christ, through whose imputed merit alone they are saved. And second, Milton's typology in this second quatrain is *artistically* successful because the analogy of Hebraic purification subsumes and advances the symbolic implications of the allusion to Alcestis and, at the same time, anticipates the full Christian salvation of the sestet. Although Alcestis did not die in childbirth, the image of purification is nonetheless appropriate to her case, for (as we learn at the end of the *Alcestis*) her restoration is incomplete until sub-sequent purification releases her from consecration to Dis: "You are not allowed to hear her speak until she has been dedicated to the nether gods and the third day comes" (1144–46). In associating Alcestis with Mosaic law, the symbolic value of the pagan allusion is extended beyond the opening quatrain; and indeed, as Fitzroy Pyle has suggested, it may have been the recollection of these lines from Euripides which led Milton to "think of 'purification in the old Law' as instrumental in his wife's apparent release."[20] Moreover, if the purification simile looks back to Alcestis, it just as clearly points forward to the Christian image of the sestet—for, typologically, the rite of purification described in Leviticus xii, 4–8, prefigures the purification of Mary in Luke ii, 21–24.

In the last six lines of the sonnet, type yields to truth and the two proleptic similes of the preceding lines are gathered up in the vision of the final movement. As Ulreich points out, the imagery moves "from simile (*'like* Alcestis,' '*as* whom') to concrete, metaphorical presence; and from the mere outward shape of a dream to the inward reality of vision."[21] However, the figural postulates of the opening quatrains are not abandoned but are rather subsumed and transformed: both mythic, physical salvation (Alcestis) and ritualistic purgation (Mosaic law) are transfigured and spiritualized in the angelic apparition who comes "vested all in white, pure as her mind." By the divine alchemy of grace, the external and ceremonial purity of lines 5–6 has been refined into inward, spiritual innocence: "pure as her mind." And the Saint's veil and white robes, which link her with Alcestis, are also the symbols of her eternal sanctification: "And to her was granted that she should be arrayed in fine linen, clean and white: for the fine linen is the righteousness of saints" (Revelation xix, 8).

Once the sonnet's tripartite typological ascent from pagan myth to Christian truth has been established, there still remains a further point of considerable importance, namely, what is the *artistic purpose* of the poem's typology? Like the vision itself, the development within the poem is internal: the *real* subject is not the "late espoused Saint" herself but Milton's growing perception of her. Since the apparition is a *saint,* she cannot change or evolve or develop; having been once "made white in the blood of the Lamb" (Revelation vii, 14), she is immutable and static. The progression implied in the tripartite symbolic crescendo leading from type to truth is, therefore, that of the *poet's* growth toward vision. The "late espoused Saint" is the catalyst of the vision, and the images used to depict her are, in reality, symbols of the poet's gradual accommodation to visionary experience. Like stepping from a darkened room into the full effulgence of a summer noon, human sight (or insight) requires time to adapt to the radiance of Truth. Initially, the vision appears "pale and faint" and the poet even doubts what he sees; gradually, however, as inward mists are purged, partial vision evolves into full mystic apprehension and, poetically, simile yields to firm metaphoric presence: "Her face was vail'd, yet to my fancied sight, / Love, sweetness, goodness, in her person shin'd / So clear, as in no face with more delight." Unlike Admetus, who needed the veil removed before he was able to identify Alcestis, Milton recognizes his wife by the heavenly virtues shining so clearly in her face that the veil is no impediment. The point I would emphasize is this: the subject of *Sonnet XXIII* is, in fact, Milton's own growth toward vision—a growth described in a symbolic ascent from pagan myth to Christian truth; it follows, therefore, that the *structure* of the poem mirrors its theme, and that the sonnet is itself an analogue of the very experience it records.

But it is just at this moment of clearest vision when, by a sudden peripeteia, reality obtrudes on dream and the apparition is lost: "I wak'd, she fled, and day brought back my night."[22] A lesser poet would have sentimentalized this moment or made it an anticlimax; Milton does neither. The reversal in the last line, while arresting, is not entirely unexpected; it has been prepared for all along. As I noted earlier, Milton juxtaposes the themes of loss and reunion from the opening line, so that throughout the sonnet a dialectical tension is established between exoteric experience and ascending esoteric understanding, between mortal reality (characterized by temporal loss) and immortal reality (characterized by eternal reunion). Thus, while the last line emphasizes the desolation of blindness and physical separation, its hopelessness is balanced and qualified by the spiritual insights gained in the preceding lines, which promise a restoration beyond time and an eternity of unhindered communion: "once more I trust to have / Full sight of her in Heaven without restraint."

Milton's last sonnet is, then, a highly wrought production. Balancing loss against restoration, despair against triumph in delicate equilibrium, the poem traces an evolving definition of salvation ascending from flesh to spirit in three interdependent stages: pagan, Hebraic, and Christian. Taking as its point of departure the fiction of Alcestis' rescue and restoration by Hercules, Milton's mythopoeic imagination works typologically to transform fictive symbol into spiritual reality and simile into metaphor. The crucial point is that the allusion to Alcestis is not rejected but assimilated, not exploded but exploited. For, while the pagan myth is *literally* untrue, the sonnet's imagery demonstrates that *symbolically* the restoration of Alcestis is an appropriate analogue to the poet's affirmation of spiritual reunion "in Heaven." The envisaged reunion, however, is to be neither immediate nor earthly and, as the heavenly apparition bends to embrace the dreamer, he wakes and the vision is lost. Within the Christian context of the poem, the return to reality, while poignant and moving—doubly so because of Milton's blindness—is neither wholly debilitating nor cause for despair. The desolation of the Eurydice-like loss is balanced against and tempered by the consolatory assurance of an Alcestis-like restoration.

While *Sonnet XXIII* is one of the most personal of Milton's poems, it is also one of the most highly crafted. What makes the sonnet impressive is its harmonious blending of manner and matter: art imposes form and control on biography, and biography imparts emotional force to the patterns of art. More efficaciously than any other of his sonnets, Milton's last stands as an eloquent refutation of that "lively saying" of Samuel Johnson who, when asked by a friend why the poet of *Paradise Lost* "should write such poor Sonnets," responded with habitual dogmatism: "Milton, Madam, was a genius that could cut a Colossus from a rock; but could not carve heads upon cherry-stones."[23] Modern readers have usually found this saying too lively by half.

University of Western Australia

NOTES

1. "Understanding Milton," *Hopkins Review*, IV (1951), 21–22.

2. Mueller, "The Theme and Imagery of Milton's Last Sonnet," *Archiv fur das Studium der neueren Sprachen und Literaturen*, CCI (1964–65), 267; Williamson, "A Reading of Milton's Twenty-Third Sonnet," *Milton Studies*, IV, ed. James D. Simmonds (Pittsburgh, 1972), p. 147.

3. "Typological Symbolism in Milton's Sonnet XXIII," *Milton Quarterly*, VIII (1974), 8.

4. Williamson, "A Reading," p. 143.

5. Ll. 354–68. The translation is mine.

6. In *Alcestis*, 357–62, Euripides appears to be drawing on an earlier version of the myth in which Orpheus succeeded in restoring his wife to life: cf. C. M. Bowra, "Orpheus and Eurydice," *Classical Quarterly*, n.s. II (1952), 119.

7. T. B. Stroup ("Aeneas' Vision of Creusa and Milton's Twenty-Third Sonnet," *PQ*, XXXIX [1960], 125–26) argues that the Alcestis allusion is inappropriate and cannot be applied to the sonnet's closing lines, since Alcestis is restored while Milton's wife is not; however, as I hope to show, the Alcestis-Eurydice nexus in Milton's imagery extends the allusive force of the Alcestis analogy through to the poem's conclusion.

8. Plato, *Symposium*, 179 b–d; Lucian, *Mortuorum Dialogi*, 23.3; Plutarch, *Amatores*, 17.

9. "Milton and the Descent to Light," in *Milton: Modern Essays in Criticism*, ed. A. E. Barker (Oxford, 1965), p. 181. See also C. W. Mayerson, "The Orpheus Image in *Lycidas*," *PMLA*, LXIV (1949), 189–207.

10. Plato, *Symposium,* 179 b–c; Hyginus, *Fabula* 51; Boccaccio, *Genealogia Deorum Gentilium,* XIII, 1; Chaucer, *Troilus and Criseyde,* V, 1527–33, and also ll. 75–76 of the Prologue to *The Man of Law's Tale;* Spenser, *Virgil's Gnat,* 425–27.

11. *The Works of Geoffrey Chaucer,* ed. F. N. Robinson, 2d ed. (Boston, 1957), 144–52; line references are to the "G" text.

12. Plato's *Symposium* was also known as the *Agathonis Convivium* ("Agathon's Feast") since the dramatic setting of the dialogue is the house of Agathon, an Attic tragedian.

13. See also Euripides' *Alcestis,* 1037–1122, where Admetus fails to recognize his wife until Heracles removes her veil.

14. Robinson, *Works of Chaucer,* p. 840.

15. Pico, *Commento,* III, viii, as quoted in Edgar Wind, *Pagan Mysteries in the Renaissance,* rev. ed. (London, 1967), pp. 156–57.

16. For Proserpine-Eve-Mary, see IV, 268–324, and V, 385–87; for Deucalion-Noah-Christ, see XI, 9–14, 719–901, and XII, 1–7, 356–465. The Hercules-Samson-Christ triad is discussed briefly by F. M. Krouse, *Milton's Samson and the Christian Tradition* (Princeton, 1949), pp. 44–45.

17. Ulreich, "Typological Symbolism," p. 8.

18. Alexander Ross, *Mystagogus Poeticus* (London, 1648), p. 169. In fact, Ross makes this point even more forcefully and (for present purposes) perhaps more relevantly when he writes in his section on Admetus that "in hell the soul should have continued for ever, if Christ our *Alcides* had not delivered it from thence" (1647 edition, p. 8).

19. Williamson, "A Reading," p. 143.

20. Pyle, "Milton's Sonnet on his 'Late Espoused Saint,'" *RES,* XXV (1949), 59.

21. Ulreich, "Typological Symbolism," p. 7.

22. So many analogues have been suggested for *Sonnet XXIII* and especially for its concluding line that one hesitates to offer yet another; however, some striking parallels in Petrarch's *Sonetto CCLXXVI* would seem to merit at least a footnote.

> Poi che la vista angelica, serena,
> Per subita partenza in gran dolore
> Lasciato à l'alma, e 'n tenebroso orrore,
> Cerco parlando d'allentar mia pena.
> Giusto duol certo a lamentar mi mena;
> Sassel chi n'è cagione, e sallo Amore;
> Ch'altro rimedio non avea 'l mio core
> Contra i fastidi', onde la vita è piena.
> Questo un, morte, m'à tolto la tua mano.
> E tu che copri, e guardi, e ài or teco,
> Felice terra, quel bel viso umano,
> Me dove lasci, sconsolato e cieco,
> Poscia che 'l dolce e amoroso e piano
> Lume degli occhi miei non è piú meco?

The clear and angelic face of Laura (*la vista angelica, serena*) and the adjectival catalogue of her virtues (*dolce e amoroso e piano*) recall the clear, radiant face of Milton's wife and the nearly verbatim description of her purity: "Love, sweetness, goodness." Moreover, Laura's sudden departure (*subita partenza*), which leaves the poet comfortless and blind (*sconsolato e cieco*) because bereft of the light of his eyes (*Lume degli occhi miei*), reminds one in its own diffuse way of that poignant moment in the last line of Milton's sonnet. (Petrarch's sonnet is reproduced from *Le Rime di Francesco Petrarca*, ed. N. Zingarelli [Bologna, 1964], pp. 1253–55.)

23. Boswell, *Life of Johnson* (Oxford, 1965), p. 1301.

MILTON'S "THORN IN THE FLESH": PAULINE DIDACTICISM IN *SONNET XIX*

Gary A. Stringer

I

ALMOST WITHOUT exception since the appearance of Smart's classic edition of Milton's sonnets in 1921, critics have accepted "When I Consider" primarily as a lyrical eruption from the depths of Milton's psyche.[1] Prompted by the insistently specific phrase "Ere half my days," this tacit assumption has fueled perennial interest in the problem of dating the sonnet and has invested the poem with a wide array of supposed biographical implications.[2] But those issues, interesting as they are, have obscured the fact that the sonnet is not essentially lyric; rather it reaches toward the narrative and the dramatic, an esthetic object consciously and decisively separated from its creator. Whatever perplexity or agony of soul he may have endured in confronting his blindness, Milton does not use this sonnet's scanty plot of ground to work out his private feelings; his brow was not furrowed, as the reader's presumably is, at the question in line 7. To put it another way, the poem does not comprise a unique, subjective meditation;[3] it is instead the consciously confected image of a spiritual question moved and answered, more like Herbert's "The Collar" than Donne's "Batter My Heart."

All of which is to say that this sonnet, derived in part from biblical parables, is itself a kind of parable, distanced from the author by devices grammatical, rhetorical, and semantic. In addition to Joseph Pequigney, who adopts the expedient of a purely fictive speaker in the octave in order to jump the dating impasse, several critics have sensed a tone of detachment in the poem, but none has quite managed to account for this feeling. Roger L. Slakey, for example, observed: "the fact that the poem is in the present tense might suggest that the situation is repeated and that *when* is whenever,"[4] thus touching the essential grammatical point. But Slakey does not appreciate the generic implications of his insight, for if the poem denotes repeated experience, it cannot be lyric. Working against the present-tense verbs, the suggestion of recurrence generalizes the event and thus objectifies it for Milton. We must therefore reclassify the sonnet, despite the verb structure and the personal pronouns, for in implying the reiteration of conflict, Milton in effect "prolongs and broods upon himself as the centre of an epical event" and sets that event in the middle distance between the reader and himself.[5]

Having thus thrust his experience to arm's length, Milton enjoys the narrative poet's freedom to direct his material to whatever end he chooses, and reading the sonnet in this light reveals that his primary purpose is didactic. He structures the poem on an antithetical pattern after the standard Italian fashion, showing a resolved tension that may be defined by such paired opposites as "I"-Patience, question-answer, complex-plain, rebellion-trust, and error-truth. The result, as I have suggested above, is a parable designed for Everyman's moral instruction.

Not recognizing this sonnet's public, didactic character, critics have had much difficulty with the allusion in the octave to the parable of the talents. The determination to dig up Milton's private spiritual records has evoked numerous learned applications of the parable to the poet's supposed state of mind, but the accumulated results of these labors are inconclusive, ranging from the one polar position of identifying Milton with the unprofitable third servant to the other of divorcing the poet from that sluggardly outcast absolutely.[6] The absence of general consensus on this crucial point suggests the misdirection of critical effort: interpretation of the parable has not clarified the meaning of the poem, in short, because it has erroneously assumed the identity of the poet with the speaker in the octave. If we avoid that pitfall, however, we can see that the "I" in the poem voices a complaint that Milton the man would have regarded as absurd, for Milton the author clearly shows it to be so.

The intrusive word *fondly* is our first clue in this matter. It has generally been argued that the foolishness of the speaker's question " 'Doth God exact day-labor, light denied' " consists in a discrepancy between human thought and a higher wisdom expounded by Patience, and this in a sense is true. But simple logic shows that the persona's question is also intrinsically foolish. Lines 1–7 contain a series of kernel propositions, all of which derive from either common sense or scriptural doctrine, that leads to a definite and unmistakable conclusion: God gives us light; God requires us to work; we must have light if we are to work; God has deprived me of light. The logically necessary end of this argument is, *ergo*, God does not

require me to work. By his question, however, the speaker suggests
the contrary conclusion and thereby threatens to abuse the process
of reason. Accordingly, upon intervening to justify God's ways, Patience does not so much supplant wisdom of the human order with
that of the divine as correct the protester's error in logic. For in
substance, Patience's answer, " 'They also serve who only stand and
wait,' " is precisely the conclusion required by the premises the
speaker has articulated, a conclusion he foolishly (illogically) tries to
deny.

Milton's artful manipulation of the poem's syntax furnishes further evidence of his distance from the plaintiff in the octave and
marks the unreliability of that speaker's response to experience.
Taylor Stoehr asserts that the troubled syntax of the octave reflects
anger and "gives the poem a perilous suspense, which the straightforward structure of the sestet then disperses and transcends."[7] We
may well agree with Stoehr's reaction to the lesson of Patience, but I
think he partly misconstrues the emotion, and hence the function of
syntax, in the octave. More than the rising tension of increasing
anger, the sinuous, overstuffed period of the first speaker connotes
confusion and an inability to grasp facts surehandedly. This vexed
syntax, in short, is the formal equivalent of the tangled thought it
embodies, a sophism that Milton, on firm biblical ground, shortly
labels a "murmur."[8]

I therefore suggest that here, as so skillfully elsewhere, Milton
has contrived to put into his protagonist's mouth a deliberate and
self-evident paralogism, a chain of specious reasoning that the
author of a handbook of logic would hardly have expected to be
charged with. If the reader is deceived into taking the problem
seriously, so much the worse for his moral and rational preten-
sions—he merely reveals his own frailty and need of instruction.
What he is meant to notice is the all-too-human absurdity of the
grumbler's murmur against God and the patience, "that whereby we
acquiesce in . . . [his] promises,"[9] that lays such foolishness to rest. If
he merely perceives one man's struggle and its eventual resolution,
failing to discern a moral for his own life, he trivializes the sonnet
and misses Milton's main point.

II

Were "When I Consider" primarily an intimate confession of
spiritual failure, it would perhaps be unique among Milton's poems,
for, as Parker has said, Milton's characteristic tone is that of a man
addressing others, frequently, one might add, with a magisterial

edge in his voice. This tone is accounted for, in large measure, by the "half-classical, half-Calvinistic" conviction that he had been especially commissioned, among the elect, as a clarion voice to proclaim God's truth.[10] The educative intent I suggested above has (at least) the virtue of harmonizing *Sonnet XIX* with the dominant tenor of Milton's life. Turning to the sestet, I should like to examine further evidence that this poem springs from the same confidence in self and God that Milton evinces elsewhere. This information resides in the sonnet's matter rather than its structure, requiring us to analyze the soil Milton has so carefully marked off and tilled.

The personification of Patience, whose prevenient interruption pacifies the repiner, is the means by which Milton chooses to dramatize the promise of Isaiah xxix, 24, "they that murmured shall learn doctrine." And his use of this figure amounts to more than a mere defensive attempt to throw a "cloak of impersonality over what has up to this been naked self-exposure";[11] indeed, the objectification of characters is a ubiquitous, apparently indispensable technique of the epic poet. In addition to the greater sense of immediacy provided the audience, the device affords the author a mask through which to speak not in his proper voice. So Milton divorces himself from the murmur in the octave; so he steps back from the answer of the sestet—in the first case to dissociate himself from a fatuous distrust, in the second to distance himself modestly from the definitive pronouncement of right reason. That decorum dictates such a withdrawal becomes clear when we recognize what Dale Herron has called a "prophetic, visionary tone" in the sestet as Milton's adoption of not only the hortatory manner, but also the verbal substance of Pauline doctrine.[12]

Allusions to the apostle's words have previously been noted in the "stand and wait" of Patience's exhortation. J. L. Jackson and W. E. Weese see here the definition of an active Christian posture that finds its authority in Paul's emphatic admonition to the Ephesians to "put on the whole armour of God, that ye may be able to stand against the wiles of the devil."[13] To this may be added the probable Pauline warrant for the phrase from lines 5–6, "present / My true account." Anticipating Milton's reference in *An Apology* to his "certaine account" (CM, III, p. 282), these words recall Paul's warning in Romans xiv, 12, "So then every one of us shall give account of himself to God." Instructive as they are, however, these links between the sonnet and Paul would assume much less importance were they not undergirded by an allusion that towers over them in significance: almost the whole of the sestet derives directly from the apostle's sermon to the Athenian philosophers on Mars' hill recorded in Acts, chapter xvii.

Noting that the "too superstitious" Athenians have included in their devotions an altar "To the Unknown God," the apostle seizes the opportunity to testify of that deity and proceeds with a basic definition of God and his nature: "God that made the world and all things therein, seeing that he is Lord of heaven and earth, dwelleth not in temples made with hands; Neither is worshipped with men's hands, as though he needed any thing, seeing he giveth to all life, and breath, and all things" (verses 24–25).[14] It may be that Milton draws upon scholastic angelology for his elaboration of God's servants into multitudinous ranks of messengers and waiters,[15] but this Pauline text is clearly the seed from which stems Patience's central theme: " 'God doth not need / Either man's work or his own gifts; who best / Bear his mild yoke, they serve him best; his State / Is Kingly.' " Patience's rejoinder to the persona's question, then, bears not only the weight of reason, but also the authority of Scripture.[16]

Of considerably greater import is the behind-the-scenes relation of poet to apostle to which these allusive lines point. One does not, of course, have to recognize the present reference to make the connection, since Milton inscribed two albums—Christopher Arnold's in 1651, Johannes Zollikofer's in 1656—with Paul's testimony of a "strength . . . made perfect in weakness" (2 Corinthians xii, 9), a text he also employed in the *Second Defense* to rebut the nasty *ad hominem* of Alexander More.[17] In fact, the repeated recourse to the passage from 2 Corinthians is more instructive of Milton's attitude toward the apostle than is his allusion to the sermon in Acts, since the former exists in the context of Paul's self-abasing account of his enigmatic "thorn in the flesh" (verse 7). This was certainly a weakness with which Milton could sympathize; I believe it was a physical malady with which he could directly identify.

In the long history of speculation about the nature of Paul's affliction, almost every conceivable trouble has been suspected at one time or another. In Milton's recent past, for example, Luther had recorded three distinct opinions on the subject: persecution (1519), persecution and spiritual trials (1535), and, finally, only spiritual trials "which no Papist has understood."[18] If Luther gloried in thus aspersing the earlier Papist ascetics, who had seen in the apostle's *stimulus carnis* an admission of carnal longings, he followed even earlier Catholic expositors in suggesting persecutions. The Greek Fathers—Chrysostom, Theophylact, Theodoret, Oecumenius—as well as Saint Ambrose and Erasmus, understood Paul's obscure

lament as a reference to suffering at the hands of enemies.[19] Persecutions, in fact, had been among the alternative explanations summarized by Jerome at the close of the fourth century as (1) the
apostle's "carnal preaching of the Gospel, as addressed to babes; (2)
His mean personal appearance; (3) Some bodily malady . . . ; (4)
Persecutions endured by him."[20]

Post-Enlightenment critics have been inclined to render Paul's
figure "thorn in the flesh" more or less literally, supposing that only
a physical malady could have given rise to such a poignant metaphor.
Among the suggestions of renal trouble, gout, colic, hemorrhoids,
Maltese fever, epilepsy, and neurasthenia, the possibility of eye
trouble—perhaps ophthalmia or partial blindness—is of particular
interest to the student of Milton.[21] The argument for this interpretation correlates three other texts with the passage from 2 Corinthians, chapter xii: Paul's allusion to a humiliating weakness in
Galatia to which his audience had responded so compassionately
that he observes, "If it had been possible, ye would have plucked out
your own eyes, and have given them to me" (Galatians iv, 15); his
valedictory reference in that same epistle to the large size of the
characters written with his own hand (vi, 11); and his withdrawal of a
sharp rebuke to Ananias the high priest on grounds that he "wist
not . . . that he was the high priest" (Acts xxiii, 5)—a retraction most
simply and plausibly explained by poor vision. Moreover, to some
expositors the conclusion suggested by these passages takes on
added appeal in the light of the apostle's initial experience of blindness at the time of his conversion.[22]

Taken in isolation, of course, modern interpretations of Paul's
"thorn" bear only indirectly upon our knowledge of how the question was understood in the seventeenth century. They assume much
more significance, however, when we remember that, in settling
upon some physical ailment, current expositors echo one of the very
earliest identifications on record. In his *De Pudicitia* (ca. 208),
Tertullian writes: "He [Paul] declares that there was given him a
stake, an Angel of Satan, by whom he was buffeted, lest he should
uplift himself . . . that is by a pain, as they say, in his ear or in his
head."[23] Tertullian's casual phrase "as they say" suggests a source in
popular legend, perhaps reaching back to Paul's own lifetime. His
comment is thus endowed with a simple, undogmatic authority that
largely disappeared at the hands of the medieval allegorizers and
hagiographers, who tended to project their own weaknesses onto
Paul and see in his temptation "a more or less perfect reflexion of the
trials which beset their own lives."[24] Directed by modern principles

of exegesis, recent commentators have pursued literal explanations aimed at recovering the same historical fact in which the early oral tradition originated. Thus, in reviving an ancient concern, these latter-day critics provide insights that carry retroactive significance. And this principle is worth noting in the present instance, for although Milton would perhaps not have been led by the critical tradition to suspect eye trouble in the apostle's case, he did have access to all the primary evidence upon which arguments about that affliction are based, and he was not reluctant to interpret Scripture independently.[25]

The likelihood that Milton identified himself and Paul as fellow sufferers, alike in the nature as well as the significance of their trials, emerges distinctly from the autobiographical section of the *Second Defense*. Defending himself against Salmasius and others who had attributed his affliction to God's displeasure, he responds that, on the contrary, he has "experienced singular marks of the divine regard" and observes further that blindness is a misfortune "which has been known to happen to the most distinguished and virtuous persons in history." He then enumerates a list of such individuals, including Tiresias, Timoleon of Corinth, Appius Claudius, Dandolo of Venice, Jerome Zanchius, the "partriarch Isaac," and "perhaps also his son Jacob." At this point Milton breaks off the list to protest that he had knowingly spent the last of his sight in the pursuit of liberty and declares that, given a choice, he would "prefer my blindness to yours [that of the attacker]; yours," he charges,

is a cloud spread over the mind, which darkens both the light of reason and conscience; mine keeps from my view only the colored surfaces of things, while it leaves me at liberty to contemplate the beauty and stability of virtue and truth. How many things are there besides which I would not willingly see; how many which I must see against my will; and how few which I feel any anxiety to see! There is, as the apostle has remarked, a way to strength through weakness.[26]

The passage speaks for itself: here, in the cool, left-handed prose of autobiography, Milton acclaims his own sense of God's favor, attests the willing sacrifice of his sight for liberty and truth, affirms an increased intensity of inner light, and directly links this image of himself with Paul, whom he puts at the very end of a catalogue of blind seers and prophets climactically arranged. If he does not actually specify the nature of Paul's malady, he had a strong precedent in Paul's own silence on the point, and why this precedent should have carried such weight is at least partly explained by the implication that he has in some mysterious way been chosen to assume the apostle's mantle in a latter day. This identification stands, it seems to me, no matter how Milton may have interpreted Paul's malady, and it imports a great deal about Milton's public posture in his later career. In order to understand the poet-prophet relationship more clearly, we need to look closely at the twelfth chapter of 2 Corinthians, where Paul refers to his "thorn."

After chronicling in chapter xi the perils he has suffered for the Gospel, Paul testifies in chapter xii of "visions and revelations of the Lord." Referring to himself in the third person, he says that he "knew a man in Christ above fourteen years ago" who was "caught up to the third heaven" where he "heard unspeakable words, which it is not lawful for a man to utter." In order that such "abundance of revelations" should not cause him to be "exalted above measure," he continues, there was given to him a "thorn in the flesh, the messenger of Satan to buffet" him. Although the Lord denied his plea to have the thorn removed, Paul avers, he did offer the consolatory promise, "My grace is sufficient for thee: for my strength is made perfect in weakness." Paul accordingly submits to God's will: "Most gladly therefore will I rather glory in my infirmities that the power of Christ may rest upon me. Therefore I take pleasure in infirmities, in reproaches, in necessities, in persecutions, in distresses for Christ's sake: for when I am weak, then am I strong."

This is clearly a seminal text—both for its precise relation to the *Second Defense* and for the wider understanding it provides of Milton's mature conception of his role as poet-teacher. As my summaries show, the parallels between these particular autobiographical reflections extend considerably beyond the common affirmation of strength through weakness. Except for labeling his malady a divinely permitted countercheck to pride (which he perhaps forgoes in respect of that very sin), Milton explicitly echoes every major point of the Pauline statement: both allude to physical losses willingly sustained in the service of truth; both profess a recompense of higher wisdom; both repose on the paradox of a divine power that turns frailty to strength. Further, Milton even came to "glory" in his "infirmities" as a symbol of divine inspiration, believing that the truth revealed to him was not only lawful, but needful for man to utter "in Prose or Rhyme."[27] Indeed, if Milton did not actually see himself as an avatar of the Pauline essence, it seems undeniable that he felt a unique kinship with the apostle's spirit and deliberately emulated his manner.

Thus led to a broader consideration of Milton's debt to Paul by his adaptation of the sermon at Athens in *Sonnet XIX*, we are alerted to Pauline echoes in the poem that would hardly reverberate outside this critical context. In the same chapter of 2 Corinthians, for example, Paul proposes his third visit to Corinth and assures his readers that he will not impose on their generosity: "And I will very gladly spend and be spent for you" (verse 15). One is inevitably reminded of the first line of the sonnet. Furthermore, the Lord's promise to the afflicted apostle, "My grace is sufficient for thee" (verse 9), so exactly embodies the truth from which patience springs that one wonders whether the phrase did not beget the figure in the poem. Even without these suggestions, of course, it seems clear enough that "When I Consider" is deeply imbued with Pauline substance and purpose, but the possibility of direct verbal and thematic allusions in the poem to 2 Corinthians, chapter xii, offers a tantalizing analogy that very closely parallels the sonnet in both form and content. As he writes, Paul looks back on the man he once was; he tells of the thorn with which he had been afflicted, a torment he still bears, and recounts his past (but now ceased) efforts to dispute with God by praying that it be removed. He then explains how his agony had been assuaged and his murmuring silenced by the Lord's intervention with the promise of sufficient grace. Now confident that his every weakness will be turned to strength, he proceeds to exhort the fickle Corinthians, intending the account he has rendered as both a lesson in Christian living and a warrant of his apostolic mission. Though Milton's devices for distancing himself from his experience are not quite so obvious as Paul's use of the past tense and the third-person pronoun, they are no less effective, and the sonnet's rhetorical and conceptual structure, as well as its didactic end, resembles Paul's example exactly.

III

As I have argued above, the basic mode of *Sonnet XIX* is narrative, and any reading that overlooks this fact will be critically inconsistent or incomplete. But the organized concert of emotion and idea which is the poem obviously does have its material cause in the chaotic noise of feeling and notion within the poet's mind. My point is simply that we have generally failed to distinguish that origin from the poem shaped out of it. We are led to neglect this distinction, of course, by the fact that Milton is here telling his own story, not that of, say, Adam or Samson. His consideration of how his light is spent ere half his days inevitably raises biographical questions. Interestingly, the recognition that these details are treated in the narrative manner described above enables us to understand their significance more easily. For instance, once we see that Milton has used his affliction and his triumph over it as a parable to illustrate how one may foolishly question God's ways and the trust one should rather exhibit, we are free to interpret the phrase "light is spent" in its apparent sense as a metaphor for blindness. The same is true of the allusion to "that one Talent which is death to hide," which looks like a plain reference to his ability to write. Aware of Milton's distance from the persona in the poem, we need not thrash about for ways to reconcile the putative desperation or bitterness of the octave with other biographical evidence that imports the contrary.

The date of composition is the most vexing biographical question about the sonnet, and I will not contend that affixing the proper generic label leads automatically to a ready and easy solution. It is true, however, that the prevalent trend of reading the poem as a lyric lament has tended to complicate rather than simplify the matter. Or perhaps the determination to date the poem has obscured the generic issue. However it is, critics have sought arduously, sometimes even frantically, for interpretations that can accommodate the demanding phrase "Ere half my days," which has recently compelled almost unanimous acceptance as a literal biographical reference. The rub, of course, is that no reconciliation of the established date of Milton's total blindness and his (actual or predictable) life span is possible. Hence commentators are constrained either to posit an abnormal life expectancy for the poet or to construe the reference to loss of light in some strained or remote sense. Those who select the first alternative turn either to elements in Milton's personal history, noting that his father endured to the age of eighty-four, or to irregular codes of longevity that bear scriptural or other venerable sanction.[28] Adherents of the second alternative either construe the loss of "light" biologically as a broad allusion to the general period (of some eight or ten years) during which Milton's sight progressively failed or interpret the phrase loosely to denote some conjectural period of depression or imaginative privation that Milton passed through in the early 1640s.[29] But even the proposers of such theories seem uneasy with them, sensing the need for something simpler.

Another solution to the problem, which has the advantage of preserving both the biographical reliability of "Ere half my days" and a literal understanding of the loss of light, turns on the periodization of Milton's presumed seventy years from 1608 to 1678. This possibility was first suggested by D. C. Dorian in 1952, when he tendered the notion that Milton meant "working days."[30] But Dorian's suggestion died for lack of real substance, since he failed to provide an authoritative paradigm of life with clear-cut divisions: if we do not know which are a man's "working days," we cannot determine which of Milton's years fell into that category. Recently, however, James Sims has shared with me a suggestion that supplies precisely what Dorian lacked.

Sims writes of the Renaissance commonplace "that full maturity was reached at 30, not 21, or 18," a tradition rooted in the authority of Scripture.[31] The New Testament indicates that Jesus began his public ministry at thirty (Luke iii, 23) and in so doing followed illustrious predecessors from the Old Testament. King David, according to 2 Samuel v, 4, "was thirty years old when he began to reign, and he reigned forty years." Before David, Joseph had begun his work as an officer of Pharaoh at thirty (Genesis xli, 46), a fact which prompted the editors of the Geneva Bible to comment that "his age is mencioned . . . to shewe that his autoritie came of God."[32] The actual cornerstone of the tradition, of course, rested on the divine sanction of thirty as the age at which the sons of Aaron could fully enter the priesthood. On Numbers iv, 3, which relates the Lord's instructions to Moses regarding this matter, the Genevan editors offer the following gloss: "The Leuites were nombred after thre sorts: first at a moneth olde when thei were consecrate to the Lord, next at 25 yere old when they were apoited to serve in the Tabernacle, & at 30 yere old to beare the burthens of the Tabernacle."

This Old Testament instrument is surely capable of combing the largest biographical tangle out of the sonnet: if his time of divine service began in 1638 at the age of thirty and should have extended for forty years, Milton was indeed, in late 1651 or early 1652 (or even in 1655), blind before he had spent half his days of mature service. Utility on one point does not guarantee general validity in a case of such hoary complexity, of course, but the implications of this biblical explanation ramify rewardingly. For one thing, this theory legitimates Milton's early rustication at Horton and Hammersmith as a spiritual retreat preparatory to entering active service, incidentally clarifying his puzzling comment in *Sonnet VII* that, at the age of twenty-four, he was merely "to manhood . . . arriv'd so near." More broadly, a Levitical solution to the biographical puzzle accords perfectly with Milton's known penchant for equating the poet with priest as moral teacher. Those who have borne with me through the full discussion above will therefore understand my enthusiasm for it.

University of Southern Mississippi

NOTES

1. See John S. Smart, *The Sonnets of Milton* (Glasgow, 1921), p. 108; and the summary of criticism in A. S. P. Woodhouse and Douglas Bush, *A Variorum Commentary on the Poems of John Milton* (New York, 1972), vol. II, pp. 442–69; to which may be added Thomas B. Stroup, " 'When I Consider': Milton's Sonnet XIX," *SP*, LXIX (1972), 242–58; and Dixon Fiske, "Milton in the Middle of Life: Sonnet XIX," *ELH*, XLI (1974), 37–49, who also read the poem as lyric. Though several scholars refer to a "speaker" in the sonnet, only Joseph Pequigney ("Milton's Sonnet XIX Reconsidered," *TSLL*, VIII [1967], 485–98) has programmatically distinguished that speaker from the poet.

2. William Riley Parker's discussion of the sonnet in *Milton: A Biography* (Oxford, 1968), vol. I, pp. 468–72, and vol. II, pp. 1042–43, touches on most of these issues, and I shall have occasion below to consider some of them, particularly the sonnet's date, in more detail. Throughout my discussion I quote Milton's poetry from *John Milton: Complete Poems and Major Prose*, ed. Merritt Y. Hughes (New York, 1957).

3. Citing Louis L. Martz's *Poetry of Meditation* (New Haven, 1954), pp. 13, 38–39, Stroup labels *Sonnet XIX* a "notable example of the meditation as a literary genre" (" 'When I Consider,' " p. 245). I shall argue that "When I Consider" stands in a mediate relation to Milton, imaging a devout state, but not tracing the moment-by-moment achievement of it; the poem is a history of devotion, not a stage script for it.

4. "Milton's Sonnet 'On His Blindness,' " *ELH*, XXVII (1960), 128.

5. In the two words *fondly* and *murmur*, of course, we witness momentary closure between poet and poem, and these instances throw into sharp relief Milton's general disengagement from the material by revealing his self-conscious judgment of it. The quoted definition of the narrative mode is from James Joyce, *A Portrait of the Artist as a Young Man* (New York, 1964), p. 214.

6. For example, J. L. Potter, in "Milton's 'Talent' Sonnet and Barnabe Barnes," *N&Q*, IV (1957), 447, takes the first view, while John F. Huntley, "The Ecology and Anatomy of Criticism: Milton's Sonnet 19 and the Bee Simile in 'Paradise Lost' I.768–76," *JAAC*, XXIV (1965), 387, argues the second.

7. "Syntax and Poetic Form in Milton's Sonnets," *ES*, XLV (1964), 293.

8. E. A. J. Honigmann (*Milton's Sonnets* [London, 1966], p. 175) notes that "murmur" is biblical. The word is invariably pejorative in the Authorized Version, as in, for example, Exodus xv, 24; Psalm cvi, 25; and Luke v, 30. Milton comments on the sin of murmuring in *Christian Doctrine* (*The Works of John Milton*, ed. F. A. Patterson [New York, 1931–40], vol. XVII, pp. 230–31, subsequently cited as CM).

9. CM, XVII, p. 67.

10. See Parker, *Milton*, vol. I, p. vii.

11. Fitzroy Pyle, "Milton's First Sonnet on his Blindness," *RES*, IX (1958), 380.

12. "Poetic Vision in Two Sonnets of Milton," *Milton Newsletter*, II (1968), 26. Herron holds that Milton here identifies "his own fervor with Christ's."

13. " '. . . Who Only Stand and Wait': Milton's Sonnet 'On His Blindness,' " *MLN*, LXXII (1957), 91–93.

14. The translators of the New English Bible render verse 25: "It is not because he lacks anything that he accepts service at men's hands." In thus changing the "is worshipped" of the Authorized Version to "accepts service," they suggest further unifying elements in the sestet that derive from Milton's knowledge of Greek. The verb *therapeuō*, translated "worshipped" only this once in the King James New Testament, stems from the same root that gives *therapon*, "attendant, servant" (see Hebrews iii, 5, AV). Thus, the primary burden of Patience's declaration here—the concept of service, explicitly articulated in the last line of the sonnet—links with Paul's sermon at Athens through the Greek.

15. Harry F. Robins, "Milton's First Sonnet on His Blindness," *RES*, VII (1956), 363–66, catches in the sestet a reference to the active and contemplative angelic orders distinguished by the scholastics and argues that Milton here associates himself with the latter (higher) order.

16. As Honigmann, *Milton's Sonnets*, p. 176, and others have noted, the "mild yoke" of line 11 refers to Jesus' words in Matthew xi, 30, "my yoke is easy."

17. See J. Milton French, ed., *The Life Records of John Milton* (New Brunswick, N.J., 1949–58), vol. III, pp. 104–05, vol. IV, pp. 118–19; CM, VIII, p. 73.

18. J. B. Lightfoot, "St. Paul's Infirmity in the Flesh," in *St. Paul's Epistle to the Galatians* (London, 1866), p. 186, n. 1. For convenience, I shall refer readers to such discussions as this of Lightfoot's rather than to the actual texts of the many authors whose opinions he surveys.

19. See Hugh Pope, "What Was St. Paul's Infirmity?" *Irish Theological Quarterly*, X (1915), 420, and Lightfoot, "St. Paul's Infirmity," p. 184.

20. Quoted in Lightfoot, "St. Paul's Infirmity," p. 185. These and many other suggestions were gathered in Milton's generation by Matthew Poole, *Synopsis Criticorum aliorumque Sacrae Scripturae Interpretum* (London, 1669–76), vol. IV, pp. 651–52.

21. See Pope, "What Was St. Paul's Infirmity?", pp. 418–19; Lightfoot, "St. Paul's Infirmity," p. 188; and Reginald Glanville, "The Predominance of Ear Over Eye in the Experience of St. Paul," *The London Quarterly and Holborn Review*, 1955, pp. 293–97.

22. I had put this evidence together some time before undertaking the present essay. When I began investigating the history of commentary on Paul's infirmity, I discovered John Brown's "St. Paul's Thorn in the Flesh. What Was It?" (in *Spare Hours*, 1st ser. [Boston, 1882], pp. 397–418), an essay that marshals exactly the same evidence—to the same end. The coincidental similarity of our positions indicates the inherent plausibility of the argument and suggests the possibility that others, including Milton, could have reached the same conclusion. Obviously, the case for any particular identification of Paul's malady is purely circumstantial and is likely to remain so, since he understandably avoided literal reference to an embarrassing affliction of which his original audience had personal knowledge.

23. Quoted from Pope, "What Was St. Paul's Infirmity?", p. 423. Cf. the translation in Alexander Roberts and James Donaldson, eds., *The Ante-Nicene Fathers:*

Translations of the Writings of the Fathers down to A.D. 325 (Grand Rapids, 1951), vol. IV, p. 87.

24. Lightfoot, "St. Paul's Infirmity," p. 186.

25. See John Paul Pritchard, "The Fathers of the Church in the Works of John Milton," *Classical Journal*, XXXIII (1937–38), 79–87, for a convenient survey of Milton's gleanings from the Fathers, including Tertullian. Interestingly, Poole nearly suggests Paul's blindness in his commentary on Galatians iv, 15, citing "Seneca in Oedipode" as a parallel instance of plucking out eyes.

26. I quote here from the translation in F. A. Patterson, ed., *The Student's Milton* (New York, 1930), pp. 1139–41. Cf. CM, VII, pp. 19, 63–73.

27. The scholars who have noted how Milton eventually transmuted his blindness into a symbol of poetic inspiration and special grace are legion. See, for example, Ernest Sirluck, "Milton's Idle Right Hand," *JEGP*, LX (1961), 771, n. 51, and Jackson Cope, *The Metaphoric Structure of "Paradise Lost"* (Baltimore, 1962), pp. 149–64.

28. See, for example, Parker, "The Dating of Milton's Sonnets on Blindness," *PMLA*, LXXIII (1958), 199; John T. Shawcross, "Milton's Sonnet 19: Its Date of Authorship and Its Interpretation," *N&Q*, IV (1957), 443; and Emile Saillens, *TLS*, October 6, 1961, p. 672.

29. Honigmann, *Milton's Sonnets*, pp. 172–73, surmises "that his power of vision (light) is worn out (spent), though not yet totally destroyed," and suggests a date "shortly before his birthday on 9 December 1644." Lysander Kemp, "On a Sonnet By Milton," *Hopkins Review*, VI (1952–53), 82, takes the loss of light as the failure of inspiration and dates the poem in 1642. Fiske, "Milton in the Middle of Life," discusses a Dantean tradition in which the years from twenty-five to forty-five constitute man's middle age, when reason is supposed to "assert itself, conquer appetite, and be perfected" (p. 40).

30. "Milton's 'On His Blindness,' " *Explicator*, X (1951–52), item 16.

31. Quoted from a personal letter that has helped me on several points in this essay. Having briefly sketched his theory of the sonnet's date for his article on "Milton and the Bible" in the forthcoming *Milton Encyclopedia*, Sims has graciously allowed me to develop it more fully here.

32. I have used the facsimile of the 1560 Geneva Bible edited by Lloyd E. Berry (Madison, Wis., 1969).

OUTRAGEOUS NOISE AND THE SOVEREIGN VOICE: SATAN, SIN, AND SYNTAX IN *SONNET XIX* AND BOOK VI OF *PARADISE LOST*

Stephen Wigler

THE DIFFERENCE in reputation between Milton's *Sonnet XIX* ("When I consider . . .") and his depiction of the War in Heaven in Book VI of *Paradise Lost* is almost as pronounced as the stylistic and generic differences that distinguish the occasional sonnet from epic narrative. In some ways, "When I consider . . ." is Milton's most moving and accessible achievement, and it is almost universally admired and loved.[1] The War in Heaven, however, is usually considered one of the least successful episodes in *Paradise Lost*. Most readers endorse Dr. Johnson's opinion that its "confusion of spirit and matter" fills the whole narrative with "incongruity."[2] Paradoxically, however, Milton's affecting little poem on his blindness and his extravagantly written epic battle illuminate each other.[3] The protagonist of the one and the antagonist of the other suggest that confusion of the individual voice or word with God's sovereign voice or Word is an important aspect of the satanic personality.

The sonnet breaks naturally into two slightly unequal divisions, with a question raised in the "octave," abbreviated to seven and two-fifths lines, and an answer given in the correspondingly lengthened "sestet":

> When I consider how my light is spent,
> E'er half my days, in this dark world and wide,
> And that one Talent which is death to hide,
> Lodg'd with me useless, though my Soul more bent
> To serve therewith my Maker, and present
> My true account, least he returning chide,
> Doth God exact day-labour, light deny'd,
> I fondly ask; But patience to prevent
> That murmur, soon replies, God doth not need

155

Either man's work or his own gifts, who best
Bear his milde yoak, they serve him best, his State
Is Kingly. Thousands at his bidding speed
And post o're Land and Ocean without rest:
They also serve who only stand and waite.[4]

Readers of the octave probably respond sympathetically to the poem's blind protagonist as he struggles with the sense of personal waste .emphasized by details like "spent," "useless," "death to hide," and "deny'd."[5] The sestet subtly transforms this response: the reader discovers that the octave is dominated by egocentricity and fruitless bitterness. The first-person pronouns *I*, *me*, and *my* occur eight times. In the sestet, the first person does not appear at all, but "God" and pronouns to which he is antecedent occur six times. Although the narrator's physical blindness is irremediable, he moves from blindness of the spirit in the octave to spiritual sightedness in the magnificent cosmic vista of the sestet.

The turn in his point of view seems to begin with the protagonist's discovery that his question ("Doth God exact daylabour, light deny'd") is foolish ("fondly ask[ed]"). Whether the answer is yes or no (and it can be either), it is improper to raise the question at all. The protagonist's problem is that he exaggerates the importance of his human works to his "Maker"; he has to learn that God "doth not need / Either man's work or his own gifts . . . his State / Is Kingly." He rather resembles Satan, whose overweening pride blinds him to the Messiah's supremacy. If the protagonist of "When I consider . . . " thinks that God cannot do without his works, then he is not far from behaving as if he were God. If Satan's blindness to the supremacy of the Word induces him to challenge God in battle, then the protagonist's blindness leads him—in his question—to challenge God in words.

An undiscussed (so far as I can tell) but nonetheless remarkable feature of *Sonnet XIX* is that syntactic ambiguity at the end of the octave—to whom does the floating clause "Doth God exact daylabour, light deny'd" refer?—permits the reader to discover that he shares in the protagonist's satanic behavior. It is easy to share the resentment, frustration, and bitterness (powerfully suggested by the peremptory question) toward a master insufficiently appreciative of the suffering and sacrifices of his loyal servant.[6] But the point of the sestet, of course, is that man must always be prepared to "only stande and waite," and to strive toward what Milton elsewhere calls "the better fortitude of Patience and Heroic Martyrdom."[7] This is precisely what the protagonist and his audience begin to learn in the abrupt "I fondly ask."

These three words turn the poem around completely. They undermine the speaker's self-pity and emphasize the complacent inadequacy of his auditors' sympathy. Strange as it seems, the statement's power can be partly explained by its revelation of the identity of the speaker of line 7 as the protagonist rather than his Maker. The last half of line 6 is "least he returning chide," and "chide" is followed only by a comma, not by the full stop that many modern editors insert.[8] Thus, there is nothing to prevent reading line 7 as God's chiding of the protagonist. Moreover, since one is reading sympathetically rather than critically, it is possible to scan "Doth God exact day-labour, light deny'd" without recognizing that these words chide God rather than the other way around.[9] The resentful tone of the question is exactly what one expects from the protagonist's disappointed master. In the microsecond that it takes to read "I fondly ask," the syntactic ambiguity is resolved, the audience recognizes that they have been reading incorrectly, and, like the protagonist, they also learn that they have been thinking improperly. The sonnet's first six lines seduce its readers into sharing the self-pity which partially disguises the protagonist's pride. The mistake in improperly understanding the syntax of line 7 is theirs and not the protagonist's. They, not he, have slipped their syntactic feet into God's syntactic shoes, but their mistake is analogous to his. To complain about the existential necessity of serving by standing and waiting is to question God's authority and thereby to assume that our voices are as meaningful as his. This mistaken attitude is understandably human, but it is also satanic: it recapitulates the arch-fiend's refusal to honor and obey God by refusing to wait, or attend ceremoniously, on the Word. As the sonnet's sestet beautifully demonstrates, however, it is fortunately given to fallen human beings, as it is not to fallen angels, not merely to recognize error, but also to learn from it.

If *Sonnet XIX* turns upon the speaker and his audience's mutual recognition that the confusion of human words with God's words is satanic, then the War in Heaven might be said to demonstrate a similarly satanic attempt to substitute for the Word. Understanding the importances of, and the differences between, words and the Word explains some of the ludicrous language and comic grotesquery which has annoyed readers of *Paradise Lost* for generations.

God's supremacy is substantially expressed by his Son's "divine

compassion," his "love without end, and without measure grace";
but his power is expressed by the Son's creative agency as his Logos,
his "omnific Word": "So spake th' Almightie, and to what he
spake / His Word, the filial Godhead, gave effect" (VII, 174–75).
This leads one to suspect that Satan's challenge to God's power and
his rivalry with the Son will manifest themselves by his attempt to
persuade himself and the other angels that his words are as powerful
as his Word. Book VII clearly demonstrates the synonymity of the
Son's articulation and of Creation. His language is powerful because
it is the truth. His words *are* what they signify:

> Let ther be Light, said God, and forthwith Light
> Ethereal, first of things, quintessence pure
> Sprung from the Deep.   (VII, 243–45)

Satan, on the other hand, is a deceiver who is utterly incapable of
using words honestly. His ironic duplicity is the index to his weakness, and Satan's efforts in battle are an unintentional parody of the
omnific Word. Instead of the significant sounds of language, he
"creates" the meaningless sounds of destruction which Milton calls
"outragious noise."

The identification of truth with honestly articulated language
and of falsehood with inarticulate brute force is suggested by God's
praise for Abdiel:

> Servant of God, well done, well hast thou fought
> The better fight, who single hast maintain'd
> Against revolted multitudes the Cause
> Of Truth, in word mightier than they in Armes.   (VI, 29–32)

Heaven has never heard anything but the harmony of language and
music, but Satan's falsehood introduces the dissonance of mere
noise and sound:

> now storming furie rose,
> And clamour such as heard in Heav'n till now
> Was never, Arms on Armour clashing bray'd
> Horrible discord, and the madding wheels
> Of brazen Chariots rag'd; dire was the noise
> Of conflict.   (VI, 207–12)

Satanic sound and fury signify nothing, however, and the rebels fare
badly. On the following night, Satan reassures his disappointed
followers by informing them of newly invented devices (gunpowder
and cannon) which will equal what Satan mistakenly believes to be
God's ultimate power—the thunderbolt:

> These in thir dark Nativitie the Deep
> Shall yield us pregnant with infernal flame,
> Which into hollow Engins long and round
> Thick-rammd, at th'other bore with touch of fire
> Dilated and infuriate shall send forth
> From far with thundring noise among our foes
> Such implements of mischief as shall dash
> To pieces, and orewhelm whatever stands
> Adverse, that they shall fear we have disarmd
> The Thunderer of his only dreaded bolt.   (VI, 482–91)

In his depravity, noise is all Satan seems to hear, and noise is certainly all that he is able to produce.

As the rebel angels prepare to discharge their noisy cannon into the ranks of the unfallen angels, their speeches become extravagantly self-indulgent:

> Vanguard, to Right and Left the Front unfould;
> That all may see who hate us, how we seek
> Peace and composure, and with open brest
> Stand readie to receive them, if they like
> Our overture, and turn not back perverse;
> But that I doubt, however witness Heaven,
> Heav'n witness thou anon, while we discharge
> Freely our part; yee who appointed stand
> Do as you have in charge, and briefly touch
> What we propound, and loud that all may hear.
> (VI, 558–67)

Walter Savage Landor cleverly remarked that the first overt crime of the fallen angels was to sin against language, but he may have been unaware of the strategic purpose of the word play.[10] Puns like those on "discharge" and "loud" are painfully labored, and the pun on "touch" has been made so often (479, 485, 520) that it seems equally obvious. Satan's language ceases to be a tool of communication and regresses to the level of primitive aggression.

Raphael's description of the attacking cannon might also characterize satanic speech:

>   thir mouthes
> With hideous orifice gap't on us wide,
> Portending hollow truce; at each behind
> A Seraph stood, and in his hand a Reed
> Stood waving tipt with fire.
>
>   .   .   .   .
>
> From those deep throated Engins belcht, whose roar

> Emboweld with outragious noise the Air,
> And all her entrails tore, disgorging foule
> Thir devilish glut.   (VI, 576–80, 586–89)

With its indecorously low diction and its sustained physiological
imagery, this passage offers an analogy with infantile intestinal and
anal aggression that seems to have stepped out of the pages of
Freud.[11] But the analogy with infantile behavior is particularly apt,
because one of the distinctions between adults and children is the
child's tendency to treat words as part of himself and his relative
inability to use language abstractly to relate to the external world.[12]
Blinded by narcissistic pride and false elation, the fallen angels
reduce language to belching and farting. Nonetheless, they believe
their ludicrous efforts have matched the power of God:

>   eternal might
> To match with thir inventions they presum'd
> So easie, and of his Thunder made a scorn.   (VI, 630–32)

They do not congratulate themselves for long; their opponents
retaliate by hurling mountains. Soon, heaven's landscape is flying
back and forth before the reader's incredulous eyes, and the narrative lapses completely into unrelieved grotesquery and unbearable
noise:

> So Hills amid the Air encounterd Hills
> Hurl'd to and fro with jaculation dire,
> That under ground they fought in dismal shade;
> Infernal noise; Warr seem'd a civil Game
> To this uproar.   (VI, 664–68)

As the action of the poem threatens to leave language behind, God
decides that the "wild work in Heav'n" has gone far enough and
sends his Word to resolve the confusion and chaos. The style
changes to a more exalted and steadier level, as the Son demonstrates the restorative powers of the Word:

> At his command the uprooted Hills retir'd
> Each to his place, they heard his voice and went
> Obsequious, Heav'n his wonted face renewd,
> And with fresh Flourets Hill and Valley smil'd. (VI, 781–84)

Upon seeing this, the devils grieve "to see his Glorie," and we
realize that God's Word is almighty, not because he commands the
thunderbolt (as the fallen angels believe), but because he is the
Truth; and any words that pretend to the contrary and attempt to
substitute themselves by either force or guile are merely "barbarous

dissonance" (VII, 32), "savage clamor" (VII, 36), and "unsufferable noise" (VI, 867).

It is interesting to speculate about what permits the speaker and the audience of "When I consider . . ." to recognize that they have mistaken their human voices for their Maker's voice and to learn from error, whereas Satan and his angels only persist in their folly. It is not simply that the human beings realize their error, and that the angels do not. As his asides reveal, Satan often recognizes his self-delusion, and the speaker's recognition of the foolishness of his question does not automatically ensure his recovery. At the end of Book IX of *Paradise Lost,* for example, Adam also recognizes that he has listened to Eve's words and ignored God's ("Was shee thy God, that her thou didst obey / Before his voice?"), but this recognition only makes his self-contempt and his hatred for Eve more pronounced. Like the egocentric protagonist of the sonnet, Adam's condition is expressed in part by fear of his Maker's chiding voice:

> I heard thee in the Garden, and of thy voice
> Affraid, being naked, hid myself. To whom
> The gracious Judge without revile repli'd.
>   My voice thou oft has heard, and hast not fear'd,
> But still rejoic't, how is it now become
> So dreadful to thee?   (X, 116–21)

Satan, the speaker, and Adam recognize that they have transgressed, and they torture themselves by continually measuring themselves as they *are* by what they *were* and by their failed promise. As victims of their own past, all three reside in "the hell within" of Samson's "what once I was, and what am now" (*SA*, 22). The blind protagonist of the sonnet is haunted by memories of sight, Adam's present is poisoned by former joys, and Satan's situation is the terrible reality of which the others are merely images. Their shame and despair, of course, are a failure of imagination. Because *they* cannot forgive themselves, they assume that *he* either cannot or will not. Milton seems to suggest, however, that one learns to forgive oneself by first having been forgiven by another. Adam escapes unending self-punishment because the Son's judgment is followed by paternal forgiveness and compassion:

>   pitying how they stood
> Before him naked to the aire, that now
> Must suffer change, disdain'd not to begin
> Thenceforth the form of servant to assume,
> As when he wash'd his servants feet so now

As Father of his Familie he clad
Thir nakedness with Skins of Beasts, or slain,
Or as the Snake with youthful Coate repaid;
And thought not much to cloth his Enemies:
Nor hee thir outward only with the Skins
Of Beasts, but inward nakedness, much more
Opprobrious, but with his robe of righteousness,
Araying cover'd from his Father's sight.   (X, 211–23)

This enables Adam in turn to forgive himself and to forgive Eve:

Remember with what mild
And gracious temper he both heard and judg'd
Without wrath or reviling; wee expected
Immediate dissolution.

.   .   .   .

Undoubtedly he will relent and turn
From his displeasure; in whose look serene,
When angry most he seem'd and most severe,
What else but favour, grace and mercie shon?
(X, 1046–49, 1093–96)

Unlike Adam, of course, Satan has never been forgiven, nor ever will be, for reasons God enunciates in Book III.

Studies of child behavior suggest that the formation of the personality is completed by the infant's internalization of his parents.[13] If the parent is judging but nonetheless loving and compassionate, then the child presumably acquires the healthy capacity not only to govern himself but to forgive himself when he fails to do so. In Sonnet XIX, the protagonist's growth from self-absorption and self-pity to an impersonal contemplation of celestial beings, from egocentric concern to theocentric awareness, and from the "dark world and wide" to the inspired vision of the angelic thousands, shows the psychological development necessary for fruitful maturity. The sestet opens with the introduction of patience, a personified new quality in the speaker that suggests an internalized voice rather than a personified abstraction.[14] In seeing things patiently the narrator sees them with new objectivity and mature wisdom. In terms less psychological and more theological, a graced and illumined part of his soul answers the complaining query of his previously depressed soul.

The protagonist learns to recognize God, not as the unforgiving domestic taskmaster of the parable of the talents, but as a forgiving heavenly king whose relations to his subjects cannot be conceived in the merely human financial terms he had mistakenly attributed to him. The visionary crescendo of lines 12–13 and the calm simplicity of the coda tell us that although his depression may be renewed, he has the unmistakable capacity to transcend personal anguish by accepting patient suffering as service which uplifts, rather than demeans, the human condition.[15]

From ambiguous syntax in a personal sonnet that momentarily encourages confusion between human and divine words, and from an epic battle in which infernal noise pretends to be heaven's harmonious and sovereign voice, we seem to have moved to a discussion of the capacity for self-forgiveness. We have not strayed so far as it appears. The argument of Milton's life was to "justify the ways of God to men," and he struggles with the problem of reconciling men to the fact that their own disobedience "brought death into the world, and all our woe." The woe is psychological as well as physical: How is man to live with his shame? Milton's insight was that whether men berate themselves (as Adam and the sonnet's protagonist do) or resort to violence against fellow creatures (as Satan does), they are prompted by an interior voice which urges an unforgiving sense of their own unworthiness. This paralyzing voice compounds suffering by not permitting the better fortitude of patience and clearly imprisons man within himself. Since Christ liberates man from bondage, this voice is not the Word, but the voice of Satan. The Word freely forgives us, and, by freely choosing incarnation, teaches us not only self-forgiveness but mature self-love. If we form the hell within by internalizing the unforgiving voice of Satan, then we form the paradise within by internalizing the forgiving voice of Christ.[16] Like the protagonist of *Sonnet XIX*, we demonstrate that we hear and understand the Word when we liberate ourselves from the bondage of what once we were by freely forgiving ourselves for what we have become, and by agreeing patiently to wait.

The University of Rochester

NOTES

1. Some authorities suggest that Milton may have written *Sonnet XIX* as early as 1642, but most favor 1651–1655. The poet was not totally blind until 1652. Milton's actual blindness and the poem's date, however, are relevant neither to my argument,

nor, I think, to the sonnet itself. See particularly Joseph Pequigney's "Milton's Sonnet XIX Reconsidered," *TSLL*, IX (1967), 485–98.

2. There are significant exceptions. Arnold Stein's recognition of the Battle in Heaven as dramatic farce rather than heroic drama, *Answerable Style* (Minneapolis, 1953), pp. 17–37, was followed by other defenses of Book VI by Joseph Summers, *The Muse's Method* (Cambridge, Mass., 1962), pp. 112–46; and Stanley Fish, *Surprised by Sin* (New York, 1967), pp. 158–207. If one can draw conclusions from one's own students, however, most initial encounters with the War in Heaven tend to agree with the negative evaluations of John Peter, *A Critique of "Paradise Lost"* (New York, 1960), pp. 63–84; and J. B. Broadbent, *Some Graver Subject* (London, 1960), pp. 218–34.

3. After Fish's study, this statement, however paradoxical, should no longer be surprising. Like Fish, I liken great things to small and interpret Book VI in the context of *Sonnet XIX*. Fish fastens upon the sonnet's conclusion, however, while I choose to elaborate about its center. For a more significant interpretive difference, see my last note.

4. My text is the Columbia University Press edition, *The Works of John Milton*, ed. Frank Allen Patterson et al. (New York, 1931–38), 18 vols. All references are to this edition.

5. See Pequigney, "Milton's Sonnet XIX Reconsidered," p. 488.

6. Paul Goodman speaks of "despair at the deprivation and inaction, mounting to almost anger and insolence" (*The Structure of Literature* [Chicago, 1954], p. 205).

7. Thomas Stroup states that patience is Milton's central theme, and he argues for the centricity of *Sonnet XIX* in Milton's canon: "It is a seminal poem, a veritable seed pod of considerations from which are sown and harvested in later works some of the poet's fundamental convictions" ("When I consider: Milton's Sonnet XIX," *SP*, LXIX [1972], 244).

8. Douglas Bush, *Complete Poetical Works* (Boston, 1965), and Merritt Y. Hughes, *Complete Poems and Major Prose* (New York, 1957), insert a semicolon after "chide" and place the following line within quotation marks. Bush also supplies a question mark after "deny'd." These emendations make it possible to read without mistaking the syntax—and without experiencing part of the poem Milton wrote.

9. Skeptics who object that "God" is the second word in the line and that, therefore, the speaker cannot be mistaken for God, forget God's fondness for referring to himself in the third person: "Servant of God, well done . . . for this was all thy care / To stand approved in the sight of God" (*PL* VI, 29, 35–36).

10. *The Complete Works,* ed. T. Earle Welby (London, 1927–36), vol. V, p. 258.

11. *Three Essays on Sexuality,* vol. VII of *The Standard Edition* (London, 1953), pp. 173–206. Of course, devils were often portrayed defecating or vomiting. See Norman Cohn, *The Pursuit of the Millennium* (London, 1957), fig. 2.

12. The child only gradually learns that noises are used as symbols of things and to transcend the infantile omnipotence of thought which attributes to words the ability to conjure up the things with which they are associated. Instead of using magical language and thought to imitate reality (as Satan does), the fully mature adult uses symbolic language and thought to control, and even to create, reality (as the reader sees the Son do). Psychologists have observed that certain words retain their original magical power: the blasphemous or obscene words, for example, which adults as well as children regressively identify with the body parts and functions for which they stand. See Sigmund Freud, "The Antithetical Sense of Primal Words," in his *Collected Papers* (London, 1926), vol. IV, pp. 184–91; Otto Fenichel, *The Psycho-*

analytic Theory of Neurosis (New York, 1945), pp. 46 ff., 295 ff., 312 ff., 437; and Sandor Ferenczi, *Sex in Psychoanalysis* (New York, 1950), pp. 132–53.

13. See particularly pp. 48–108 and 189–274 of Erik Erikson's *Childhood and Society,* 2d ed. (New York, 1963).

14. Pequigney, "Milton's Sonnet XIX Reconsidered," p. 489.

15. See ibid., p. 495, and Fish, *Surprised by Sin,* pp. 196–207.

16. My reading of Milton is indebted to Stanley Fish, *Surprised by Sin,* but I take exception to his painful characterization of the experience of reading *Paradise Lost:* "the poem is a profoundly disturbing experience which produces something akin to a neurosis; the natural inclination to read on vies with a fear of repeating old errors and encountering new frustrations . . . submitting to the style of the poem is an act of self-humiliation" (p. 207). But Milton asks that his readers learn to humiliate themselves in order that they may live with diminished pain as well as with diminished pride. He speaks of the indwelling "Spirit" as a "comforter," and one suspects that Milton might detect in Fish's voice not only a great deal of his own thought, but also a little of Satan's.

THE EDUCATION OF THE FAITHFUL IN MILTON'S PIEDMONTESE SONNET

Nicholas R. Jones

R EADING MILTON's sonnet "On the Late Massacre in Piemont" as an expression of the poet-statesman's personal dismay over the atrocities of a Catholic tyrant, a process encouraged by a knowledge of the circumstances of its composition, blinds the reader to the sonnet's larger rhetorical and thematic nature. To some degree, of course, the voice of the poem is Milton's own, and its subject therefore one of personal importance: the intensity of the complaint matches what we might expect of Milton, confronted with news of such a disaster. Without robbing the sonnet of its biographical appeal, however, a reader can go beyond the local and individual meaning. Thematically, the sonnet treats more than mid-seventeenth-century politics: it deals with a specific example of the efficacy of faith in relation to wisdom and zeal. Rhetorically, the sonnet is more than an exercise in "personal relief": it dramatically humanizes its themes through the creation of a fictitious speaker whose monologue involves and moves the reader.[1] The personal components of struggle and relief transcend their personal origins and produce a statement of universal meaning and impact.

For a closer analysis of the character and growth of the speaker, a text of the sonnet is essential.

On the Late Massacre in Piemont

Avenge, O Lord, thy slaughter'd Saints, whose bones
    Lie scatter'd on the Alpine mountains cold,
    Ev'n them who kept thy truth so pure of old
    When all our Fathers worship't Stocks and Stones,
Forget not: in thy book record their groans
    Who were thy Sheep and in their ancient Fold
    Slain by the bloody *Piemontese* that roll'd
    Mother with Infant down the Rocks. Their moans
The Vales redoubl'd to the Hills, and they
    To Heav'n. Their martyr'd blood and ashes sow
    O'er all th'*Italian* fields where still doth sway

167

The triple Tyrant: that from these may grow
A hundredfold, who having learnt thy way
Early may fly the *Babylonian* woe.[2]

 The sonnet presents a nameless, fictitious character involved in
the universal process of religious self-education. Although his faith
remains essentially stable, providing the basis for a steadily religious interpretation of experience, his wisdom grows from a temporary state of indignation into a more balanced and durable state of
charity. The harsh zeal of the opening lines, a prayer for vengeance
on the enemies of the church, develops into a more profound feeling
of compassion, expressed in a prayer for conversion. The poem, so
ordering the emotions of its speaker, vividly demonstrates its
theme—the operation of faith in the establishment of God's kingdom
on earth.

 The speaker's continuing faith manifests itself through the uni-
fied rhetorical intention of his poetic speech. The sonnet, though a
poem of growth, is seamless in its fabric. Compared to the almost
conversational variety of other sonnets by Milton, such as "To Mr.
Cyriack Skinner upon his Blindness," the Piedmontese sonnet conveys a uniformly intense concern. The syntax, with its "three request
structures," binds the poem together in parallel and mounting
supplications.[3] The imagery—hard, penetrating, and extreme—also
unifies the poem with its implications of a world of bare, uncompromising strife: "bones," "mountains cold," "groans," "woe."[4] Finally, although Milton chooses the sonnet form with its compart-
mental quatrains, octet, and sestet—a form which so often emphasizes the shifts and divisions of its subject matter—he avoids any of
the expected breaks of thought. This speaker does not cut off his
syntax at the crucial fourth and eighth lines; here, and throughout
the sestet, the enjambment ensures that the poem be read as one
continuous utterance rather than a collection of diverse attitudes.[5]
Kester Svendsen has noted that the extraordinarily intense movement of this sonnet is organically related to just such matters of
"conscious artistry," that the awareness of Milton's control over the
technical details of the sonnet enables the reader to "preserve
aesthetic distance."[6] The nature and purpose of that "aesthetic distance" is of interest here—how the personal is made universal.

 Directed by these unities—syntactical, imagistic, and formal
—the reader may consider the poem as a single rhetorical unit,
specifically as an example of prayer (or deesis, in the language of the
rhetorician).[7] The immediately established tone of supplication re-

mains unbroken except for a brief sentence of description (8–10). Again and again, the supplications follow the pattern of the first request: calling for action, asserting or implying the presence of the divine audience, and recounting the events of the massacre. They are not so much separate requests as amplifications of one underlying pattern of prayer, the attempt to move a specific audience by direct petitions.

The rhetoric of prayer, of course, has its thematic complement in faith. The speech which takes the form of such a supplication to God reflects an inner condition of belief in his promises and power. In *The Christian Doctrine*, Milton outlines the relationship between prayer and faith: "Supplication is that act whereby under the guidance of the Holy Spirit we reverently ask of God things lawful, either for ourselves or others, through faith in Christ."[8] Prayer is a form of worship; worship consists of good works; and the essential form of good works is their accordance with faith. "For it is faith that justifies, not agreement with the decalogue; and that which justifies can alone render any work good; none therefore of our works can be good, but by faith" (p. 9).

Doctrinally, a true prayer is a good work in accordance with faith. The question arises, then, of the authenticity of this sonnet-prayer. Certainly the initial request might seem too zealous to be a true prayer, for is not the speaker demanding a vengeance which should be the Lord's alone? "Among errors under the head of prayer may be classed rash imprecations, whereby we invoke God or the devil to destroy any particular person or thing" (p. 103). Several factors in this case, however, combine to remove the label of "error." First, to "avenge" does not necessarily mean to destroy. Second, the apparent rashness of the sudden opening may be an abruptness only of expression and not of thought. Milton does acknowledge that in considered prayers it is lawful "to call down curses publicly on the enemies of God and the church" (p. 99). Finally, the unity of the poem's expression, which I outlined earlier, moderates this first request by linking it with the later ones, making them all part of one continuing prayer. The last expression of that prayer (the final supplication: "that from these may grow . . .") certainly fulfills Milton's own criteria for a true prayer: it asks "things lawful" (conversion and salvation); it asks them "under the guidance of the Holy Spirit" (that is, it involves "calling into action . . . the gift of the Holy Ghost" within the speaker); it prays reverently (with purity and charity, promptly, humbly, and earnestly); and, most important, it prays through faith in Christ's promises (pp. 81–105).

There are many varieties of faith, of which this sonnet spans at least two: hatred of the enemies of God's church and desire for the expansion of his kingdom. The first prayer—perhaps rash, certainly abrupt, fierce, and indignant—develops into the assured, hopeful prayer at the end of the poem. Concentrating on the elements of change, Milton energizes the religious experience through the speaker, primarily by attention to his growing wisdom. This important narrative demonstration of change occurs only because the speaker believes in the promise of God; through faith, his understanding grows in the knowledge of God's will. In *The Christian Doctrine*, analyzing the causes of good works and virtue (including prayer), Milton identifies faith as the foundation of all development, citing St. Peter: "add to your faith virtue" (p. 5; 2 Peter i, 5). There is a significant doctrinal foundation for the attributes of growth in the persona of a religious poem.

Milton's comments on wisdom in *The Christian Doctrine* offer a useful working definition for a close examination of the development of this sonnet's speaker: "Wisdom is that whereby we earnestly search after the will of God, learn it with all diligence, and govern all our actions according to its rule" (p. 27). The sonnet parallels this sequence. *Searching* is the movement of the poem, a subtle process in which an angry zeal considers and reconsiders the event of the massacre. *Learning* is the effect of the search, a demonstration of knowledge through mature and assured language. Finally, *acting* by the rule of God's will (a separate step in Milton's doctrinal exposition) immediately accompanies the preparatory stages of quest and education: the contemplative and active stages are simultaneous. Thus, growing in wisdom, the speaker demonstrates the unity of faith and action in language, a unity which lies at the root of the concept of religious poetry.

The growth of wisdom has its starting point in the first four lines of the sonnet. In them, the speaker, intensely denouncing the massacre, is separated by anger from the wiser response of compassionate charity. His language, cold and awkward after the splendid first outburst, reflects an initial detachment from God's will.

The speaker seems in his first request ("Avenge, O Lord, thy slaughter'd Saints") to be a part of the popular English zeal of 1655, generated in immediate response to the brutal murder and displacement of Italian Protestants.[9] As E. A. J. Honigmann has shown, an intense nationalistic indignation filled the newspaper accounts and inflammatory narratives of the atrocities.[10] The speaker's outburst bears some resemblance to the passionate outrage of the Protector Cromwell, who supplemented his letters of protest with plans for vengeance in the form of military action against the Duke of Savoy.[11] The speaker's righteous anger allows him no time for the amenities of a more meditative prayer—the leisurely invocation, the narrative of circumstances, the careful requests. His demand in the sonnet's first clause reflects a notion of immediate, tangible retribution, a naive providentialism. Surely it is God's will to avenge this massacre! Yet, unknown to the speaker, the search for the appropriate response is just beginning. Only as he understands the event in fuller, sympathetic detail will he learn what specific vengeance God might intend.

Immediately after the intense first clause, there is a strange loss of warmth. Depending at first upon an easy, popular emotion, the speaker now reveals his essential detachment from the event. After the vehemence of "Avenge, O Lord, thy slaughter'd Saints," the next two lines give an impression of chill clarity. With its direct sensory impact, the phrase "Alpine mountains cold" operates by connotation to express the speaker's feelings. He sees the massacre with a detached and "cold" anger: the atrocities are catalogued in his mind, not as present realities, but only as past events. They are ready as evidence of injustice but not as objects of grief or charity. They are present in knowledge but not yet in spirit. In retrospect, the reader can see that even in that intense first clause the massacre stands at one remove from the speaker: he chooses a verb form bound to the past tense ("slaughter'd") instead of, for example, a substantive form ("the slaughter") of indeterminate tense and therefore capable of a closer temporal relationship to the speaker.

The search for God's will, with the consequent growth of wisdom through faith, occurs only indirectly in these first lines. Although the speaker appropriately chooses to review the events and implications of the massacre, the naive elements of self-righteous and nationalistic anger which characterize his first attitude cause him to digress from a true Christian search. The image of scattered bones, for example, accentuates the attitude of detachment, expressing cruelty with vivid details but without an immediate sensation of involvement. Here are no suffering victims, no felt terrors, not even corpses, but "bones"—an image grim enough but lacking a necessary quality of sympathy with human life. The homeless wandering of the oppressed Protestants, which might have provided a strong impulse of pity, assumes only a very indirect expression: not people, not the faithful Waldensians, but "bones / Lie scatter'd." All together the lines describe a tableau—a static and dehumanized image of past action.

The dehumanized clarity is once again evident in attitude and diction as the speaker amplifies the concept of "Saints": "Ev'n them who kept thy truth so pure of old." The emphasis upon the religious history of these early Protestants, derived from the speaker's initial anger, is of course crucial to his argument: it was obviously a major component of the popular outrage. Yet once again an essentially active subject assumes a static quality. The monosyllabic words, supporting with their rhythmic simplicity the concept of primitive purity, make the victims seem part of an antique and unapproachable world of innocence.

Line 4 contrasts the early enlightenment of the Waldensians with the relatively late Reformation in England. At this transitional point in the sonnet—the end of the introduction, as it were—the speaker confirms his detachment from the situation and at the same time reveals a movement which is to lead him closer to it. The theme of English idolatry is relevant to the indignation of the speaker, but as a serious argument it is awkward and out of place. The ludicrous alliteration ("Stocks and Stones") resembles the bitter language of sectarian controversy, a literary pursuit far removed from poetic prayer. This picture of idolatry, another static tableau, further extends the already static effect of the previous line, but there is a major difference: with the introduction of awareness of the self (the English Protestant and his history), the earnest search for God's will has begun. The criticism of self-righteous anger (reminding English Protestants that their Reformation was long delayed) has a humanizing effect on the speaker's own naive emotion. His development of the events of the massacre now begins to broaden as he becomes aware of his own inadequate assessment of the event and his hasty demand for a providential response from God.

At the end of this fourth line, an abrupt discontinuity, the most prominent rhythmic feature of the sonnet, signals with its awkward displacement of thought the upswing of self-awareness and the resulting growth in wisdom. The belated addition of the imperative verb "Forget not" converts the third and fourth lines, which seemed to be a clause in apposition to "Saints," into a direct object, forming a new and unexpected request (to paraphrase: "do not forget them who kept thy truth so pure of old"). Syntactically, the third and fourth lines, stretched from each end, undergo a severe tension which, for me, recurs at every reading of the poem. Semantically as well as rhythmically there is a jolt: of these two parallel requests ("Avenge . . . Forget not"), the second is unexpectedly mild. The strong, unreflective anger of the first has disintegrated; its facile unity has vanished in expansion and self-awareness. The speaker begins the second quatrain no longer sure of what to ask of God. Out of his unsettledness comes a germ of sincerity: he demands not retribution but remembrance, a wiser request for a mortal consciousness. For God needs no reminders of his knowledge or will; it is man who must labor to "Forget not," to achieve and maintain a close sympathy with the event.

It is no accident that the phrase which so jars the syntax should use the figure of litotes, expressing memory by the negation of forgetfulness. The two contraries epitomize a crucial reversal. Forgetting—drifting in aimless anger—has been the pattern of thought of the first quatrain. Now, the slower process of remembering begins with the summoning of details that are capable of an intense personal application: the speaker initiates the earnest search "after the will of God." Already in the fifth line the anticlimax of "Forget not" begins to focus more sharply. From an indeterminate sense of infuriating wrong the speaking voice turns to the specifics of human response: "their groans." The contrast of the sensual and active re-creation with the silent, static tableaux of the first lines implies that the event is now imaginatively remembered, although the speaker is still far from a full knowledge of God's will.

Rhetorically, the last three lines of the octave constitute the general figure of enargia, or vivid and objective description. There are no prayers or demands, no obvious signs of sympathy or emotion. This section, shocking in its details but free from pathos, accomplishes a major transition from naive and self-willed narrowness to wisdom. The change occurs between the two separated rhyme words of the second quatrain, between "their groans" and, four lines later, "Their moans." Without the blinding anger of "Avenge, O Lord," the event becomes approachable. The image of "Sheep," a metaphor extending the inarticulateness of the "groans," invites more emotional involvement than its initial equivalent, "Saints." Vulnerability becomes so intensely realized that the static images develop into vivid action, as if a still photograph had suddenly become a moving picture. These "moans" are as yet only remembered from the past, but the temporal detachment of memory grows ever smaller as the poem moves toward fulfillment. While the verbs, of course, retain their past-tense forms, the powerful substantive phrases move the action toward the present tense of the mind's sympathy. From the almost archeological condition of "their ancient fold," the speaker moves to the less distant image of "the bloody *Piemontese*"—the enemies of the faithful still covered with badges of slaughter. From there the progression of sympathy—still without any explicit figures of emotion—leads to a sharply horrifying image, "Mother with Infant down the Rocks." It is a continuing, immediate image, for though it is governed by a verb in the past tense, "roll'd," that verb's situation in the preceding line diminishes its effective control. Pathos is now wisely excluded because the speaker's consciousness is wholly directed away from himself and toward the event; he is involved in discovering not his own desires but God's will.

At the end of the octave the transitional image of "moans" is strongly present in the mind of the speaker. From his sudden political anger at the beginning of the sonnet, the speaker has wandered into the paths of cold argument, only gradually and indirectly developing a fuller human sorrow. His present emotion resembles the anger of the first line in its intensity but differs in containing the seeds of its fulfillment. The anger of the eighth line has assimilated some important developments: a retraction from vengeance, a sense of personal misdirection, and an image of human cruelty.

In the sentence beginning "Their moans," the speaker seems suspended in the absence of will. The octave gives over to the sestet without a break in syntax, entering a quiet moment of reflection and growth in which the slow Virgilian image of echoing sounds matches the suspension of emotion.[12] The speaker now holds his conscious desires and his anger away from the discourse while the divine order reasserts itself in spiritual guidance. Although this sentence tells of a moment of intense horror, it is nonetheless a moment of quiet grace as the natural world, with all its impatience, cold disengagement, and brutality, gives way to the transcendent. The figure of ascensus (also called climax) here incorporates a literal ascent "To heaven," so subtly worked as not to impose but to permit a spiritual motion. The mystery attendant on the fulfillment of prayer partly justifies the arresting plainness of the accompanying zeugma: there is no verb to tell exactly how this motion to heaven occurs. At this point, the violent willfullness in the imperative forms of the beginning of the sonnet has developed into a more peaceful state of verbless transformation.

In the final sentence of the sonnet the speaking voice returns to a modified form of his initial demand. Now, however, instead of an uncompromising demand for vengeance, there are three gentle and ambiguous petitions. The event of the massacre still appears in the past tense, for the meditative interval of sympathetic perception has given way to the call for action. This use of the past tense, however, has none of the chill of the initial tableau. These "blood and ashes" are more intimate, more nearly connected with the episode itself, than "bones": with "blood," for example, the reader senses the lost life in the very act of spilling. The historical precision of "slaughter'd" has developed into a far richer concept, "martyr'd," viewing the time-bound massacre in the light of eternity. The harsh cry of vengeance has modulated, through the increasing sympathy of consideration, into a plea for growth. The final requests might still include the military vengeance which the sonnet's beginning implies (the possible allusion to the myth of Cadmus makes one think that "Italian fields" could mean the battlefields of an English invasion of Savoy), but the two major, unmistakable allusions of this passage are more indicative of faith than of revenge. As many have pointed out, these primary references are to the parable of the sower (Matthew xiii, 3–9) and to the apothegm of Tertullian, "the blood of martyrs is the seed of the Church."[13]

The extraordinary richness of the last five lines conveys the assurance, synthetic power, and newfound eloquence of the speaking voice. From faith has emerged the wisdom which seeks and acts upon God's will. After the intense and confused exposition and the moment of reflective stillness comes this assimilation of contemplation and action, of meditation and prayer. From the awkward shifts of the first lines the voice has grown to a mature assonance and a flexible but not mannered use of enjambment. From the hasty pinpointing of topics in the first lines the voice has engaged a complex of simultaneous emotions and thoughts. Victim and victor now are bound together; though "the triple tyrant" is still excluded from any thought of grace, the prayer for conversion dissolves the purely national and sectarian impulse of the opening lines. Most important, the prescriptive demand has become acceptance of God's will. A political solution with its need for partisan cruelty is no longer relevant.

The Piedmontese sonnet is a characteristically Miltonic prayer, calling for education of the conscience, looking toward an action of self-sacrifice, and leading eventually to individual salvation. The process of the sonnet—education—becomes the subject of its concluding prayer. It is finally more than a personal outcry: it is a poem about the education of the faithful, a rhetorical demonstration of how the wisdom to recognize and conform to God's will can grow only in the presence of faith.

Oberlin College

NOTES

1. The quoted phrase is from William Riley Parker, *Milton: A Biography* (Oxford, 1968), vol. I, p. 460. See also Lawrence W. Hyman, "Milton's 'On the Late Massacre in Piedmont,' " *ELN*, III (1965), 27, for the statement that the poem represents Milton's own "struggle to overcome his shock at the ways of God to those just men who follow His way."

2. *John Milton: Complete Poems and Major Prose,* ed. Merritt Y. Hughes (New York, 1957).

3. Taylor Stoehr, "Syntax and Poetic Form in Milton's Sonnets," *ES*, XLV (1964), 299–301.

4. Kester Svendsen, "Milton's Sonnet on the Massacre in Piedmont," *Shakespeare Association Bulletin*, XX (1945), 147–55.

5. For consideration of the nature of the unity of a sonnet with respect to its boldness of form, see F. T. Prince, *The Italian Element in Milton's Verse* (Oxford, 1954), esp. pp. 89–107.

6. "Milton's Sonnet," p. 154.

7. The rhetorical terminology used here and elsewhere in this essay is catalogued by Richard A. Lanham in *A Handbook of Rhetorical Terms* (Berkeley and Los Angeles, 1969), and by Sister Miriam Joseph in *Shakespeare's Use of the Arts of Language* (New York, 1947).

8. *The Works of John Milton,* ed. Frank Allen Patterson et al. (New York, 1934), vol. XVII, p. 81. Subsequent references to *The Christian Doctrine* are to this volume and are given by page number in the text.

9. A summary of the historical background may be found in John S. Smart, *The Sonnets of Milton* (1921; rpt. ed., Oxford, 1966), pp. 87–93.

10. *Milton's Sonnets* (New York, 1966), pp. 164–66.

11. Smart, *Sonnets of Milton,* pp. 91–92.

12. The Virgilian echo is noted in A. S. P. Woodhouse and Douglas Bush, *The Minor English Poems: A Variorum Commentary on the Poems of John Milton* (New York, 1972), vol. II, p. 440.

13. Ibid.

MILTON ON THE PROVINCE
OF RHETORIC

Irene Samuel

I hate when vice can bolt her arguments,
And virtue has no tongue to check her pride.
                                   —The Lady in *Comus*, 760–61

Nature and laws would be in ill case if slavery were eloquent
and liberty mute.   —*First Defense*

W HEN MILTON compared Satan-in-the-serpent, about to
launch his delusive harangue at Eve, to "some orator renowned / In Athens or free Rome, where eloquence / Flourished,
since mute" (*PL* IX, 670–72), he was hardly equating eloquence with
trickery, denigrating the oratorical skill in which Athens and free
Rome excelled, or congratulating later times on having grown vir-
tuously tongue-tied. It is a hopeful sign in Milton studies that commentators no longer accept as valid every misleading word given
Satan to utter; it is less hopeful that some now read Milton as
assigning to deliberate misleaders the entire province of rhetoric.
Like the distrust of learning that supposedly overtook him in his
later years, his supposed distrust of rhetoric has been foisted on him
by those unwilling to make distinctions such as he himself habitually made.[1] Too thoroughly a man of the Renaissance ever to suppose that ignorance of any valid learning could improve mankind,
Milton, along with Renaissance humanists generally, regarded rhetoric, rightly understood and used, as a valid branch of learning.

What the passage in Book IX shows is the poet's knowledge of
the ancient art, and knowledge too of how the trickster may misuse
it.[2] Against the remark that Satan's preliminary bit of *actio* calls to
mind—how, with effective speakers of antiquity, "each
part, / Motion, each act won audience ere the tongue"
(673–74)—may be set the comment in the Tractate *Of Education* that
a proper training in the "organic arts" would have a number of
beneficial effects on public speakers:

177

There would then also appear in pulpits other visages, other gestures, and stuff otherwise wrought than what we now sit under, oft times to as great a trial of our patience as any other that they preach to us. (CM, IV, p. 287)

That Satan, skilled in *actio,* abuses his skill is an argument, not against *actio,* but against Satan, as his abuse of the whole rhetorical art argues not it, but him, evil. John Steadman has amply shown that Satan abuses the rhetorical art, pointing out in detail the fallacious arguments and trickster's devices Milton assigns him, a *dianoia* befitting the satanic *ethos.*[3]

Needless to say, Milton scorned the false and the misused in any art. But no one assumes that his contempt for "our common rhymers and play-writers" (*Of Education,* CM, IV, p. 286) speaks a contempt for verse and drama, or his disdain for the logic choppers of the universities a disdain for logical thought. As little may the reference to Satan's false eloquence in *Paradise Regained* as "the persuasive rhetoric / That sleekt his tongue" (IV, 4–5) be taken to signify that Milton consigned all effort at persuasion to the devil. To "make persuasion do the work of fear" is the Savior's own intention in *Paradise Regained* (I, 223); the ugly word in the phrase on Satan is neither *persuasive,* nor *rhetoric,* but *sleekt.* Art directed to evil ends Milton of course detested, along with the bad art that prides itself on its artisticality and the inadequate art that does not know how to pursue its own ends; but he confused none of these with art itself.[4]

Rhetoric he took to be one of the "organic arts," those studies which are instruments to the production of something beyond themselves, and always so to be regarded. The view accords with the best tradition of rhetorical theory from at least as far back as Aristotle, although it has doubtless sometimes been obscured by the confusions of muddled theorists. Even the exaltation of rhetoric in the Renaissance that made it, as Paul Oscar Kristeller has observed, "the professional core and favorite subject of humanist learning" took it as instrumental to the production of the eloquent writer-speaker who was to function as guide to a society.[5] And Milton, though far too much of his time to disparage what humanism valued so highly, accorded it a humbler role, always aware that the "organic arts" are properly not central, but ancillary.

Donald Lemen Clark and Harris Francis Fletcher have made clear how thoroughly grounded in rhetoric Milton was at St. Paul's and again at Cambridge.[6] And John Major has traced Milton's references to rhetoric throughout his work.[7] The Cambridge prolusions demonstrate how effortlessly the young Milton applied the rhetorical principles he had assimilated, only surprised that his less agile-minded fellow students could not do the same.[8] So, too, his controversial writings reveal a continuing awareness of rhetorical theory. According to Merritt Y. Hughes, "It is on Milton's occasional outbursts against the taste of his opponents that we have mainly to rely for his evidently strong and clear ideas about the rhetorical principles which governed his prose."[9] Mainly, perhaps, but not entirely, for there is also enough positive statement scattered through the prose to demonstrate the rhetorical principles that guided Milton in constructing his own arguments as well as in refuting his opponents.[10]

What is amply known and demonstrated of Milton's training and the nature of rhetoric down through the ages we need not rehearse. But we must consider what Milton took rhetoric to be. We know that he produced a Ramist grammar and a Ramist logic. Was he also Ramistic in his rhetorical theory? From the discussion in the tractate *Of Education* it would seem not; for there the final course, clearly rhetorical in its purposes, though it includes logic and poetics with rhetoric, is planned thus:

And now, lastly, will be the time to read with them those organic arts, which enable men to discourse and write perspicuously, elegantly, and according to the fitted style of lofty, mean, or lowly. Logic, therefore, so much as is useful, is to be referred to this due place with all her well-couch't heads and topics, until it be time to open her contracted palm into a graceful and ornate rhetoric, taught out of the rule of Plato, Aristotle, Phalereus, Cicero, Hermogenes, Longinus. To which poetry would be made subsequent, or indeed rather precedent. . . .

From hence, and not till now, will be the right season of forming them to be able writers and composers in every excellent matter, when they shall be thus fraught with an universal insight into things. Or whether they be to speak in parliament or council, honor and attention would be waiting on their lips. There would then also appear in pulpits other visages, other gestures, and stuff otherwise wrought than what we now sit under, ofttimes to as great a trial of our patience as any other they preach to us. (CM, IV, pp. 286–87)

It is evidently traditional rather than Ramistic rhetoric that is to be taught in all its five parts: *inventio, dispositio, elocutio, actio, memoria;* and yet it is not an entirely conventional rhetoric that lists Plato as a text along with Aristotle, Phalereus, Cicero, Hermogenes, and Longinus. For although *Phaedrus* defines the scope and parts of rhetoric almost as Aristotle proceeded to work them out in his treatise, the Platonic Socrates there and elsewhere in the dialogues spends far more time questioning whether rhetoric is an art at all than elaborating its aims and methods. Or is the inclusion of Plato itself conventional?

His questioning of rhetoric certainly became part of the rhetorical tradition. Aristotle touches the matter briefly in his opening section (*Rhetoric* I. 1–2), showing his awareness of the kinds of issue the Platonic dialogues had raised. Is rhetoric an art at all? Does it prescribe any and every means of persuasion? Should judges allow themselves to be swayed by anything more than the facts of a case? Is not the very effort to sway by other means the merest trickery, the cookerylike flattery Socrates had called it in *Gorgias*? Aristotle answers that since the sources of persuasion can be codified and are therefore available, they ought to be available to good men as well as to evil. In much the same way, Cicero takes up and answers objections to rhetoric as a study (*De Oratore* I. 80–96, 166–204). Quintilian again rehearses the attack on rhetoric and amplifies its defense (V. Preface. 1–5). And Longinus, too, though only in connection with excellence of style, deals with the question whether an art is involved at all and whether it can be taught (*On the Sublime*, 1–7).

Clearly Plato heads the list of texts in order to open the whole question of what rhetoric should be and aim at and do. Most of the texts in the list somehow enforce the Platonic teachings on these matters, and Longinus would drive it home with his wholly Platonic insistence that literary excellence stems first and foremost from greatness of soul.

In any event, from the author of a Ramist *Logic* the whole passage in the tractate raises problems. The logic taught is evidently to be Ramistic, the phrase "so much as is useful" summarizing both Milton's distaste for the excesses he had observed at Cambridge and the emphatic statement in the preface to his own text. There, explaining that his purpose is to treat the art and its applications "for those who have need," he insists:

For those who have need, I say, for I do not require that those whose native abilities are active and strong should torture themselves in this analytic sort of exercise with too much labor and misery. For art is used for the purpose of aiding nature, not of hindering it; when it is employed too anxiously and too subtly, and especially where it is unnecessary, it blunts rather than sharpens capacities. (CM, XI, p. 7)

Logic is therefore reduced in the tractate to her "well-coucht heads and topics," as Ramists reduced it. But Ramist logic implies Ramist rhetoric.

Indeed, in his *Logic* Milton uses the standard Ramist definition of rhetoric as "ars bene dicendi"[11] and the standard Ramist division of its parts into *elocutio* and *actio*.[12] He accepts the Ramist view that traditional writers err in making rhetoric include *inventio, dispositio*, and *memoria*, which properly belong to logic (CM, XI, p. 323). But the texts listed in the tractate deal largely with these very matters. Nor can we argue that Milton was a Ramist only when he compiled his *Logic* and his *Accidence Commenced Grammar*. His agreement with Ramism started early[13] and is evident at least through his writing of *Animadversions*,[14] when he refers Bishop Hall to Downham's Ramist *Logic* to learn how to think and argue better. The chief influence of Ramus on Milton's thought is not, however, in the assignment of their different matter to different arts (the so-called law of justice of the Ramist method),[15] but in the interrelation of logic and rhetoric. Where Aristotle was content to take the two as akin, where Cicero and Quintilian made logic subserve rhetoric and were concerned with it only to the extent that it could, Ramus redefined logic to make it the necessary base of all coherent discourse. What is involved in the Ramist assignment to logic of invention and disposition, long known as two main branches of rhetoric, is the insistence that all discourse be logical, both in the grounds of its arguments and in their arrangement. Ramus was renowned for using literature to illustrate his dialectical principles, and Milton follows that known model in choosing the illustrative materials for his Ramist *Logic*. Indeed, if for him one main virtue of Ramist logic is that it is a minimal logic, another is that it emphasizes the need of logic in, and its decisive importance for, all discourse. That Milton has logic precede both rhetoric and poetics in his educational plan is the best possible demonstration of his continued Ramism: clearly a highly logical *inventio* and *dispositio* are to be studied before any attention is given to *elocutio* and *actio* or the issues of poetics.

The emphasis on logic, on reasoned argument as the proper basis, characterizes Milton's views on all matters usually subsumed under rhetoric. That is why he shows a consistent preference for deliberative over epideictic and forensic oratory, a consistent preference for logical over ethical and pathetic proof, and a consistent preference among modes of proof for the artistic over the inartistic.[16]

To take the first matter first: his taste assuredly was not for controversy. The familiar passage in the *Reason of Church Government* can hardly be doubted; he makes the point insistently: "to every good and peaceable man it must in nature needs be a hateful thing to be the displeaser and molester of thousands; much better would it like him doubtless to be the messenger of gladness and contentment, which is his chief intended business to all mankind" (CM, III, p. 231). And again: "I may deserve of charitable readers to be credited that neither envy nor gall hath entered me upon this controversy, but the enforcement of conscience only and a preventive fear lest the omitting of this duty should be against me when I would store up to myself the good provision of peaceful hours" (pp. 233–34). The enforced disputations of his Cambridge years gave him a lasting distaste for anything involving the contentious. His preference was for poetry, for exploration of ideas, for the process of learning that builds steadily toward positive achievement. Controversy he thought largely negative, at its best a clearing away of error that the positive building might start, and of its very nature a thing that can seldom be at its best. Human affairs with their habitual muddle make the distinction hard to apply: to persuade others almost inevitably involves contending with opponents. And from the first, Milton's prose led him straight into the thick of dispute. Though his subject is deliberative, the course that reformation of the church should take in England, he inevitably crosses into the epideictic realm of blame and the forensic realm of accusation.

Even so, the greater part of even his most forensic works, *Eikonoklastes* and the *Defenses,* concerns itself with lasting issues more than with praise, blame, accusation, and defense. And it is well to remember that all these works were in a sense imposed tasks. What he wrote wholly of his own choice was consistently in the deliberative vein, advising on a course of action, not attacking or defending. Here too the evidence of his prose is insistent. In *Hirelings,* he ends his advice: "If I be not heard nor believed, the event will bear me witness to have spoken truth; and I in the meanwhile have borne my witness, not out of season, to the church and to my country" (CM, VI, p. 100). So again in *A Free Commonwealth* he offers his counsel: "with all hazard I have ventured what I thought my duty to speak in season, and to forewarn my country in time" (CM, VI, p. 148). And again in *Of True Religion:* "I thought it no less than a common duty to lend my hand, how unable soever, to so good a purpose" (CM, VI, p. 165). Unfortunately, the speculative arguments in which Milton engaged involved persons as well as issues, wrongs that had been done as well as decisions to be taken for the future. And unlike the fellow whom Dr. Johnson famously put down, Milton when he is contentious leaves no one dubious as to what he is being contentious about. But no honest-minded reader can fail to observe that however much praise and blame, accusation and defense employed Milton's oratorical skill, his steady preference was for deliberation.

So again with ethical and pathetic as opposed to logical proof. He knows that these are available as means to persuade, and he knows that at times he must use them. Of course when the argument is about himself—as it so often became in his opponents' attacks— we can hardly say that he is resorting to ethical proof. In the *Apology for Smectymnuus*, for example, where he has to refute the character that the confutant has drawn of him, he speaks at some length of himself, his education, his habits, purposes, and tastes— but all with an awareness that such elaborate self-presentation has its danger of tastelessness: he has been brought by his opponent to the odious necessity "to enter into mine own praises" lest it "harm the truth for me to reason in her behalf, so long as I should suffer my honest estimation to lie unpurged from these insolent suspicions" (CM, III, pp. 296–97). Although he must clear his character first, his main concern is to *reason*. So too, whenever he presents himself as the kind of person whom his readers may trust, or his opponents as the kind they ought not, he does not rely on such means of persuasion, known and accepted commonly in rhetoric as ethical proof, but turns his and his readers' attention away from these to the substantial questions at issue. As for pathetic proof, though all language necessarily involves some degree of feeling and hence most use of language necessarily to some extent plays on feeling, Milton is at some pains to avoid emotional appeals himself; certainly he avoids the kind that he recognizes and attacks in his opponents.[17]

Out of the same preference for reasoned argument, Milton prefers among modes of proof what has been known since Aristotle as the artistic or artificial to the inartistic or inartificial. Of the most common form of inartistic proof, the appeal to testimony, particularly the testimony of authorities, he is consistently skeptical. It is not only that he incorporated in his *Logic* the Ramist view of testimony: "I commonly attribute to testimony very little power for proof in investigations of the deepest truth and nature of things" (CM, XI, p. 283); he seems almost to equate "inartificial" with unreliable when

he uses the term in *Tetrachordon* and apologetically explains his
offering such inherently questionable proof at all:

Although testimony be in logic an argument rightly called 'inartificial,' and
doth not solidly fetch the truth by multiplicity of authors, nor argue a thing
false by the few that hold so; yet seeing most men from their youth so
accustom as not to scan reason nor clearly to apprehend it, but to trust for that
the names and numbers of such as have got, and many times undeservedly,
the reputation among them to know much; and because there is a vulgar also
of teachers who are as blindly by whom they fancy led as they lead the
people, it will not be amiss for them who had rather list themselves under
this weaker sort and follow authorities to take notice that this opinion which
I bring hath been favored and by some of those affirmed who in their time
were able to carry what they taught, had they urged it, through all Christen-
dom, or to have left it such a credit with all good men as they who could not
boldly use the opinion would have feared to censure it. (CM, IV, p. 206)

The passage sums up Milton's view of reliance on authorities in
place of arguments. Aristotle, aware that there is never likely to be a
lack of testimony of some sort for a speaker to offer in favor of any
position, concerned himself only with how the speaker may use it
effectively. Milton's concern is rather with the validity of testimony
in itself. He too resorts to citations of authorities, but regularly—as
here—distinguishes between reliance on the mere names of those
who can be marshaled in a given cause and the use of their arguments. Again, it is not simply that he disparages the "authorities" his
opponents may cite, as when he refers to the "calumnious dun-
ceries" of Lombard and Gratian in *The Doctrine and Discipline of
Divorce* (CM, III, p. 505) or adjures his readers in the *Apology for
Smectymnuus:* "be not deceived . . . by men that would overawe
your ears with big names and huge tomes that contradict and repeal
one another because they can cram a margin with citations. Do but
winnow their chaff from their wheat, ye shall see their great heap
shrink and wax thin past belief" (CM, III, p. 358). For then it would
be easy to argue that Milton has learned from Aristotle and other
rhetorical theorists how to discredit witnesses on the opposing side.
The important point is that he regularly takes pains to show that the
authorities he cites not only are on his side but have reason on theirs.
Thus, in his address "To the Parliament of England" prefixed to his
translation of *The Judgment of Martin Bucer*—the whole of which
may, as a translation, be considered a resort in a sense to the inartificial proof of testimony—he explains that his purpose in the work is
"to let his [Bucer's] authority and unanswerable reasons be vulgarly

known, that either his name or the force of his doctrine may work a wholesome effect" (CM, IV, p. 9). He is habitually careful to argue the truth, the reasonableness, of what is said by his witnesses, not letting the argument rest on who said it. Thus he subordinates authorities to the valid reasons they offer in a phrase in *Tetrachordon:* "authorities contributing reason withal [are] a good confirmation and a welcome" (CM, IV, p. 230); and even so he offers them only as "confirmation," not primary evidence, his "unexpected witnesses," not his "instructors." A "petty fog of witnesses" is for him no proper means of persuasion, nor even evidence of much good sense: "To heap . . . unconvincing citations . . . argues not much learning nor judgment, but the lost labor of much unprofitable reading" (*Hirelings,* CM, VI, p. 65). Over and over he derides the habit of relying on testimonies and authorities, using such phrases as "this fond argument of antiquity" (ibid.), "that indigested heap and fry of authors which they call antiquity" (*Of Prelatical Episcopacy,* CM, III, p. 82), and warns against "the inconvenience we fall into by using ourselves to be guided by these kind of testimonies" (ibid., p. 101). Yet Milton is not simply, as Thomas Kranidas suggests, an antitraditionalist.[18] He is aware that there is more than one tradition (even, we may note, in the possibilities of the epic poem);[19] he is aware too that tradition can be misused to shift reliance from what is valuable in it, its soundness when it is sound (when authorities have in fact worked out for the rest of us, as their heirs, something of truth), to what is valueless, the mere weight of names. An impressive passage in *Of Reformation* makes clear why he found it necessary to argue so often against the resort to authorities. The "native worth" of "spotless truth," he writes,

is now become of such a low esteem that she is like to find small credit with us for what she can say, unless she can bring a ticket from Cranmer, Latimer, and Ridley, or prove herself a retainer to Constantine and wear his badge. More tolerable it were for the church of God that all these names were utterly abolished like the brazen serpent than that men's fond opinion should thus idolize them and the heavenly truth be thus captivated. (CM, III, p. 10)[20]

What disturbs Milton is that for most men reasoned argument is of far less force than the testimony of supposed authorities; even when the authorities are sound, reliance on them can be damaging to truth, since it does not demand the exercise of reason.[21]

Hence, when in arguing for an uncommon view Milton feels it advisable himself to cite authorities, he habitually shows a discomfort: "But herein the satisfaction of others hath been studied, not the gaining of more assurance to mine own persuasion" (*Tetrachordon,* CM, IV, p. 230); "lest this which I affirm be thought my single opinion, I shall add sufficient testimony" (*Free Commonwealth,* CM, VI, p. 128). He knows, of course, how to make his own witnesses outweigh his opponents': "we shall abound with testimonies to make appear that men may yet more fully know the difference between Protestant divines and these pulpit-firebrands" (*Tenure,* CM, V, p. 46). He knows how to argue "first the insufficiency, next the inconvenience, and lastly the impiety of these gay testimonies" (*Of Prelatical Episcopacy,* CM, III, p. 83), how to undercut completely the force of the testimony of numbers: "You take the voice of the beggarly refugees for the voice of the people" (*Second Defense,* CM, VIII, p. 177). But the very knowledge of how easily witnesses may be piled up on any side of a question makes Milton prefer to draw a new argument from such disagreement:

But as to those before them, which I cited first (and with an easy search, for many more might be added) as they there stand, without more in number, being the best and chief of Protestant divines, we may follow them for faithful guides and without doubting may receive them as witnesses abundant of what we here affirm. . . . If any one shall go about by bringing other testimonies to disable these, or by bringing these against themselves in other cited passages of their books, he will not only fail to make good that false and impudent assertion of those mutinous ministers . . . but will prove rather what perhaps he intended not, that the judgment of divines, if it be so various and inconstant to itself, is not considerable or to be esteemed at all. (*Tenure,* CM, V, pp. 57–58)

Against witnesses other witnesses can be brought, and sometimes, alas, some can be brought to witness against themselves. Of what value, then, are such appeals, except to show the frailty of those appealed to for their testimony?

Milton, for all the frequency with which he cites testimony, particularly that of his preferred poets, never deludes himself that such citation can take the place of reasoned argument. Even the authority of the Bible is not offered except as a demonstration of what the Bible itself says, especially against those who distortedly cite other authorities: "Thus while we leave the Bible to gad after these traditions of the ancients, we hear the ancients themselves confessing that what knowledge they had in this point was such as they had gathered from the Bible" (*Of Prelatical Episcopacy,* CM, III, p. 86). But he is more likely to support even biblical citation with "reasons." Unlike those who cite "fragments of old martyrologies and legends to distract and stagger the multitude of credulous readers" (ibid., p. 82), he hesitates to gain credence by using the very authority of Scripture, and not merely because Scripture too may be misread and thus misused to support views contrary to its obvious purport, but because the only valid kind of argument is "artificial," the kind reason works out, whether through enthymeme or syllogism, through induction or example. The passage from the *Logic* which I quoted earlier on testimony goes on:

I commonly attribute to testimony very little power for proof in investigations of the deepest truth and nature of things; this would seem to apply to divine as well as human testimony. . . . Divine testimony affirms or denies that a thing is so and brings about that I believe; it does not prove, it does not teach, it does not cause me to know or understand why things are so, unless it also brings forward reasons. (*Logic*, CM, XI, p. 283)

That is the Ramist position, though some Ramists were careful, in explaining the point about divine testimony in *Dialecticae Institutiones,* to argue that Ramus meant the pagan gods, whose testimony might more properly be called diabolical than divine. Milton does not hedge: at issue is not the source of the testimony but the validity of testimony itself as argument. If even divine testimony can only command faith but not effectively prove "unless it also brings forward reasons," reasons are the *only* effective proofs. The proper ground of rhetoric then, even in terms of its effort to persuade, must be logic.

We can quickly gauge how far Milton's Ramist doctrine takes him from the common Renaissance view of testimony by glancing at two of the commentators on Aristotle's *Rhetoric* most widely read in the era, Alessandro Piccolomini and Pietro Vettori. Both are concerned merely to clarify or amplify what Aristotle says.[22] Like Aristotle himself, and like texts on rhetoric generally, neither Vettori nor Piccolomini shows the slightest concern that the citation of witnesses may get us no nearer to the truth of a matter. But for Milton, far more even than for most who followed Ramus in making logic essential to rhetoric, getting at the truth of a matter was the central concern, no less important than getting others to see it as true. His acceptance of rhetoric is not in question; what distinguishes his acceptance is his consciousness that, unless tested and verified by the art that seeks truth, all the devices of persuasion can be so many handicaps to a serious inquirer and persuader of others to undertake the hard task of serious and thoughtful inquiry.

Not that Milton was uniformly successful in his use of the art of persuasion. I refer here not to the effect on whatever audience he reached or sought to reach in the seventeenth century—that is, not to whether he won his "case"—but to the skill with which he uses the art, or—to put it conversely, as Aristotle suggests—to the effect on an "ideal judge." Effects on readers inevitably vary with the readers' own predisposition to credit or doubt the case to be proved. But that Milton aimed at rational persuasion is evident as early as *Of Reformation:* "But I shall chiefly endeavor to declare those causes that hinder the forwarding of true discipline, which are among ourselves. Orderly proceeding will divide our inquiry into our forefathers' days and into our times" (CM, III, p. 7). And he does indeed offer the history of England's reformation in an orderly fashion. He offers, too, answers to his opponents' arguments: "But it will be said, these men were martyrs. What then? Though every true Christian will be a martyr when he is called to it, not presently does it follow that every one suffering for religion is, without exception" (p. 9). He quotes the testimony of Paul to confirm his argument: "St. Paul writes that 'a man may give his body to be burnt (meaning for religion), and yet not have charity': he is not therefore above all possibility of erring because he burns for some points of truth" (pp. 9–10). Martyrdom is simply no proof of the martyr's religious creed, or all manner of creeds would by now have been proved true: people have suffered and died to bear "witness" to the most opposed beliefs, as we all know. The argument too obviously aims at the rational to need further analysis here.

So too with Milton's next argument: "Now to proceed, whatsoever the bishops were, it seems they themselves were unsatisfied in matters of religion as they then stood"—or why did they (Cranmer, Latimer, and Ridley, among others) appoint a commission to "frame ecclesiastical constitutions"? And he offers further evidence that what England then arrived at in the way of church reform is by no means final: "Lastly, we all know by examples, that exact reformation is not perfected at the first push, and those unwieldy times of Edward VI may hold some plea by this excuse" (p. 11). Milton has, so to speak, *too much* logic here: he does not want to limit his line of reasoning to just what will answer opponents; he wants also to be fair. The argument requires only that he prove the initial reformation of the English church incomplete; but in his fair-mindedness he is concerned lest anyone think he is blaming the original reformers for

not achieving all necessary reforms. And thence back to the central
point: that these men were bishops *and* martyrs cannot prove the
rightness of episcopacy: "It was not episcopacy that wrought in them
the heavenly fortitude of martyrdom, as little is it that martyrdom can
make good episcopacy" (p. 11). Far otherwise: it was their being
bishops that produced their errors: "But it was episcopacy that led
the good and holy men, through the temptation of the enemy, and the
snare of this present world, to many blameworthy and oppobrious
actions" (p. 11). And episcopacy still has the same effect on church-
men: it debases even the best of them, so that even the "most learned
and seeming religious of our ministers," once they get to be bishops,
rarely keep even their learning—and then only "by some potent
sway of nature" (p. 11). The argument is intricate—and far from over
when Milton comments on the effect episcopacy has on those who
become "bishops." He proceeds to deny that what his opponents
call "bishops" are properly speaking bishops at all; that is, he proceeds to a redefinition of the key term.[23]

So far Milton has accepted his opponents' use of the word, and
argued from their own assumption that a bishop is someone called a
bishop. Now he cuts the ground from under them—they do not even
know what the word *bishop* means:

He that, enabled with gifts from God, and the lawful and primitive choice of
the church assembled in convenient number, faithfully from that time forward feeds his parochial flock, has his coequal and compresbyterial power to
ordain ministers and deacons by public prayer and vote of Christ's congre-
gation in like sort as he himself was ordained, and is a true apostolic bishop.
(p. 12)

We may not agree with the argument, but that it is step-by-step an
argument logically pursued we cannot question: some of the steps
are compressed, at least one of the enthymemes being compressed
into two adjectives and a conjunction, "coequal and compresbyterial"; but even that compression is clearly an argument
logically grounded: bishops may ordain ministers and deacons;
presbyters may ordain ministers and deacons; bishops therefore
constitute no distinct order of the clergy on the ground of their power
of ordination. But what of those entitled bishops? They are chiefly
distinguished by pride of the special chair and haughty palace, pomp
of worldly place and power. Such "bishops" are no fit overseers of
the church at all, so that in a summary enthymeme "he that makes

him bishop makes him no bishop." Then comes the example of St. Martin to enforce that enthymeme. And so the argument proceeds.

Of course, Milton does not follow any single pattern of argument: there is no single pattern for all arguments. There are, however, classes or kinds of argument: the enthymeme (or compressed deduction); the example (or compressed induction); common materials of argument (the topics); and common procedures (chronological sequence, division into issues, definition and distinction, and the like). And, of course, Milton does not always argue with equal caution, calm, or even rationality (though daring and emotion are not necessarily at odds with reason). But assuredly he did not spend his time hopping up and down on the same square inch of ground in *any* of his controversial prose works, even the most inept, so that where the incautious or overingenious may assert a redundance, as, say, in the headings of *The Reason of Church Government,* Book I, chapters 1 and 2, the careful and scrupulous will observe a clear progression. Chapter 1 is headed "That Church government is prescribed in the Gospel, and that to say otherwise is unsound"; chapter 2, "That Church government is set down in holy Scripture, and that to say otherwise is untrue." The *Gospel* is, of course, the New Testament; whereas *Holy Scripture* includes both the Old and New Testaments; *unsound* signifies unhealthy, not grounded in reason; whereas *untrue* signifies contrary to fact. Any reader who cannot understand why Milton makes the first step that the New Testament does indeed prescribe a form of church government, and only then proceeds to the facts of the organization explicitly set forth in the Old Testament and its partly implicit, partly explicit modification in the New, is simply ignoring Milton's patent concern to refute the arguments advanced by advocates of a hierarchical church structure. And anyone who does not see why he calls *unsound* their argument that the New Testament says nothing at all about how the church should be organized, while he reserves *untrue* for their doubly erroneous argument that the New Testament by implication sanctions the continuity into Christian times of a *hierarchical* priesthood that the Old Testament *established,* is simply refusing to make distinctions that would have been second nature to Milton, trained at St. Paul's and at Cambridge in logic and rhetoric.

To have to spell out such obviousnesses is boring. Milton does not spell them out but assumes his readers' ability to move along with him. And move along we do—whether to agreement or not is beside the point. The argument may not persuade, but hardly because it is stuck fast in one same assertion. Milton in fact is generally rather good at summarizing the stages of his argument, as he does here in the final sentences of chapter 1 and chapter 2. That he himself detested the tediousness of repetition anyone may know who looks up the word (or its antonym *variety*) in, say, the index to the Columbia edition of his works; when he had to answer a repetitious argument, he both answered it and called it repetitious, as witness long stretches of *Eikonoklastes* and the *Defenses*.

But my argument does not concern Milton's use of rhetoric in his controversial prose, much less in his poetry, nor even the entire body of rhetorical principle set forth piecemeal in his work. To discuss that would involve a book in itself. My concern here is only to demonstrate his full respect for an art in which he himself was thoroughly grounded and which he expected his readers also to know. The contemporary critic who never uses the word *rhetoric* without prefacing it with *mere* is himself using bad rhetoric of a sort in which Milton never indulged. Regarding the art of persuasion, he was both astute and informed: his constant invention for all the misleading speakers in his poems of the best possible arguments, not the most easily demolished, is so successful that they have often misled naive and careless readers, even when they are decisively answered by honest argument within the poems themselves. Satan in *Paradise Lost* is only the most notable example. Even honestly searching inquirers in *Comus, Paradise Lost,* and *Samson Agonistes,* presented in the imperfections of *dianoia* corresponding to the imperfections of their *ethos,* can mislead the hasty scanner of Milton's lines who comes to them unaware of the poet's subtle fidelity in the mimesis of his agents. The responsibility is ours, not Milton's.

He consistently recognized the risks implicit in his undertakings; hence his prayer for an audience fit however few. In his controversial prose, too, he recognized his risks, though the issues at stake struck him as important enough to warrant his taking all manner of risk. And once, at least, undertaking possibly his greatest risk, that of offending the very side on which he thought England's hopes rested of attaining a total separation of church and state—and therewith a true freedom of conscience, and a government of sound law, not dependent on monarchical whim—he wrote into the prefatory

address "To Parliament" in the *Doctrine and Discipline of Divorce*
what may stand as the summary of his rhetorical theory and practice:
"I seek not to seduce the simple and illiterate. My errand is to find
out the choicest and the learnedest who have this high gift of wisdom
to answer solidly or to be convinced."

Atlanta, Georgia

NOTES

1. Compare the disparagement of bad rhetoric in *Works of John Milton*, ed. Frank
Allen Patterson et al. (New York, 1931–38), V, pp. 5, 104, and VI, p. 151, for example,
with the exaltation of eloquence in III, p. 186, or VIII, pp. 159–61. All references,
unless otherwise noted, are to this edition, hereafter cited as CM.

2. So with the condemnation of bad invention, misused aphorisms, and false
argument from tropes in CM, III, pp. 47, 171.

3. See "Milton's Rhetoric: Satan and the 'Unjust Discourse,' " *Milton Studies*, I,
ed. James D. Simmonds (Pittsburgh, 1969), pp. 67–91; and "*Ethos* and *Dianoia:*
Character and Rhetoric in *Paradise Lost*," in *Language and Style in Milton*, ed.
Ronald D. Emma and John T. Shawcross (New York, 1967), pp. 193–232.

4. For Milton's early use of rhetorical principle see, for example, CM, III, p. 96,
and for his late use CM, VIII, p. 13.

5. *Eight Philosophers of the Italian Renaissance* (Stanford, 1964), p. 34; see also
p. 153.

6. See *John Milton at St. Paul's School* (New York, 1948), pp. 4–15, 147–51; and
The Intellectual Development of John Milton (Urbana, 1961), vol. II, pp. 201–70.

7. "Milton's View of Rhetoric," *Studies in Philology*, LXIV (1967), 685–711.

8. See the use of commonplaces on rhetoric in CM, XII, pp. 119, 149–51, 159,
163–65, 211, 249, 253.

9. Introduction to *Complete Prose Works of John Milton*, ed. Don M. Wolfe et al.
(New Haven, 1953–), hereafter cited as YP, III, p. 138.

10. See, for example, the letter to Philaras, CM, XII, pp. 57–59.

11. For Milton's early use of Ramus see his letter to Young, CM, XII, p. 5. Wilbur
Samuel Howell, *Logic and Rhetoric in England, 1500–1700* (Princeton, 1956), p. 281,
notes that both Milton's tutors at Cambridge were Ramists. For the stock Ramist
definition of rhetoric see Omer Talon, *Rhetorica, e Petri Rami . . . praelectionibus
observata*, the opening sentence. (I have used the edition printed in Frankfurt-am-
Main in 1575.) Among English Ramists who repeat the definition see, for example,
Anthony Wotton, *The Art of Logick. Gathered . . . by . . . Ramus* (London, 1626);
Alexander Richardson, *The Logicians School-Master* (London, 1629); Charles Butler,
Rhetoricae Libri Duo (London, 1629); and Hanserdus Knollys, *Rhetoricae Adum-
bratio* (London, 1663). Cf. Howell, *Logic and Rhetoric*, pp. 262–63.

12. Butler varies this to "Elocutio & Pronunciatio."

13. See his letter of March 26, 1625, CM, XII, p. 5.

14. CM, III, pp. 115, 135.

15. On Ramus and Ramism see Walter J. Ong, S.J., *Ramus* (Cambridge, Mass., 1958), and his introduction to the photographic reprint of Ramus, *Collectaneae praefationes, epistolae, orationes* from the Marburg 1599 edition. Cf. Howell, *Logic and Rhetoric*, p. 187.

16. See, for example, *Prolusion VI* (CM, XII, pp. 219–21) and *Reason of Church Government* (CM, III, p. 272).

17. Cf. Merritt Y. Hughes, introduction to YP, III, p. 136.

18. "A View of Milton and the Traditional," *Milton Studies*, I, ed. James D. Simmonds (Pittsburgh, 1969), pp. 15–29.

19. As in *Reason of Church Government* (CM, III, p. 237) and *PL* IX, 13–43.

20. Milton uses another kind of inartificial proof, the oath, to begin the passage (CM, III, p. 10) but obviously does not rely on it to replace rational argument.

21. That is how a man becomes a "heretic in the truth" according to *Areopagitica* (CM, IV, p. 333).

22. See Piccolomini, *Copiosissima Parafrase* (Venice, 1565), pp. 47, 305, 311–12; and Vettori, *Commentarii* (Florence, 1548), pp. 221–24.

23. The use of definition as a form of argument is at least as old as Socrates, but Milton rests his case on definitions and redefinitions of key terms with a regularity that speaks his conviction on the right relation of rhetoric to logic. See, for example, *Of Reformation* and *Of Prelatical Episcopacy* on *bishop; Animadversions* on *presbyter* and *ordination; Tetrachordon* and *Doctrine and Discipline of Divorce* on *marriage; Tenure of Kings and Magistrates* on *king* and *tyrant; Eikonoklastes* on *commonwealth; Treatise of Civil Power* on *civil* and *religious authority, blasphemy, heresy, inward man,* and *evangelical religion; Of True Religion, Heresy, and Schism* on those three terms; as well as the familiar definitions of *education* in *Of Education, censorship* in *Areopagitica,* and all terms involved in *De Doctrina Christiana.* And see *Defensio Secunda* on calling things "by their right names" (CM, VIII, p. 147).

MILTON, ASCHAM, AND
THE RHETORIC OF
THE DIVORCE CONTROVERSY

John M. Perlette

WHEN MILTON set forth his arguments proposing an expanded conception of the legitimate grounds for divorce,
he hoped to establish a dialogue. But the "fair and christianly"
discussion which he called for in the preface to *The Judgment of
Martin Bucer* (1644) failed to develop. In its stead limped the
anonymous *Answer* (1644); otherwise, the only responses were silence or outright condemnation. Recently, however, a brief essay,
"Of Marriage," written in 1647–1648 by Anthony Ascham but apparently never published, has come to light.[1] This enigmatic little
treatise, now Ascham's earliest known work, raises several interesting questions, not least among them whether it might be in some
sense an oblique response to Milton.

But if the work is an enigma, its author is even more so. Not a
great deal is known about Ascham; variously tutor by appointment of
Parliament to James, Duke of York, perhaps propagandist for that
Parliament and finally its ill-fated ambassador to Madrid, Ascham
was stabbed to death there by royalist exiles in 1650.[2] All but forgotten for the next three hundred years, Ascham has over the past
two decades received increasing attention from political historians
interested in his theories of the legitimacy of de facto government,
and he serves as a major background figure in one literary study,
John M. Wallace's *Destiny His Choice: The Loyalism of Andrew
Marvell*.[3] Wallace, J. G. A. Pocock, and others present Ascham as a
spokesman for the English Everyman trying casuistically but sin-
cerely to reason his way out of the personal dilemma brought on by
the political and constitutional dilemmas of the late 1640s. Pocock
finds Ascham "presenting the individual as constantly faced with
conflicting demands for allegiance, dilemmas of choice which, since
they are incapable of moral resolution, ought not to have been forced
upon him." Hence he wittily but aptly sums Ascham up by saying,

"He might be described as the Captain Yossarian of the English Revolution, and his works collectively as the *Catch 22*."[4] Those works (probably some half-dozen, though no one is certain how many are his) have been variously interpreted. One certainty, however, is that almost all the known activities and writings of Ascham are political. "Of Marriage," then, creates even more problems. For one, why is the theoretical and practical politician Ascham interested in writing on marriage and divorce in 1647–1648? And beyond that, what can Ascham's treatise tell us about the politics and rhetoric of the divorce issue?

I shall suggest here that Milton's argument provided one of the stimuli to the composition of Ascham's treatise. But such a relationship between "Of Marriage" and *The Doctrine and Discipline of Divorce* prompts a larger inquiry. What would account for Ascham's interest in the divorce question, and what can it tell us about Milton? In the final sections of this essay I suggest that "Of Marriage" is not only a refutation of divorce but also a political document in its own right, and that Ascham's "disguised" rhetoric operates at several levels. What appears to be a casual excursus on marriage is actually an argument against divorce, and that argument is both an end in itself and the means to a broader political end. But most significantly, the political aspects of "Of Marriage" allow us to view the arguments of *The Doctrine and Discipline* from a new rhetorical perspective.

I

"Of Marriage" constitutes, however indirectly, a refutation of Milton's divorce thesis, in spite of the fact that the essay's rhetorical "reply" motif is almost entirely obscured. Ascham carefully avoids the typical methods of the "animadversion" or any appearance of polemic. He never mentions Milton (or any other proponent of divorce); he never directly quotes him; he never undertakes an obviously systematic refutation of his argument. Nevertheless, though he tells us he is writing "Of Marriage in General," his emphasis throughout the essay falls decidedly upon the need for the marital relationship to endure and upon the impossibility of divorce.

The chronology of events supports the contention that "Of Marriage" was written with Milton's work in mind. Ascham probably wrote his essay in the autumn or early winter of 1647–1648.[5] Hence it is contemporaneous with an overt and significant attack on Milton, that of the Sion College Presbyterian Synod of December 14, 1647.[6] This list of "Errors, Heresies, and Blasphemies" quoted Milton's divorce thesis verbatim. The only other work mentioned therein in connection with marriage was the anonymous pamphlet *Little Non-Such*.[7] The omission of any reference to other works which could be construed as supporting the legitimacy of divorce, such as John Selden's *Uxor Ebraica* (1646), is indicative of Milton's dominance of the topic.

More important, the treatises of Milton and Ascham intersect in a range from verbal echoes through specific arguments to general principles ultimately transcending the divorce question. Some verbal affinities, especially when taken in the aggregate and in conjunction with other evidence, point directly to *The Doctrine and Discipline*. For example, the formal statement of Milton's divorce thesis had stipulated *"that there be mutuall consent"* (p. 242). Ascham, in the first paragraph of his essay, recognizes that "It should seeme to bee a rough contract which may not cease by mutual Dissent (as all other doe)" (fol. 1). At another point, Milton argues that to forbid divorce "is to make an Idol of mariage, . . . to make it a transcendent command, above both the second and the first Table, which is a most prodigious doctrine" (p. 276). But Ascham answers: "it were therefore a grosse imputation of imprudence in God to thinke hee prouided not for the maintenance of [marriage] in *the* Decalogue, as well as for other lesser things, or to conceiue the place of its injunction any where ells then in the front of the Second Table" (fol. 38). A final verbal echo, one which needs no comment for those who are familiar with Milton's prose, occurs when Ascham characterizes the right to divorce as "this pretence of Liberty" (fol. 31).

The true seventeenth-century polemist grants his antagonist nothing. Ascham, perhaps in keeping with his reasonable, non-polemic pose, agrees with Milton quite frequently. For example, Ascham affirms the spirit of Milton's "meet and happy conversation" when he characterizes marriage as "the Partnership of a more communicatiue life," a "ffellowship of souls and bodies" (fols. 1–2), and "a perfect communion both of body and minde" (fol. 7). Both men also express the notion that this sensitive appreciation of the more transcendent qualities of marriage is a privilege not within the grasp of all. And Ascham is perfectly willing, on the other hand, to grant that "the evil and the affliction" attendant upon a bad marriage, which Milton repeatedly makes so much of, can create a disaster. At several points in *The Doctrine and Discipline*, Milton adds as a subsidiary consideration the effects of marriage on the well-being of "the Common-Wealth," linking "all hope of true Reformation in the state" with the "carefull education of our children" (pp. 229–30). On the importance of marriage to the Commonwealth, Ascham could not concur more heartily, but with a totally different emphasis. Ironically, solicitude for the "carefull education of our children" leads directly to a major flaw in Milton's case.

Much of Milton's argument for divorce rests upon the assertion that the provision of spiritual benefits and consolation is a necessary end, even the primary end, of marriage. Though Ascham shared to some extent Milton's lofty vision, he implies that even in a perfect marriage "the mynde (as *saint* Paul saith) [1 Corinthians, chap. vii] must needs suffer some Diuision, neither party being wholly it selfe, nor free, but as it were bound to spend much of that attention and tyme, in mutual compleasance, which is due to God" (fols. 2–3). Therefore, spiritual qualities, however desirable, cannot be the primary end of an institution which, by its very nature, partially frustrates or detracts from them. A quest for spiritual perfection "would oblige all men and Women to an vnmarried Life, if they were not diuerted from it by a pure Instinct of propagation" (fol. 3). The necessary end of marriage must lie elsewhere, and all nature indicates that it is to be found in the procreation and nurture of offspring. The condition of man is such that the fulfillment of this duty requires an unbreakable marriage contract: "and this is compleate marriage; Especially when wee contract for the Durance of it, which is necessary as well for the childes sake as the Mothers" (fol. 7). This concern for "the childes sake," seemingly appended as a mere afterthought, is actually the thesis that Ascham discusses and defends in "Of Marriage." The enduring obligation of parents to their children and the consequent impossibility of divorce recur throughout Ascham's argument, within both the individual chapters and the work as a whole, culminating in chapter 5, "Of the Education of Children."

The specific, pragmatic arguments of each writer are complemented by arguments at the level of general principles. To the recognized reason for divorce, "naturall frigidity," Milton sought to add the other "natural" reasons of "*indisposition, unfitnes, or contrariety of mind, arising from a cause in nature unchangable*" (p. 242). The assertion that fundamental differences of character guarantee the failure of certain matches (or mismatches) is presented as one application of a cosmological principle true of all creation, that "there is indeed a twofold Seminary or stock in nature, from whence are deriv'd the issues of love and hatred distinctly flowing through the whole masse of created things" (p. 272). This posits the existence of immutable categories in nature, permanently dividing the forces of love and hate, of harmony and discord. To attempt to

cross these boundaries by forcing the association of natural antip-
athies is to court disaster.

Ascham's treatise advances another, and equally reverent, cosmological principle through which the operations of nature can be
differently interpreted. To Milton's static concept of permanently
divided, immutably fixed categories, Ascham opposes the familiar
Renaissance principle of *discordia concors*. This dynamic concept
posits an ongoing process in nature creating harmony from the clash
of those very discords of which Milton spoke. Ascham says:

> The world Continues its order and vnity amongst the continual Alterations
> and Contrarieties of the Elements; and Nature suffers not in theis combats
> but renforces hirselfe for hir productions in the opposite seasons: The same
> may happen in some familyes, in which opposite humors may bee corrected
> by theyr contrarieties, and the Avarice of one may qualify the prodigall
> profusion of the other; the drought of the Earth and moysture of the Water
> forme but one Globe, and presse together in *the* same center, the same
> Infinite Wisdome which Hath allyed things of soe different Natures,
> marryes allsoe humors as Contrary in vs, that soe by the mixture they may
> bee the better temperd. (fols. 28–29)

Characteristically, Ascham concludes this section of his argument by advocating patience in a simple but forceful reassertion of a
position which Milton had anticipated and dismissed: "there remains then noe other expedient for Remedy but Patience and a fixt
resolution not to quarrel more with this condition then wee would
with our selues, for being made of contrary humors" (fol. 30). Milton
repeatedly rejected the appeal for Patience: "God sends remedies,
as well as evills; under which he who lies and groans, that may
lawfully acquitt himself, is accessory to his own ruin" (p. 341). In the
dialectic, these sharply contrasting positions begin on common
ground, argument from natural law,[8] but they veer off in opposite
directions almost at once.

One principal point of divergence is illustrated by the concept
of "necessity." For Ascham, various forces in nature, depicted as
being largely external to man, create circumstances, situations,
"events" which are beyond one's control. Nature itself is a force
which single-mindedly works to achieve its own ends, regardless of
man's desires. It is nature's "pure Instinct of propagation" which
guides us into marriage, and "Heerein therfore wee worke more for
Natures Ends then *our* owne" (fol. 5). Therefore Ascham, facing the
inevitable with traditional Stoic doctrine, concludes: "The Wiseman
is calld the Artificer of his owne happines, because hee adjusts his
desires to the necessity of Events, and mooues chearfully through

that way, through which hee would otherwise bee sullenly dragd"
(fol. 36).[9] As opposed to Ascham's concept of an external, often
hostile, necessity of events, Milton considers necessities to be those
internal requirements of fallen man, unfailingly provided for by an
equitable, charitable God. The legitimation of divorce is just such a
necessary provision. In Paradise, Milton argues, marriage was perfect and therefore indissoluble. But since in the fallen world mar-
riages will fall short of perfection, the law of divorce "was granted to
apparent necessities, as being of unquestionable right and reason in
the Law of nature" (p. 313). Milton even goes so far as to say that "of
those three ends [of marriage] which God appointed, that to him is
greatest which is most necessary: and mariage is then most brok'n to
him, when he utterly wants the fruition of that which he most sought
therin, whether it were religious, civill, or corporall society" (p. 269).

In Milton's view, then, necessities, internal requirements, and
legitimate desires are almost synonymous, and there is no reason to
suppose that these desires should be subject to frustration: "the
waies of God . . . are equal, easy, and not burdensome; nor do they
ever crosse the just and reasonable desires of men, nor involve this
our portion of mortall life, into a necessity of sadnes and malecon-
tent" (p. 342). Ascham must have found this unbounded optimism
nearly incomprehensible, for his own position is precisely the contrary: "but the euill which torments you is as it were necessary in the
state of the World, in which wee haue not a reall choice betwixt a
good and an euill, but only that betwixt two Euils wee may choose
the lesse" (fol. 27). And he views the consideration of man's desires
as pure folly, first because in the scale of events they count for so
little, but also because to seek their fulfillment in this world is to
pursue a chimera: "ffor noe man yeat euer enjoyd soe high a content,
but hee could possibly imagine to himselfe something of the same
kinde a degree higher and the missing of this (which in right reason
wee should not haue expected) is that which indiscreetly breeds
Anxiety" (fol. 5). In Ascham's world, evil is inevitable; in Milton's it
is remediable, if only we have the strength and fortitude, the wisdom
and courage to find and use those remedies which God and the
secondary law of nature must provide. We can discern in these
countersuppositions bases for the commonplace characterizations of
their proponents: Milton the revolutionary counsels actions and
reform to adjust the discrepancies inherent in nature, while Ascham
the quietist counsels patience and passive reliance upon the processes of nature itself.

Milton, of course, would amend or abandon some of these notions as his career developed, but the point to which such principles
could ultimately lead was hardly imaginable in 1643. By 1648, however, Ascham, who like Milton would transfer the principles of his
arguments on divorce to his political writings, must have noticed the
dangerous tendencies and implications of such views. The divorce
question was by no means a dead issue. Nevertheless, considering
the nearly universal rejection of Milton's divorce thesis, the relatively late date of Ascham's reply, and the developing political
situation, we must finally ask: What prompts Ascham, whose basic
interests are political (as all of his subsequent writings and known
activities indicate), to compose an apparently casual essay on marriage and divorce in the winter of 1647–1648? My answer is that "Of
Marriage" is a political work in its own right, one, however, whose
rhetoric operates indirectly, in a manner analogous to that of an
allegory, a parable, or a seventeenth-century political poem like
Denham's *Cooper's Hill*.[10] While Ascham's argument against
divorce is an important element of his rhetorical motive, his ultimate
goal transcends a refutation of divorce. Ascham employs this argument, useful in itself, as a vehicle for his characteristic precepts of
quietism and passivity which his audience might abstract and apply
directly to the immediate political situation. Partly an argument
against divorce, "Of Marriage" is more an argument against that state
of mind which could champion divorce among other reforms ecclesiastical, domestic, and civil. Significantly, then, "Of Marriage"
serves as a reflector by which Milton's rhetoric can be viewed from a
new perspective.

II

Before considering the details of the arguments, we might notice the larger matter of form.[11] The particular rhetorical forms that
Milton and Ascham employ are significant in that they subtly
complement the utmost principles of the respective arguments
which they figure forth. The opposed positions we have been exam-
ining determine these forms and are reflected in them. From start to
finish, the movement of *The Doctrine and Discipline* indicates that
its mode of persuasion is deliberative.[12] Openly hortatory and expressing a strong sense of an urgent public matter, it finds its end in a
politically (in the broadest sense) expedient action and its audience
in the members of Parliament and the Assembly or those with the
power to influence them. Milton's use of an obviously deliberative

form is significant in its own right. Aristotle has written: "Clearly counsel can only be given on matters about which people deliberate; matters, namely, that ultimately depend on ourselves, and which we have it in our power to set going" (*Rhet.* 1359a). Thus, in the divorce argument, Milton's choice of form, his employment of an openly deliberative mode to exhort a radical change for the improvement of the condition of man, is in itself an assertion of faith in the nature of man as agent capable in no small measure of controlling his destiny. Milton's premises, as we have seen, repeatedly asserted such a role for man.

But it should also be noted that, in the divorce tracts, Milton was implicitly advocating a daring and radical expansion of the domain of deliberative rhetoric itself. To the field of debate, where men made decisions and took action upon contingencies, matters of choice, matters thought properly to be within man's power to decide, Milton brought a question which most men considered not a matter of choice at all, but a matter of necessity.[13] The thrusting of such an issue into the deliberative mode constitutes in itself an implicit but powerful argument: the form implies the crucial assumption that the matter is arbitrary, not necessary. On the other hand, the refusal of the learned community to debate the issue was, from a rhetorical point of view, a devastating answer in its own right. It was not that its members did not take Milton seriously; all the evidence suggests that they did. They refused to reply because to do so would have been to admit that the matter was debatable, and by the mere fact of such an admission, the status of the prohibitions of divorce would have been reduced from absolute truth to the merely probable or expedient. They barred the gates to the province of rhetoric by pretending that the issue was beyond question.

Unlike Milton, Ascham is much more circumspect about his intentions and purposes. I have located his thesis in his statement that "a perfect communion" of man and woman, in both body and mind, "is compleate marriage; Especially when wee contract for the Durance of it, which is necessary as well for the childes sake as the Mothers." Yet this isolated thesis is an inadequate, because incomplete, formal principle.[14] The question still remains: To what end, for what purpose, does he prove it? Lacking any declaration of intent or intimations of urgency, and given its casual, even disinterested survey of various aspects of marriage, Ascham's treatise might be classified as an epideictic exercise, a literary composition, an essay which does not appear to have any immediate, practical purpose.

But this epideictic pose which Ascham adopts would simply be a further extension of his decision not to use the form of the polemical reply, and would explain in large part his tactic of simply reasserting without elaboration points which Milton had anticipated and elaborately refuted in *The Doctrine and Discipline*. Ascham does not argue the points, because he too wants to maintain the pretense that they are incontrovertible. He wants to make assertions rather than devise refutations. But in the final analysis, he is disguising an essentially deliberative intent, for he must have known that these traditional values and beliefs which he was reasserting had in fact been questioned and subordinated to other values by Milton. Through his epideictic pose, then, he is able to have simultaneously the best of both modes. On the one hand, he has his reply, and on the other, he has the benefit of appearing not to have replied at all. Thus, he avoids making a "rhetorical" issue of the question of divorce; his basic ploy is an attempt (much like that of those who simply refused to argue) to make the entire issue appear to be beyond the scope of deliberative rhetoric.

The relationship between form and the other elements of argument is no less intimate in Ascham's case than it was in Milton's. Ascham's specific arguments rest upon the presupposition that "The Wiseman . . . adjusts his desires to the necessity of Events." That supposition controls the form itself of his rhetoric in "Of Marriage." With the weight of tradition and rhetorical inertia on his side, Ascham could safely assert that marriage (and even marital problems) and the customary prohibition of divorce are the necessary and inevitable results of the laws of God, of nature, and of nations. And as Aristotle noted with regard to deliberative rhetoric: "Concerning things which exist or will exist inevitably, or which cannot possibly exist or take place, no counsel can be given" (*Rhet.* 1359a). Hence, Ascham discusses marriage and divorce as though his concerns were theoretical *(cognitionis)* rather than practical *(actionis)*,[15] matters which could be discussed but not debated. Thus, the epideictic pose complements his doctrine of acceptance and passivity; once again the form itself is a powerful argument.

However, this leaves Ascham's rhetoric straddling not only the epideictic-deliberative fence but also the Stoic paradox: What does one do when one can do nothing? In spite of necessity or events, what remains in man's power is his attitude, and it is to the matter of attitude that Ascham ultimately addresses himself. At this level he is indeed giving counsel, and his intentions become most genuinely deliberative, though still not openly so. But in order to understand fully the method and implications of his argument, we must probe a bit more deeply into Milton's.

III

Implicit in Milton's choice of rhetorical form and premises is the assumption that man can control and improve the circumstances of his life. Implicit in Ascham's rhetorical choices is a denial that man's power extends so far. One crucial premise that we have not yet noticed is typical of Milton: "For all sense and reason and equity reclaimes that any Law or Cov'nant how solemn or strait soever, either between God and man, or man and man, though of Gods joyning, should bind against a prime and principall scope of its own institution, and of both or either party cov'nanting" (p. 245). Ernest Sirluck, recognizing the central function of this premise in Milton's treatise, has called it an "axiom."[16] Taken at face value, the assumption is quite secure; no law should operate against its own ends. Vulnerable here are its implications, for in order to apply this axiom to the argument for divorce, two assumptions must be made: first, that the ends of marriage can be adequately and unequivocally known; second, that an indisputable hierarchy of these ends can be established. Milton labored at length to establish both. Against the first, Ascham asserts that we are in no position to determine what ends are best for us, that God and nature act and we of necessity follow passively, working "more for Natures Ends than our owne." Against the second he argues, as we have seen, by admitting the ends which Milton identified, but then inverting the hierarchy of ends or values which Milton attempted to establish.

However, Milton's application to marriage and divorce of the axiom that no "Law or Cov'nant . . . should bind against a prime and principall scope of its own institution" finally leads to a problem of far greater import. In the preface "To the Parlament," added to the second edition of *The Doctrine and Discipline*, Milton related his own conclusions about divorce to the recent political actions of Parliament:

Advise yee well, supreme Senat, if charity be thus excluded and expulst, how yee will defend the untainted honour of your own actions and proceedings: He who marries, intends as little to conspire his own ruine, as he that swears Allegiance: and as a whole people is in proportion to an ill Government, so is one man to an ill mariage. If they against any authority, Covnant, or Statute, may by the soveraign edict of charity, save not only their lives, but honest liberties from unworthy bondage, as well may he against any private Covnant, which hee never enter'd to his mischief, redeem himself from unsupportable disturbances to honest peace, and just contentment. (p. 229)

A comparison of this passage with the full context in which Milton's axiom subsequently appears (p. 245) clearly reveals that these two examples are put forth, in a preliminary statement, as consequences of that principle.[17] Sirluck calls this passage "a remarkable and pregnant analogy between divorce and political reformation," adding: "It was obviously excellent rhetoric for Milton to relate his own case to that of Parliament in this way."[18] But Sirluck's analysis is questionable on two counts. First, is this really an analogy? And second, whether it is analogy or something else, is it in fact "obviously excellent rhetoric"?

If Milton's argument is interpreted as an analogy, the theme consists in the statements relating to marriage ("He who marries," "One man to an ill mariage," "May he against any private Covnant . . . redeem himself"); and the *phoros*, or the elements used to support the argument, consists in the statements relating to politics ("he that swears Allegiance," "as a whole people is in proportion to an ill Government," "They . . . may . . . save not only their lives, but honest liberties"). The structure of Milton's argument here certainly gives it the appearance of being an analogy, starting out as it does with the characteristic form: "as this . . . as that," "as this . . . so that." However, the structure then shifts slightly, away from the analogical toward the more strictly logical "if . . . then" form: "If they . . . as well may he." This shift is slight, but it serves as a clue which indicates that even at this point Milton did not think of the relationship between divorce and Parliament's own proceedings as a mere analogy.

Analogy requires, first (and simply) that the *phoros* be better known or more easily understood than the theme, and second (and more subtly) that this theme and *phoros* belong to different spheres. "When the two relations encountered belong to the same sphere, and can be subsumed under a common structure, we have not analogy but argument by example or illustration, in which the theme and the phoros represent two particular cases of a single rule."[19] The distinction between analogy and argument by example is often difficult and sometimes impossible to make, yet I think it can be made in this case by comparing Milton's argument quoted earlier with another of his which is more clearly a case of true analogy:

There must be therfore some other example found out to shew us wherin civil policy may with warrant from God settle wickednes by law, & make that lawfull which is lawlesse. Although I doubt not but upon deeper consideration, that which is true in Physick, will be found as true in polity: that as of bad pulses those that beat most in order, are much wors then those that keep the most inordinate circuit, so of popular vices those that may be committed legally, will be more pernicious then those which are left to their own cours at peril, not under a stinted privilege to sin orderly and regularly, which is an implicit contradiction, but under due and fearles execution of punishment. (pp. 322–23)

Here Milton's analogy begins by pointing out that not one but two spheres are involved, "physick" and polity; it is obvious that only by resorting to some extreme level of abstraction could a rule be formulated (and Milton makes no effort to formulate one) which would include the two cases. On the other hand, Milton subsumes both divorce and Parliament's actions under the explicitly formulated rule that no "Law or Cov'nant . . . should bind against a prime and principall scope of its own institution." He explicitly includes both in the same sphere, since both marriage and political allegiance are actually covenants or contracts, and since both legitimation of divorce and parliamentary supremacy are elements of one process, the reformation. Far from seeing them as distinct spheres, Milton sees the two cases as being intimately, consequentially related. Therefore he can conclude: "And farewell all hope of true Reformation in the state, while such an evill as this lies undiscern'd or unregarded in the house" (pp. 229–30). The one correlates directly with the other. Sirluck himself says, of the later *Tetrachordon*, that "Milton has here gone far beyond his analogy of the preceding year between divorce and Parliament's 'own actions and proceedings.' He has completely integrated the case for divorce with that for Parliamentary supremacy: they are twin consequences of a single principle, the jurisdiction of the secondary law of nature."[20] I am suggesting here that this integration of the two cases did not need to wait for the *Tetrachordon* or, as Sirluck suggests, for Milton's "discovery" of the secondary law of nature. Milton, at least as early as the composition of "To the Parlament," already conceived of these two cases as "twin consequences of a single principle."

Therefore, to characterize as an analogy the argument relating divorce to Parliament's case is to fail to see the binding logical force which Milton evidently felt that it carried. It is no mere analogy which prompts him to begin, "Advise yee well, supreme Senat, if charity be thus excluded and expulst, how yee will defend the untainted honour of your own actions and proceedings." He is actually presenting an argument from the rule of justice: "The rule of justice requires giving identical treatment to beings or situations of the same kind. . . . The rule of justice furnishes the foundation which makes it possible to pass from earlier cases to future cases. It makes it possible to present the use of precedent in the form of a quasi-logical argument."[21] One of Milton's primary assumptions is that his divorce proposal is simply a logical extension of precedents already established in other areas of the ongoing reformation. Parliament, he says, has effectively established the precedent that a covenant may be broken when it fails to produce its proper ends, and a covenant is a covenant whether it is that of one man or of many. Those elements of the argument which seem to establish an analogy are actually designed to establish the sine qua non of the argument from the rule of justice, namely, that the essential characteristics of the situations be the same. Once this is admitted, the logic that what applies to one case applies equally to the other is impeccable.

This brings us to the second question: Is Milton's use of this argument "obviously excellent rhetoric," as Sirluck has called it? My own conclusion is that it most emphatically is not. Arguments from the rule of justice run the risk of a potential backfire, resulting not just in failure, but rather in a conclusion wholly obverse from that desired. For example, a politician under criticism for a given policy or practice might offer the rule-of-justice defense that he is only doing what his predecessors in office had done with impunity in similar situations. But if opinion against him and his policy were sufficiently aroused, the argument would backfire. It would result in the unanticipated conclusion that his predecessors too should not have been allowed to proceed as they did and establish such precedents. Or a particularly heinous criminal, condemned to death, might seek a commutation of his sentence under the rule-of-justice argument that others so sentenced had been spared. But again, if opinion against him were sufficiently vehement, the argument might produce negative results by making the "audience" question the wisdom of ever having established such precedents. The outcome, ironically, might be an upsurge of opinion in favor of rigorous execution of the death penalty, not only in this but in other cases as well. The argument can be successful only insofar as it appeals to precedents upon which there is agreement, but even this agreement can be withdrawn in the light of the most recent case. An attempt to extend a rule to a new situation may result instead in the precedents and the rule itself being perceived in a new way and consequently rejected.[22] And, it should be noted, reversals such as these will take place because of, not in spite of, the admittedly impeccable logic.

Milton's argument relating divorce and politics is even more open to this kind of reversal than is normally the case. As Sirluck's introduction to Milton's divorce tracts indicates, writers of the 1640s frequently referred to the marital covenant, whether by way of analogy or example or comparison, to support various political arguments. But no matter how marriage was used in argument, or for whatever ends, it was always presented as the more familiar case, as the known, uncontroverted fact, as the *phoros* which buttressed the theme, while the political issue was the debatable point. The political issue had little status independent of the argument, while the example of marriage was presented with the status of fact upon which agreement could be assumed. Now Milton's argument (and this is true whether it be considered an analogy or an argument from the rule of justice) is a rather dangerous attempt to reverse this status, suddenly to present the political issue as beyond question and the marital one as debatable. Thus, not only does he run the normal risk of reversal in the rule-of-justice argument (or in the interrelationship between the terms of an analogy); he greatly increases that risk by using a precedent which, if the amount of rhetoric expended in defending it is any indication, was highly questionable in itself.

Milton's linking of the case for divorce with Parliament's own case may appear to be excellent *logic*, abstractly considered, but it remains a *rhetorical* liability nevertheless. Milton's rhetoric in this pamphlet verges, at times, on the tactic of threatening. This argument is a good example of that tone. Milton almost dares Parliament to deny his conclusion. But the tighter he draws his logical noose, the less likely it is to be rhetorically effective. In the field of rhetoric (unlike, say, geometry), pursuing premises or axioms to their logical conclusions frequently results in a reductio ad absurdum. A familiar method of arguing against either a premise or a precedent is by pushing its logical extension to extremes (ironically perhaps: witness Swift's *Modest Proposal*), and watching its proponents attempt to explain that that is not what they meant at all. In 1642–1643, the Royalists used this tactic, arguing that if Parliament could take power from the king (an action based essentially on premises like Milton's axiom), then what was to prevent the people, in their turn, from taking power away from Parliament when they disagreed with it?[23] In this polemical atmosphere, given the theoretically "factual" status of matters concerning marriage and divorce, it is not at all inconceivable that something like Milton's divorce argument could have been proposed ironically in an attempt to embarrass Parliament.[24] Consequently, to present a serious argument for divorce as a logical extension of the ecclesiastical and civil elements of the reformation was a most dangerous procedure. Yet that is exactly what Milton did, not only in this one explicit argument, but in the whole spirit, tone, and form of *The Doctrine and Discipline of Divorce.*

Of course, the members of Parliament were, to a certain extent, trapped by Milton's logic; they could be expected not to repudiate their own actions. But the larger audience did not function under this limitation; it was free to repudiate past precedents or principles, as the Parliament itself would undoubtedly have recognized. If Milton's conclusion about divorce was as utterly unthinkable as it seems to have been to his contemporaries, then, by logical reciprocity, an unfavorable reaction could easily be cast back from that conclusion to the precedents and principles used to support it. The argument for divorce had a strong potential to be rhetorically damaging to any other case of which it was presented as the logical extension. Thus Milton, by linking divorce and politics, created an argument which could all too readily be turned against Parliament and the reformation, an argument whose strength was a direct function of the strength of contemporary opinion against divorce. And its potential for damage increases proportionately as it is perceived as having logical rather than merely analogical force. That is why it matters that this be recognized as a quasi-logical argument based on precedent and principle, rather than as a mere analogy.

A growing sense of frustration may have caused Milton to add the overt political material to the second edition, but it only made explicit the rhetorical weakness implicit in the first edition and inherent in both. The argument for divorce, and this particular part of it especially, contains the potential for a severely debilitating embarrassment of the very Parliament to which Milton was appealing. Given the state of contemporary opinion, asking Parliament to legitimize divorce was at best a difficult and risky undertaking; but asking Parliament to legitimize divorce as the logical consequence of its own principles and actions was an insult more to be expected from its enemies than from a friend. It is no wonder that Milton's attempt to expedite and extend the course of the reformation met with scorn, silence, and peremptory rejection among the councils to which it was addressed.

This analysis also clarifies the rhetorical potential of Ascham's treatise. I have suggested that "Of Marriage" was just as much an argument against Milton's principles as it was an argument against divorce. Our comparison of the two texts, revealing as it does so many points of direct attitudinal contrast, is enough to suggest this possibility; the rhetorical analysis reinforces it. Deliberately or not, Ascham's approach exploits the potentially embarrassing weakness in Milton's argument. He indirectly argues against Milton's premises by arguing against the "absurd" conclusion to which they lead and by simultaneously reasserting a wholly different set of his own premises. In *The Doctrine and Discipline*, Milton uses his premises as the means to an end. Ascham, in effect, reverses the normal relationship between premises and conclusions, using a readily acceptable, rhetorically "obvious" conclusion to bolster the credibility of the premises he is advancing. Nevertheless, his argument against divorce was neither rhetorically superfluous nor arbitrary. The necessity of the endurance of the marital relationship had in fact been questioned, albeit unsuccessfully. But more important, the more obvious the argument against divorce could be made to seem, the more powerful became the implicit case against the principles which had been used to support it. The argument against divorce exposed by implication the extremes ("this pretence of Liberty") to which the principles of the reformation could lead when abused. Finally, the vicissitudes of marriage were ideally paradigmatic of, and an excellent vehicle for, Ascham's quietist axioms: that we work more for nature's ends than our own, that evil is necessary in this world, that no earthly content can satisfy us, and that we must be patient and adjust our desires to the necessity of events.

At first glance, such a rhetorical motive may seem strange for Ascham, who was a supporter, as well as an employee, of Parliament. But ironically, if predictably, the Parliament of 1647–1648 was under a political attack based on the very premises it had once found useful. William Haller has described how premises used "by Parker in support of Parliament against the crown . . . were finally turned by Lilburne, Walwyn and Overton against Parliament itself." The extension of the "democratic dogma" of the Levellers led to "the logical projection of that dogma into dreams and theories of a naturalistic communism. . . . The great decision was taken when, in May, 1647, Parliament turned its back on democracy, which was the logic, if not the remedy of the revolution, and ordered the 'large petition' burnt by the common hangman."[25] Such circumstances would explain not only Ascham's motive but also his decision to avoid an openly polemical reply. He would avoid mentioning Milton and disguise his argument against divorce because he would not want the effect of his treatise to be limited to those immediate associations. It stands not only as a refutation of divorce in particular but also as a warning against all such "logical projections." Ultimately more important than the particular argument was the attitude which lay behind it. Those principles which had become dangerous to Parliament could not, of course, be openly refuted or rejected, even though they had outlived their usefulness. Ascham argues against them only indirectly, not to refute but to replace them with a more passive attitude of Stoic acceptance.

When "Of Marriage" is considered in the context of Ascham's subsequent work, its role in his effort simultaneously to control and consolidate the revolution becomes clear. His program involved the adaptation of a *via media* between extremists and reactionaries; it sought no less than to quell revolutionary excess on the one hand and to win acceptance for revolutionary accomplishments on the other. Almost immediately after composing "Of Marriage," Ascham wrote and published his more politically explicit *Discourse: Wherein is Examined, What is Particularly Lawfull during the Confusions and Revolutions of Government* (London, July 1648). Therein he described the political dilemma as he saw it:

As reforming powers in all Ages make it their chiefest worke to take down the greatest Colossuse's, or whatever else might be ombragious in the excrescencies of Civill Pomp; so some others of this Age, by a new Art of levelling, thinke nothing can be rightly mended or reformed, unlesse the whole piece ravell out to the very end, and that all intermediate greatness betwixt Kings and them, should be crumbled even to dust, where all lying levell together as in the first Chaos, Spades ought to be put even into the hands of those who were heretofore adorned only with Scepters.[26]

This attack on the "Art of levelling" occurs in a work the purpose of which is to enable the average man to suspend the question of political legitimacy and grant his allegiance to a de facto government.[27] The *Discourse*, reprinted in 1649, became a key work in the Engagement Controversy of that year. John M. Wallace, who has identified Ascham, Francis Rous, and John Dury as the forerunners of those who argued for Parliament's Oath of Engagement, has described their attitude: "The mark of an Engager was his willingness to lend his passive support to a usurper who commanded lawful things, regardless of the usurper's claim to legitimacy. He obeyed for the sake of peace, in order to prevent further bloodshed,

and he did so on the understanding that illegal government would
continue only for an interim period, until a more stable constitution
could be formed."[28]

The *Discourse,* though obviously political, uses an indirect
rhetorical strategy similar to that in "Of Marriage." It is thinly disguised as a consideration of the condition of subjects and the problems of loyalty during the Wars of the Roses and makes its point by
implication rather than by direct application to contemporary affairs.
Ascham's indirect rhetoric is further evident in his inclusion in the
Discourse of the story of Ferdinand, King of Naples. Ascham presents him as a model king who, facing imminent conquest, abdicated
rather than expose his people to ruin.[29] Wallace has pointed out that
"Ascham had related the story of Ferdinand of Naples with obvious
persuasive intent,"[30] that he "had intended his main thesis to suggest the expedience of the king's [Charles'] abdication."[31] In the
Discourse, then, as well as in "Of Marriage," we see the casuist in
Ascham at work, setting forth precepts indirectly via discussion of
the "hypothetical" extreme case. In the later work, Ascham used the
same premises (sometimes verbatim)[32] which he had used in "Of
Marriage" to urge the same attitudes of quietist acceptance, warning
his countrymen that in the face of pressing necessity and the threat of
chaos they could not afford to be overly scrupulous about cooper-
ating with a de facto government. To calm those activists who would
yet struggle either to extend the revolution or to reverse it, Ascham
proposed a Stoic passivity reflecting the classic Stoic differentiation
between that which is in our power and that which is not.[33] This
distinction informs Ascham's rhetorical stance with regard to both
marriage and political allegiance. Implicit in his choice of form, in
his choice of premises, and in his rhetorical motives is the idea that,
in the face of necessity and circumstance, choice of action is limited,
and attitude is all that a man really can manipulate.

It is interesting that Ascham apparently had intended to carve
out an audience which would accept his quietist attitude as early as
the winter of 1647–1648, as the nation hurtled toward the disasters
which lay at the end of the logical extension of the revolution. It may
be that the press of the "necessity of Events" caused Ascham to forgo
the leisurely, indirect attempt to influence attitude through the
treatise "Of Marriage" and turn to the politically explicit, if still
slightly oblique, *Discourse.*

University of Florida

NOTES

1. Discovered by Quentin Skinner and briefly discussed in his essay "The Ideological Context of Hobbes's Political Thought," *The Historical Journal,* IX (1966), 309. A unique scribal copy exists as MS Gg. I. 4 in the Cambridge University Library. A transcribed text is now available in my "Anthony Ascham's 'Of Marriage,' " *ELR,* III (1973), 284–305. Citations to the treatise in this essay will be identified parenthetically by the folio numbers which are incorporated into the transcribed text.

2. For biographical data in addition to the *DNB* entry, see Irene Coltman, *Private Men and Public Causes* (London, 1962), pp. 198–239.

3. (Cambridge, 1968). Other studies of note include Perez Zagorin, *A History of Political Thought in the English Revolution* (London, 1954), pp. 64–77; John M. Wallace, "The Cause Too Good," *JHI,* XXIV (1963), 150–54, and "The Engagement Controversy," *Bull. NYPL,* LXVIII (1964), 384–405; Quentin Skinner, "History and Ideology in the English Revolution," *The Historical Journal,* VIII (1965), 151–78, and "Conquest and Consent: Thomas Hobbes and the Engagement Controversy," in *The Interregnum: The Quest for Settlement, 1646–1660,* ed. G. E. Aylmer (Hamden, Conn., 1972), pp. 79–98; and J. A. W. Gunn, *Politics and the Public Interest in the Seventeenth Century* (London, 1968), pp. 82–87.

4. "Obligation and Authority in Two English Revolutions," Victoria University of Wellington, Dr. W. E. Collins Lecture, May 17, 1973, p. 20.

5. See my introduction to the text, *ELR,* III (1973), 285.

6. See David Masson, *The Life of John Milton* (1873) (London, 1896), vol. III, p. 673.

7. Ibid., pp. 676–78. Of *Little Non-Such,* Ernest Sirluck has pointed out that these ministers or their delegates "took as serious and heretical novelty what was intended as a parody." See Appendix C: "Little Non-Such: A Satire on Milton's Divorce Argument?", *Complete Prose Works of John Milton,* ed. Ernest Sirluck (New Haven, 1959), vol. II, p. 801. Citations to Milton's prose identified parenthetically in this essay refer to this volume, specifically to its edition of *The Doctrine and Discipline of Divorce.* All italics appear in the original.

8. Like "Scripture," the "natural law" concept was authoritative but ambiguous; see Merritt Hughes's discussion in his introduction to *Complete Prose,* vol. III, p. 68.

9. Cf. Seneca, "On Obedience to the Universal Will" (and especially the last lines of the verse therein: "Ducunt volentem fata, nolentem trahunt"), in *Epistulae Morales,* trans. Richard M. Gummere, Loeb Classical Library ed. (London, 1925), vol. III, p. 228. This doctrine not only forms the essence of Ascham's own political views but also serves as a major component of the "Loyalist" mentality; see Wallace, *Destiny His Choice,* esp. pp. 252–57.

10. See John M. Wallace, "Dryden and History: A Problem in Allegorical Reading," *ELH,* XXXVI (1969), esp. pp. 271–73; and " 'Examples Are Best Precepts': Readers and Meanings in Seventeenth Century Poetry," *Critical Inquiry,* I (1974), 273–90.

11. For some discussions of form, see Bernard Weinberg, "Formal Analysis in Poetry and Rhetoric," in *Papers in Rhetoric and Poetic,* ed. Donald C. Bryant (Iowa City, 1965), p. 36; R. S. Crane, *The Languages of Criticism and the Structure of Poetry* (1953) (Toronto, 1967), p. 197, n. 57; and Ch. Perelman and L. Olbrechts-Tyteca, *The New Rhetoric: A Treatise on Argumentation,* trans. John Wilkinson and Purcell Weaver (Notre Dame, 1969), p. 508.

12. Aristotle's system of rhetorical kinds or species, the deliberative, the epideictic, and the forensic, provides one method of broadly classifying particular forms; see *Rhetorica*, trans. W. Rhys Roberts, in *The Works of Aristotle*, ed. W. D. Ross (Oxford, 1924), vol. XI, p. 1358b. Subsequent references to Aristotle's *Rhetoric* are to this edition and will be indicated parenthetically in the text. Lane Cooper summarized the three kinds of rhetoric thus: "(1) Deliberative (political, advisory); (2) Forensic (legal); (3) Epideictic (ceremonial). These may be distinguished by their (a) divisions, (b) times, and (c) ends and aims. The (a) divisions of deliberative speaking are exhortation and dissuasion; (b) its time in the future; (c) its ends are expediency and inexpediency. The (a) divisions of forensic speaking are accusation and defense; (b) its time is the past; (c) its ends are justice and injustice. The (a) divisions of epideictic speaking are praise and blame; (b) its time is the present; (c) its ends are honor and dishonor." (*The Rhetoric of Aristotle*, trans. Lane Cooper [New York, 1932], p. xxxviii.)

13. Chilton Latham Powell's *English Domestic Relations, 1487–1653* (New York, 1917) implies that while Milton's divorce tracts are in the tradition of a long series of writings on marriage and divorce, they nevertheless constitute a radical departure from the traditional approach to the subject, treating it as a practical issue rather than a merely hypothetical question (89).

14. An isolated thesis—for example, Milton's "That indisposition, unfitness, or contrariety of mind . . . is a greater reason of divorce than naturall frigidity"—does not necessarily imply the argumentative end; Milton's thesis could be proved in order to justify a past act (forensic) or to display rhetorical skill and wit (epideictic).

15. Cicero, *Topica*, trans. H. M. Hubbell, Loeb Classical Library ed. (Cambridge, Mass., 1949), p. 445. Cf. Powell, *English Domestic Relations*, p. 89.

16. Introduction to *Complete Prose*, vol. II, p. 147. In his annotation to *The Doctrine and Discipline* in this volume (p. 229, n. 34), Lowell W. Coolidge has called attention to the political provenance of the "axiom": "That political institutions are subordinate to the ends for which they are established was a principle inevitably invoked by apologists for Parliamentary resistance to the king."

17. Coolidge's note (ibid., p. 245, n. 2) refers the reader back to these two examples.

18. Introduction to *Complete Prose*, vol. II, p. 152.

19. *The New Rhetoric*, p. 373.

20. Introduction to *Complete Prose*, vol. II, p. 157.

21. *The New Rhetoric*, pp. 218–19.

22. Ibid., p. 220.

23. See introduction to *Complete Prose*, vol. II, pp. 26–29.

24. The process, ironically, would be the same as that by which the author of *Little Non-Such* attempted to embarrass Milton. See *Complete Prose*, vol. II, p. 907.

25. *Tracts on Liberty in the Puritan Revolution, 1638–1647* (New York, 1934), vol. I, p. 7.

26. Quoted from the expanded second edition, published as *Of the Confusions and Revolutions of Goverments* [sic] (London, 1649), sig. C1^v.

27. See Zagorin, *A History of Political Thought*, pp. 64–77; Skinner, "History and Ideology"; Wallace, *Destiny His Choice*, pp. 54–58; Gunn, *Politics and the Public Interest*, pp. 82–87.

28. "The Engagement Controversy," p. 384.

29. Sig. H3^v.

30. *Destiny His Choice*, p. 83.

31. "The Engagement Controversy," p. 389.

32. Cf. the second edition, *Of the Confusions*, sig. F6ᵛ with MS fols. 4–5, 27–28.

33. For example, "The Manual of Epictetus," trans. P. E. Matheson, in *The Stoic and Epicurean Philosophers*, ed. Whitney J. Oates (New York, 1940), p. 460.

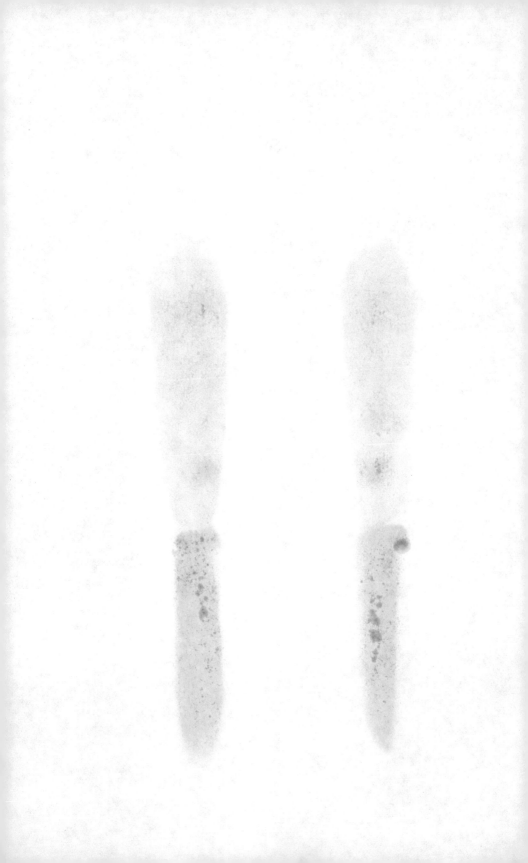